MW00466049

THE HIDDEN MESSAGES OF JESUS

How the Gnostic Gospels Change Christianity

LARRY A. ANGUS

Wasteland Press
www.wastelandpress.net
Shelbyville, KY USA

The Hidden Messages of Jesus:
How the Gnostic Gospels Change Christianity
by Larry A. Angus

Copyright © 2012 Larry A. Angus
ALL RIGHTS RESERVED

First Printing – April 2012
ISBN: 978-1-60047-699-0

Front cover image by Professor Scott Angus
www.Angusstudio.com

EXCEPT FOR BRIEF TEXT QUOTED AND APPROPRIATELY CITED IN OTHER WORKS, NO PART OF THIS BOOK MAY BE REPRODUCED IN ANY FORM, BY PHOTOCOPYING OR BY ELECTRONIC OR MECHANICAL MEANS, INCLUDING INFORMATION STORAGE OR RETRIEVAL SYSTEMS, WITHOUT PERMISSION IN WRITING FROM THE COPYRIGHT OWNER/AUTHOR.

Printed in the U.S.A.

0 1 2 3 4 5 6 7

This book is dedicated in appreciation for Elaine Pagels, Marvin Meyer, Karen King, and Bart Ehrman, all of whom have moved mountains in the arena of Christian faith.

Acknowledgments

Foremost, the greatest encouragement for writing this book has been the hundreds of persons who signed on for my "Seeking Christians Newsletters" through **gnosticschristians.com**. The response has been incredible as I was told by a literary agent there just wasn't much interest in the Gnostics. Hopefully, this book will help create some greater interest in the little understood Gnostic Gospels and also help to affirm that the Gnostics were not simply heretical Christians who believed in a secret "gnosis." Such a popular hurdle may be difficult to overcome, as it has been an effective means to silence the Gnostics and their gospels. With all the responses to the web site, it is known now that there is a different side to this story. Hopefully, this book will reveal that this so called heretical movement in early Christianity supports faith as more than what one believes but rather is an open minded, honest, seeking of truth and God — a different way to be Christian.

My readers and editors have brought invaluable insights, corrections, and suggestions to the project. Dr. Tom Boyd, a minister and professor of Philosophy and Religion at Oklahoma University wrote a thirty two page edit with a vast number of accolades. Evelyn Hamilton, Ph.D. in Religious Studies read the manuscripts many times always encouraging publication. Patricia Steiner, an instructor and artist of meditative religion has been an indefatigable and creative editor. Geologists, Allan F. Hills and Jack Bright, gave careful scrutiny to the manuscript, so I said to them, thanks for checking on its "ground, different layers of wisdom, and foundations." Jim Bennett, a former Presbyterian Executive, a layman and lawyer, suggested the title be changed from Message to "Messages." Bill Muldrow, a former missionary in Ethiopia, civil rights leader, and minister endorsed the view of many who said the book clarified the way he has always believed as a Christian. Also, appreciation goes to Carol Irwin of Manuscript Magic who carefully copyedited the book line by line. Dr. Barbara Boyd, also of Oklahoma University, insisted for footnotes; some have complained they are too extensive, but their purpose is to verify the research of this book and that the many positions within are not simply the "ideas" of the author alone. Others should be cited for encouraging its publication, but finally, not as a matter of courtesy, but as a fact of true support and love, I give thanksgiving for my wife, Gloria.

Wasteland Press may first appear as a "station" for failed literary works, but the Press is named after T.S. Elliot's great poem, "The Waste Land." Many remember its opening line, "April is the cruelest month...." His poem, heavily footnoted, offers little hope for mankind and the confusing world after World War I. My work suggests Christianity can move one beyond the wasteland of despair, but as with Elliot, not having to have the answers. Therefore, I was drawn to Wasteland Press. Wasteland recommended the highly efficient Susan Giffin for indexing. Of some significance, larger publishing companies have expressed interest if it sells well, so thanks to you have purchased this book and hopefully would recommend it to others. Wasteland was professional in every detail, and after extensive research was an outstanding choice for publication.

gnosticschristians.com / A Different Way to be Christian*

*This is the way the web site appears on most search engines — usually near the top — regarding Gnostics.

Larry A. Angus

Table of Contents

Prologue

Gnostic Christians believed that questioning one's faith was always important. To know (gnosis) Christ was to seek a deeper and honest meaning for one's life. This gnosis led to wholeness in a person's relationship to God and the world. Christ's way was a spiritual journey, encouraging persons continually to seek God and all truth. Gnosis did not mean secret knowledge but a vital relationship with Christ and God.

However, the early apostolic church, also known as the proto-orthodox, which would be favored and supported by the Emperor Constantine for political reasons, was able with his direct involvement to define what the *true* Christian should believe about Christ. Constantine's blessing confirmed the earlier teachings of Bishops, such as Irenaeus, that those who did not accept their church's literal interpretations of Christ — or questioned their beliefs — were "heretics." Understanding Christ became limited to one narrow interpretation, and the beliefs of the church were established — now with the power of the state — as the unquestionable, absolute truths of Christianity.

Over the voices of those called Gnostics, the orthodox form of Christianity not only prevailed but has continued ever since to define Christianity, foremost, as a belief system. The Gnostic Gospels show that there was, and is, a more refreshing, honest, open, spiritual, loving, and exciting way to be a Christian.

gnosticschristians.com

Often the question is asked, "How did you get interested in the Gnostics?" After I read Elaine Pagels' *The Gnostic Gospels*, when it came out in paperback in 1981, the book would not leave my mind. I kept thinking; this is intriguing — new gospels? I like honesty in religion, and Elaine's book is about being honest with the development of early Christianity. Why couldn't there be more than four authentic gospels about Jesus? When I learned the facts surrounding the choice of only four true gospels, and then, the reason for the exclusion of others, I was disturbed. It was not that I wanted other gospels to be added to the New Testament, but my question was, "why was this information and these responses to Jesus suppressed?" What became alarming was that it was fairly obvious that only one view of Jesus was to become the norm, and other understandings were to be overpowered and condemned because of the need of one group to be right and claim exclusive truth. Now, after much study, my first copy of Elaine's book looks somewhat like the tattered books and gnostic manuscripts discovered at Nag Nammadi in Egypt!

Reading *The Gnostic Gospels*, and the gospels and books found at Nag Hammadi, was a freeing experience for my faith, not because it made me a Gnostic, but because it gave support to my feeling, that as a Christian, I didn't have to have all the answers. Life is more comfortable, of course, when you have the answers. Having answers is not all that wrong or dishonest. However, when your own answer becomes *the* answer, a temptation that seems a natural part of the nature and history of mankind, and particularly so in religion, the consequence is that peace, honesty, and wisdom become more words than reality. These values become slogans to support one's beliefs; however, too often, their actualities are not that apparent in those who are boldly claiming to possess these qualities and the true faith.

In contrast, and particularly appealing to me, the gnostic approach to faith teaches that we are to seek the values of peace, honesty, and wisdom, rather than to go around bragging that we are privy to these qualities. I found the gnostic way of always seeking these higher values in one's life, and their deeper search for the great questions of our existence, a more honest way to believe and be a follower of Jesus. I was inspired because, for the Gnostics, faith was foremost a process of seeking rather than blindly accepting doctrines and unquestionable religious truths.

To be a seeking Christian raises my religious spirit because faith at the deepest level means trusting a source and energy greater than my knowledge. There is something within me that feels and believes that there is more to life than a material existence, so I am religious, and I am a Christian. As a religious person, however, it upsets me when people wear their religion on their sleeve, or push their agenda, or try to convince me their way of being religious is the only way. "I have the answer, and you need to believe as I do." Of course, there is plenty of such evangelizing today, both subtle and direct.

Interestingly, a ringing alarm from the Gnostic Gospels is that religious, dogmatic insistence dates back to the early formation of Christianity. Those with the attitude that what they believed was the only way to understand Christ and Christianity triumphed as the true way to believe and be Christian. Their loud voice and arrogance drowned out the possibility that the messages of Jesus could be heard in other meaningful ways. In essence, the response to Christ was hijacked, placed in a straightjacket, and victoriously won by one form of Christianity that insisted only they knew the truth of Christ. Faith changed from being a thoughtful follower of Christ to being a believer in a particular way of Christianity.

Early Christian writings, which are extant, provide ample testimony that the messages of Christ were diverted into a narrow system of beliefs. This system presumed that a literal acceptance of certain beliefs was the only true way to believe in Jesus. These beliefs, which included the virgin birth and promise of a bodily resurrection for believers, would define the essence of Christianity. Christianity became a collection of beliefs, and one's future, either heaven or hell, became dependent on accepting these beliefs. With the Nicene Creed declaring that Jesus was not just divine but God, who could better know the truth than Christians? Therefore, the Christian tradition became that only Christians have true religious answers about the world and God because of Christ. All are destined to hell, unless they believe in Jesus. Believe in Christ, only as the Bible teaches, and you will have the answers to life, salvation, and a wonderful life. That is not my Christ!

At one time in my life, that was my Christ. Evangelical friends had convinced me that only they had the true way to believe in Jesus and that their beliefs were those of true Christianity. The Bible contained all truth, and those who did not believe in the Bible were going to hell. However, even within their ranks, it became obvious that Christ can be interpreted differently by sincere Christians, as they began to split hairs over Bible verses, and particularly, Christian doctrines. Slowly, I began to accept that there was more than one correct way to believe and be a follower of Jesus.

Therefore, going beyond my need to declare that I had the answer for everyone, I realized that Jesus' vision of faith was more open and loving. He protested those in his own religion who believed and lived as if they had all the answers, were legalistic, and judgmental in their faith, giving the impression they were better than others. However, that was the very kind of Christianity I had embraced. I became convinced, "There is only one true religion, mine is it; all other religions are false." This claim to exclusive knowledge of God did not stop there. Such conviction, usually based on one's religious experience, became, "My version of Christianity is the true way." Well, there is something satisfying in such certainty, but the sad part is that those who become such true believers and warriors for their truth often have no concept of their posture of self-righteousness and arrogance.

Joining these passionate believers, I loved the verse in which Jesus said the way was narrow. I strongly believed I had found this beautiful, exclusive way and the truth — and was proud of it! Honestly, this certainty was helpful at that point in my development as it gave me badly needed confidence and belief in myself. Somehow Christianity had ingrained in me that I was totally corrupt, sinful, and not worth much. Gosh, it was wonderful to have the answers and be born again! So having found the light, I was out to convert and save the world. I had found true Christianity and those who just thought they were Christians needed God's truth. On the stump, I preached that because you went to a chicken house that didn't make you a chicken. The message of this "pretentious wisdom" was that just because one went to church, unless one held true beliefs and experienced the born again gospel, attendance didn't make one a Christian. Of course, this was a loving proclamation rather than a judgmental one, since it was based on God's word, and so it was I tried to convince my family, friends, and all who went to church and had not experienced being born again. My conversion experience was proof of my belief as good things started to happen. I was convinced I now had happiness, knew that God loved me, that finally I believed in myself because of Jesus, and life in general was better. Therefore, I preached if you would believe this way, great things would happen to you, as well. Repent and believe!

Then, slowly, I began to realize that after I had found the answer — whoops, I needed to repent again! My confidence had become overconfidence. I began to recognize that I was condemning all others to hell, becoming quite obnoxious, knowing it all, and unwittingly had joined the club of self-righteousness. It took about a year before my brain started to challenge my own certainty, but thank God it did, as I was becoming a person who wasn't all that honest with myself and others.

Finally, my narrow, unbending religious straw broke when I went to a prestigious Christian leadership conference. Those of us who had been filled with the Holy Spirit by special prayers were to go to a park, and convert children or whomever we met, by convincing them to accept Jesus as their Lord and Savior. My mission partner and I didn't save anyone. Then, when it came time to report, before a large crowd, she said, "Larry and I saved twenty children." Oh my! You can hear the applause, and the "praise Jesus" shouts, and then the personal accolade by the founder of the evangelical organization. Afterward, I approached this demigod of faith, and said, "Doctor," as that is what they called him, "Patty and I saved no one." With a look that I will never forget, he commented, "Larry, am I to believe you or the Holy Spirit?" Time to repent again! I walked ten miles into Minneapolis from the conference grounds and got on a Greyhound bus, swearing I would never walk into a church — except for necessities such as weddings and funerals.

Listening to this story, an atheist professor and advisor shockingly responded, "Larry, why don't you go to Yale, Harvard, or Princeton Divinity School as you do have an interest and a mind for religion. You don't have to become a Reverend!" The long and short of it was that growing up as a Presbyterian I went to Princeton, got the first Master's Degree required for the profession, and then, a second Academic Master's Degree. Ready to go for a Ph.D. in order to teach, I thought I would try a year in a church to get some firsthand experience. Finding I enjoyed working in the church, especially with youth, I never went back for the higher degree.

This book reflects my life's journey, but I have chosen not to write the book in first person because it is more than just my story. As non-fiction, the study, research, and writing have taken over five years; the attempt has been to be honest and correct. However, as you will see, the book isn't about the correct message of Jesus but seeking it. I am accepting of those who need to know the answer or answers, or somehow presume that they know the correct message of Jesus. My belief, now, is that certainty only shuts the door to faith and misses the essential message of Jesus. It is not that these folks are not Christian, in whatever form of religious or church certainty they use to proclaim their truth, but it is to say all of us need to keep that door of repentance open! Because change is often needed and sometimes required, the position of this book is that those Christians, who in the past were labeled Gnostics, can inspire a way to be Christian that says, "*We seek the truth — We don't declare it.*"

Such a faith position is uncomfortable for a lot of people, particularly as the world gets more uncertain, increasingly confusing, and even at times frightening. For some, not having to claim that their beliefs and morals are God's last word, because the Bible, their church, or some authority says so, is a relief and comfort in itself. Identifying oneself as a seeker of truth, as a Christian, rather than the holder of exclusive truth for whatever reason, is for some of us a much more honest approach with oneself, others, and the facts of the world today. The basic premise of this book is that the Gnostics were persons of faith who saw themselves as believers in Jesus, but more importantly as followers without the final answers. Gnostic Christians defined themselves as seekers! The challenge is not to accept their beliefs but to be inspired by their seeking style of Christianity.

This book is more about *how* one believes than what one believes. That is not to say that beliefs that one holds are not necessary. Beliefs are a part of the process and should be debated, but when beliefs become the final word or message, faith becomes rote and routine. The Gnostics had various beliefs and different, interesting myths. The myths of the Gnostics are both fascinating and ridiculous. Inadvertently, they raise questions about some traditional Christian myths and stories, such as the world being created in seven days. Despite the absurdity, from today's perspective of some of the gnostic myths and beliefs, all of these were secondary to faith; all were subject to change. The Gnostics did not hear Jesus preaching a set of beliefs, writing his message in stone or print, saying his followers were to insist on their beliefs as exclusive truth. Nor, did his disciples say that they were better than others because of their belief. Beyond beliefs, which all have, faith was to be dominated by trust and love in the one whom the Gnostics called the living Jesus.

This book's purpose isn't to condemn any particular church or churches in general. As a Presbyterian minister, I know firsthand that churches do tremendous good for persons and often for people in need. Socially, church membership and fellowships are helpful for many. Even evangelical organizations need to exist, and should be praised, when they turn around peoples' lives who have been going in a wrong direction. However, there is no question that churches can get sick and not be helpful. Usually that happens when some insist over and against others that only their way and beliefs are true. It can also happen when serious divisions grow when certain groups within a church begin to insist on their own personal positions and feelings – such as the minister isn't teaching the Bible or preaching the Word – as they want to hear it! For Christians and churches who believe they don't need to have all the answers or the answer, hopefully, this is a book that will bring fresh air.

The Gnostics, who were successfully discredited as heretics by the church fathers, have much to say about faith, Jesus, and God. As it turns out, these condemned heretics speak for themselves in their gospels and books, and the evidence verifies that they were sincere Christians who did not just accept the axiom, "Believe what you are told." One purpose of this book is to correct the assumption that the Gnostics were those who insisted on their own way or knew it all. Instead, by their quest to be true to themselves and honest with God, they can inspire a new way of faith and Christian identity today. Some who have read the first drafts of this book have said, "This is the way I have believed all my life." The book is more about affirmation of that way of believing and seeking and is not designed to convert one to be a Gnostic or believe in Gnosticism, but rather to be inspired by the gnostic way of faith, encourage Christians to be open to new knowledge, and embrace Christ in new light.

One notable comment is that I have chosen to capitalize the term, "Gnostics," after much consternation. To capitalize the Gnostics tends to make them one coherent group, easily explained and written off as false Christian, as the early church bishops and fathers desired. They were not one group, and a surprising revelation will be that they were, certainly at first, part of the early church and not a separate church body. Just as the Protestants were not one group, it will become clear that the Gnostics were not either, but as with the Protestants, there were some basic themes that bound them together. As will be argued in Chapter Five, titled, "Who were the Gnostics?", they were in essence the first Protestants. Therefore, since "Protestants" is normally capitalized, so in this book they will be capitalized as "Gnostics."

This decision has been a minor dilemma because some leading gnostic scholars, including Dr. Elaine Pagels and Dr. Marvin Meyer, do not capitalize these Christians, as "Gnostics." Doing likewise would be my preference; however, I have decided to capitalize their description because the majority of my readers has indicated after reading this book that they preferred capitalization. Whichever method one chooses to refer to these early Christians, the argument will be made that they were not one group, with specific and consenting beliefs and that they boldly believed that there was more than one way to believe in Jesus. Indeed, as with the Protestants, there were specific groups like the Lutherans and Presbyterians, and so it was for the gnostic movement. Therefore, for these schools, which never became denominations, I have capitalized those such as the Valentinians and Sethians.

Further, I have not capitalized gnostic when used as an *adjective,* like the adjective orthodox, which is normally not capitalized; gnostic represents a description of a way of belief. Beyond the debate, and the argument over semantics, the meaning is in the message and messages of Christ, whether one prefers, "gnostic" or "Gnostic." So it is that for those who might come to identify themselves, not as Gnostics, but as gnostic or seeking Christians.

As stated, I have attempted to be correct and honest as possible. However, even within the Gnostic Gospels there are conflicting opinions, and they are not one voice. Just as people argue over interpretations in the Bible, the same will be the case for these writings. There will be those, for example, who will claim with some support that "gnosis" means secret knowledge. Since no special hidden secrets are found in the materials and that all these secret writings are now made known for all to read, gnosis will be presented in a different understanding than has been explained or assumed traditionally. Again, history is debatable, and there is much history that is presented in the book. An example of debate might be the figure of Constantine. Certainly, there are hard, cold facts about Constantine, but people often have strong feelings if he was truly helpful to Christianity or not. Then there are issues – like the Apostles' and Nicene Creeds. Their beliefs are often emotionally and strongly supported, but reason will be given why not all, but some of their doctrines, should be questioned. Unfortunately, or fortunately, depending on one's backgrounds or affiliations, many Christian groups may be offended, but hopefully, that will raise a flag for what the Gnostics call "self examination." It may appear that there is an assault particularly on the Roman Catholic Church, but it is the position of this book that the early apostolic church was different, although the direct forerunner, of the Catholic Church. Indeed, there should be the realization that almost all churches must trace their roots back through the Catholic Church to this church that created the beliefs of the Apostles' Creed, which many evangelical and mainline churches hold sacred today. The bottom line is that the Gnostic Gospels do not attack any modern church, specifically.

Instead, they are resources that encourage those who believe that it is fair, honest, and healthy that all Christians don't have to believe the same and that Christ's intention for Christianity was much more than a battle over beliefs. Believing just anything is not the message of these gospels, either, but they support that truth is greater than the measure of anyone's mind and greater than those who arrogantly claim the corner on truth. Having read many books on the subject, and having attended many conferences, and having had conversations with many brilliant scholars, discovering many conflicting positions even among them, this book does not claim to be the only truth. The basis of seeking is that one can be mistaken, corrected, forgiven, and can change, and at the same time choose to be Christian and faithful. Although most everyone has met individual Christians, or Christian churches, or denominations that claim with certainty that "they" know the truth, the greater truth is that not we, nor others, can claim equality with God. As seekers, humility overcomes arrogance, and even so called authority, because, ultimately, only God holds the mystery of truth.

Hopefully, to be clear, I am not a Gnostic, and I am not promoting a religion called Gnosticism. There are churches that call themselves Gnostic and attempt to replicate not only the beliefs but some of the rituals mentioned in their writings. Many respond after reading my web site, where can I find a "Gnostic Church?" That is far from my intent, as these gospels do not represent a separate religion or another Christian denomination, but instead, they imply that faith is more than believing a system of beliefs and myths, even those of the Gnostics. Rather, these gospels indicate that faith is not without beliefs, but in its essence, is beyond belief. Faith is a relationship with Christ and God that is not bound by the necessity of believing certain spiritual truths or doctrines, but it is a continual process of seeking truth and God with humility, openness, and honesty. The Gnostic Gospels do not belittle the truth of Christianity, but they support a different way to be Christian.

Larry A. Angus
gnosticchristians.com, a Different Way to be Christian

Chapter One

New Discoveries of Early Christian Gospels

> Now that scholars have begun to place the sources discovered at Nag Hammadi, like newly discovered pieces of a complex puzzle, new to what we have long known from tradition, we find these remarkable texts, only now becoming widely known, are transforming what we know as Christianity. [1]
>
> - Elaine Pagels
>
> *Beyond Belief: The Secret Gospel of Thomas*

Deep in the morass of theology, there was a voice, extraordinary and beautiful, but buried in silence. This voice was different from the traditional understanding of Christianity. It did not claim absolute truth, insist on correct beliefs, doctrine, or dogma, but heard Christ saying we all have the capacity to know God by looking inward within ourselves. Knowing ourselves, and thus the world, was crucial to knowing God.

As some early Christians put these thoughts into writing, their voice was condemned as false, described as gnostic and heretical, because their "gnosis" or "knowledge" was erroneous. Considered a threat to the church, because they challenged what was called the "immoveable truth," their writings were ordered destroyed.[2] Although they did not call themselves by such a name, they were labeled as "Gnostics."[3]

In December of 1945, two years before the discovery of the Dead Sea Scrolls, this ancient gnostic voice was emancipated, unexpectedly, from a secret burial site in Egypt. Peasant farmers, working near a mountain range known as Jabal al-Tarif, accidently, unearthed an unusually large, weathered, reddish vase. Most likely hidden originally in a mountainside cave, this clay artifact was found in the talus below one of the high cliffs.[4] The discovery was made not far from the site of an ancient Christian monastery and a village named Nag Hammadi. Five hundred miles south of Alexandria, yet only a few miles west of the Nile River, this remote, unknown hamlet was destined for fame because of the contents within the vase.

The farmers, who were brothers, were digging at the base of a cliff for sabakh — a soft soil containing bird lime — used as fertilizer for their crops. Extracting the lighter soil from the rocky debris, near a sizeable boulder, the shovel of one of the brothers struck an unusual object. Since it did not break, they carefully dug around what appeared to be a tall jar, about one meter or forty inches in length, and lifted it out of the sandy soil. The jar was unadorned vase and sealed. Initially, the brothers did not want to break open the receptacle as they feared that within might be what was called in their religion a "jinn" — a wicked or evil spirit! Hoping for old coins or gold, curiosity overcame their fear and religious conviction. With one blow, the bravest shattered the mysterious clay cylinder. Dismay and disbelief struck them all. Lying amidst the rubble was their treasure, *thirteen books*. The books were bound with leather covers, dust-laden, tattered, and looked very ancient![5]

The books were written in a script the brothers could not read. They were not alone! Coptic was an ancient language, related to Egyptian Christians, and at the time of the discovery, it was a dialect only a few linguists in the world could translate. Coptic was written using all capital letters from the Greek alphabet with the addition of a few Egyptian symbols intertwined. Deeply disappointed and saddened by the jar's contents, the brothers gathered the books, (which are called "codices" or "codex" for one book) and transported them to the home of the eldest brother, Muhammad Ali.

Muhammad Ali? Yes, but, obviously, not even distantly related to the Muhammad Ali of boxing fame, yet his highly recognizable name does help one remember that of the discoverer, Muhammad Ali al-Samman. His brothers and biblical scholars grant to Muhammad the credit for uncovering one of the most significant, Christian, archeological discovery in centuries. By exhuming this cache, unintentionally and unknowingly,

Muhammad Ali al Samman brought to light new information concerning early Christianity. This new information expands our knowledge of Jesus and has the potential to change some of the understanding and views of Christianity.

Traditionally, the books of the Bible have been considered to be the only authentic stories and early documents about Jesus. As these newly found manuscripts have been analyzed and dated by biblical scholars, they yield startling information. Now, intense study by both religious and non-religious scholars has led to the opinion that many of the books were written at the same time as those in the New Testament.[6] The books contained writings named "gospels," a word that means "good news" (in Greek "*euangellions*" or the word "evangelical"). Not all the writings are classified as gospels, but most give witness to the life and meaning of Jesus Christ. The contents of these books validate that beyond the authoritative or orthodox interpretation of Christian beliefs, very early in its development, other credible and feasible understandings of Jesus and his messages existed.[7] Not belittling the power of Jesus, the teachings within these codices reveal, for some early Christians, his intent was more than establishing a religion of beliefs. Although containing new and unusual beliefs, the greater importance of these books is that the interpretation of Christianity shifts from being primarily a belief system to a dynamic spiritual journey.

These gospels teach that beliefs, although important, are secondary to one's relationship to Christ and to the one they often called God the Father/God the Mother.[8] Faith was not equivalent to what one believed, but it was a continuous process of seeking. This way of faith, hidden and covered by sand for over fifteen hundred years, challenges several widely held doctrines and many common assumptions about Christianity. Expected to be entirely mythological tales, these gospels uphold Christ and encourage faith, hope, love, and spiritual maturity — because of Jesus. The books found within the thirteen leather bound volumes are collectively known as the Gnostic Gospels."[9]

Purposely hidden for preservation and posterity by early Christian monks, the survival of these manuscripts was a miracle. Early in the development of Christianity, powerful Christians who didn't accept any teachings and meanings of Jesus, other than their own views, made bold claims that those who disagreed with them were heretics.[10] Attaining the title, Bishops of the Church, they gained enough power and authority to claim only the gospels selected by them were true and holy. Four gospels, those now in the Bible, were chosen; all other gospels were declared worthless, false, and need not exist. Unbelievably successful in establishing that the destruction of other gospels was God's will, very few of the condemned gospels could be extant and awaiting discovery. However, with the sound of a jar shattered, the imposed silence was broken, and these unorthodox gospels could speak again for themselves. In essence, they renew and revise the story of the Gnostics, and even more importantly, the early development of the history of Christianity.

The survival story of these gospels is fascinating. Even at the outset of their discovery, these fragile books easily could have been destroyed and remained unknown to the world. Shortly, after these rare gospels were freed from their hiding place and removed from the shattered jar, some pages were burned as ordinary fuel. Muhammad, years later, reported that on his arrival at home, he laid the books next to his mother's wood burning stove. The pages of these books were constructed from papyrus, a leafy reed, when pressed together becomes a form of thin, delicate paper. Ideal for kindling, Muhammad's mother used some of the pages to ignite her oven's fire. The number of pages burned is not known, but for this and other unknown reasons, many of the writings are not complete. Quite possibly, all the pages could have been burned but were spared by an unusual intervening circumstance, which would seem to have little to do with the story.

Rather than figuring out if these books had any value, Muhammad and his brothers had a more pressing agenda. They were possessed with revenging the recent murder of their father. When the brothers were able to catch the person whom they believed had killed their father, in a local tradition of retaliation known as "blood revenge," they hacked off the man's limbs, slit open his chest, and pulled out the heart from his body.[11] As prime suspects, knowing that the police would be searching their home, and most likely would seize these newly found manuscripts, Muhammad had the presence of mind to take the books to a Christian priest. With lettering on the pages being so different from their modern Egyptian language, he wondered if they might have something to do, as he said, "with the Christian people."[12]

The priest showed the books, not sure of their origin, to his brother-in-law, Mr. Raghib, who was a teacher in the village of Nag Hammadi. Mr.

Raghib, perceiving some value, took one of the leather bound books, now called Codex III, which included interesting writings identified as the *Gospel of the Egyptians* and *The Dialogue of the Savior*, to the Coptic Museum in Cairo. On October 4, 1946, the curator of the Museum bought Codex III for 250 Egyptian pounds.[13]

Mr. Raghib sold the other codices to antiquities dealers for unknown prices. A Cyprus dealer, living in Egypt, bought nine of them; one contained the most famous book, the *Gospel of Thomas*. Another book labeled Codex I, which was destined for notoriety because of its future owner, was bought by a Belgian antiquities dealer also working in Egypt.

Albert Eid, the Belgian dealer, illegally, took Codex I to the United States with the clear intention of making significant money. Several noted Universities and Foundations were not ready to purchase. The University of Michigan, which had a famous collection of papyri documents, first declined Mr. Eid's offer. Then, Carl Jung's Bollingen Foundation, which had a special interest in Egyptian antiquities, rejected the manuscript.[14] In 1949, he took the book back to Belgium where he placed Codex I in a safe deposit box in Brussels.

In the meantime, the Coptic Museum, being able to attain the codices still within Egypt, declared these books ancient, authentic manuscripts and quite unique for the study of early Christianity. Desiring to complete their collection, the Egyptian government set a 6000 pound monetary value on the smuggled, but once again, hidden and lost Codex I.[15] With a secret password for the lock box, known only by Mr. Eid, the leather bound book, still simply called Codex I, remained lost to the world and was still silent, until 1952.

Now, enter Dr. Carl Gustav Jung, the famed psychologist, and Dr. Gilles Quispel, a professor of religion at the University of Utrecht (Netherlands).[16] Close friends, they had a serious interest in the Gnostics of early Christianity. Having heard of the existence of Codex I, but not knowing of its illegal status, they approached the Bollingen Foundation to consider the purchase of the Codex. This Foundation, named after the lake by Jung's home in Switzerland, once again did not have the funds because they were currently financing other excavations in Egypt.

Another miracle — or at least an unexpected event — was to happen. An American citizen, George H. Page, living near Zurich, contributed $8000 to the Foundation for the purchase of Codex I.[17] On, May 10, 1952,

Codex I moved from Brussels to the hands of Gilles Quispel, who translated and studied it for over a year. At the celebration of Jung's 80th birthday, on November 15, 1953, he was presented, as truly a special gift, this leather bound, ancient book.[18] Codex I is now commonly referred to as the "Jung," or "Jungian," Codex.

Jung was thrilled as he believed the Gnostics, and particularly, their gnostic perspective, possessed a very honest illustration of the predicament of mankind. He is quoted as saying, "I have worked all my life to know the psyche — and these people knew already."[19] Jung believed strongly in the unconscious force in which archetypes of the mind and reality were found and formed — as did Gnostics. Jung also perceived much value in the Gnostics' use of mythology to explain the unexplainable, and more so in their quest for truth, as exemplified in one of the five books contained in his codex, the *Gospel of Truth*. Interestingly, Jung refused to identify himself as a Gnostic.[20] Why? Although inspired by what he read, he did not believe the Gnostics had all the answers nor that Gnosticism should be revived as a religion (both positions of this book). After Jung's death, the Bollingen Foundation donated Codex I to its rightful home, the Coptic Museum in Cairo.

All thirteen original Codices discovered at Nag Hammadi were now acquired by the Coptic Museum for safe keeping, study, and posterity. The monetary cost that was paid to obtain the books from the antiquities dealers within Egypt is not known, but obviously, today, the collection is priceless. Realizing their intrinsic value, the Coptic Museum and Egyptian government proclaimed the original manuscripts should never leave Egypt.[21]

Once collected, intense study by international scholars began. After facing all kinds of political and scholastic jealousies, which delayed publication in English for all the books until 1977, only those who still see the Gnostics as a threat to traditional Christianity question their authenticity. By use of the Coptic language, dating the papyrus, astonishingly, finding written dates in some of the material used to bind the leather to the pages, and other scholastic investigations, there is little debate that these gospels were translated from earlier Greek editions. With further study, they were believed to be translated by Egyptians into the Coptic language around 350-400 C.E.[22] This dating of these books is important as to their authenticity.

The dating of these gospels, when compared to the writings of the New Testament, may seem late, making their authenticity suspect. However, the most ancient documents of the New Testament, which are not simply fragments, or pieces, also date to the same period of time of the Gnostic Gospels. Most scholars accept that the New Testament Gospels were first written some thirty to sixty years after the death and resurrection of Jesus. Only translations from the originals of the gospels in the New Testament have been found, as is true, of the Gnostic writings and gospels. The earliest known and most complete manuscripts of the New Testament Gospels are:

(1) The Codex Sinaitius found in 1844 at the foot of Mt. Sinai. Interestingly, it contained two extra books, the *Epistle of Barnabas* and *The Shepherd of Hermas.* Neither became a part of the canon of the Bible.[23]

(2) The Codex Vaticanus had been in the Vatican since 1481. Some fragments of the New Testament are missing, but otherwise it is fairly complete, containing only books now in the Bible.[24]

(3) The Codex Alexandrinus, originally thought to have been found in Alexandria, was discovered in the archives of the British Museum with records indicating that it had been there since 1627. It contained two books, which would not be in the Bible, *1 Clement*, and *Psalms of Solomon.*[25]

These codices of the New Testament are dated no earlier than the fourth century.[26] What's the significance? The same dating is true for the new gospels and books found near Nag Hammadi. This makes the Gnostic Gospels as extraordinary and ancient as the known manuscripts of the New Testament.

Interestingly, the inclusion of other books, in the earliest of the New Testament collections, indicated or gave a clue that there were other written Christian resources available to early Christians, other than those in the Bible. In more recent times, even beyond the books at Nag Hammadi, other texts that didn't make it into the Biblical canon have been found in ancient garbage pits, graveyards, and caves, particularly in Egypt, because of its dry climate. These books are relevant because in the early development of Christianity, there were various, significantly, different interpretations or opinions about Christ and his messages. The most recent discovery was startling. This was a gnostic gospel not included in the books found at Nag Hammadi.

This most unusual manuscript, the *Gospel of Judas*, was found in the 1970's in an Egyptian desert cave.[27] Because of many complications explained in National Geographic's sponsored book *The Lost Gospel*, the text of this gospel was not published until 2006. The last disciple of Jesus whom one might expect to have had a gospel named after him would be the betrayer, Judas. Could this gospel not just be a later work or a hoax? The new evidence is astonishing. Radiocarbon dating by the University of Arizona yielded a time frame for this gospel between 220 C.E and 340 C.E.[28] This could be the oldest known of nearly complete ancient Christian manuscripts yet found, but the importance of its find extends beyond its dating and the book itself.

Importantly, easily overlooked, three other books were discovered along with the discovery of the *Gospel of Judas*. Two of these three books also were found_in the codices of Nag Hammadi, which affirm that these books were not singular works and underline the fact of there being more early Christian writings than normally assumed. These two books were *First Apocalypse of James* (a version of the one in Nag Hammadi) and *Letter of Peter to Philip*. The third book, not a part of the cache of Nag Hammadi, and a previously unknown manuscript, was included and given the name the *Book of Allogenes* (Allogenes means Stranger).[29]

Why the *Gospel of Judas* and the *Book of Allogenes* were not included among the books found at Nag Hammadi is unknown. What is known is that Bishop Irenaeus of Gaul mentioned in an early church document, written around 190 C.E., underscoring its early existence, that there was a book called the *Gospel of Judas*. His comment was that this false, heretical, gospel should not be read![30] Perhaps, a gospel by Judas was too shocking even for those at Nag Hammadi who collected and translated the Gnostic Gospels in Coptic. Quite likely, from Irenaeus' judgment, the early church did not take to this gospel as would become the tradition. However, if the church had allowed this gospel to circulate, it might have been a resourceful and helpful counter-force to the fierce anti-Semitic movement, often led by Christians, because Judas, a Jew from Judea, willfully, turned against Jesus. Although not a part of the Nag Hammadi collection, this gospel, by its early dating and gnostic relationship, should not be overlooked.

In stark contrast to traditional belief, the message from this gospel is that Judas' betrayal was necessary in God's plan and understood by Jesus. Judas turned Jesus over to the high priests, and to the Roman authorities, because Jesus had designated him to do so. As a respected disciple, and as some translations imply, a "favorite," Jesus chose Judas for this difficult task because his spirit was stronger than the rest.[31] Although not without textual problems and debate, this witness is a far cry from the traditional condemnation of Judas as the Jewish betrayer of Jesus. Whether one agrees with the story told in the *Gospel of Judas* is not the main message, because who knows what was the historical truth. Rather, this gospel gives evidence that there were different points of view about Judas in early Christianity. Before the discovery of this gospel, the tradition was strongly set, even though he was an original disciple, that there was nothing good to say about Judas. Now, there is, at least, some room to change or reconsider the totally negative view of Judas.

The fact that all early manuscripts were handwritten, limiting their production, makes any find of these documents remarkable. Certainly, the discovery of new manuscripts of gospels involving the Bible would be eventful and exciting. Finding what is known as Quelle or the "Q" sayings, (Quelle is the German word for source), which is believed to be the common original source for Jesus' teachings in Matthew and Luke, would be monumental. Scholars believe such a document existed because of the similarities of wording in these two gospels, but no manuscript has been found — yet.[32]

All these details may sound academic, but they lead to a revolutionary and expanded view of Jesus and Christianity. The various early manuscripts, which have been found, are astonishing, not only by their discoveries, but by the shock of additional gospels. Unsettlingly to some is that the understanding of Jesus is being extended by writings of other disciples, such as Thomas and Philip. Indeed, these original disciples, in their witness to the power of Jesus, present some details and beliefs in different ways and expose some conflicts over doctrines such as the virgin birth and a bodily resurrection. However, in spite of differing beliefs, the bottom line is that these disciples also shared a deep faith in God because of Jesus. These new gospels also do not diminish Jesus, but hold him high as Savior. Therefore, by their differences of beliefs, they do support that Christians do not have to believe in Jesus in the same way; a belief many Christians accept today.

Beyond this general realization, there is a significant historical and theological message from these gospels. The historical battles over doctrines and beliefs, which would develop intensely, have often overshadowed and misdirected the primary message of God's love preached and taught by Jesus. These new gospels have differing interpretations of beliefs, but their position is that faith is more than accepting unquestionable doctrines, and truth is more than agreeing on certain beliefs. Christian truth isn't a closed case, but an open process of debate as to what is true, because no one has the corner on truth. Arrogantly, claiming exclusive truth is not faith, not love, and not honest. Faith is a spiritual exercise that builds trust and hope; it is a relationship with God beyond specific beliefs. If given the chance to be heard, the insight to be gained by the Gnostics' voice is that the story of Christianity isn't being negated; rather, Christ's power and messages are strengthened by historical voices long silenced and hidden.

The Gnostics' voice was silenced because it tried to assert that doctrines and beliefs were secondary to faith and should be open to change. Although some church fathers implied the Gnostics weren't Christians, in order to raise their own beliefs as the only truths, Gnostics definitely believed in Jesus. Shockingly, in spite of this prejudicial judgment of unbelief, if the truth be known, within their gospels, boldly and without reservation, they often refer to Jesus as "Lord and Savior."[33] Accepting these powerful words, "Lord and Savior," as their affirmation of faith in Christ, may be more insightful than condemning them as false believers and heretics, because they did not believe doctrines, correctly. This condemnation became their fate. According to those in power in the early church, their false beliefs, and their rejection of certain true beliefs, denied them the promised gift of eternal life and heaven. In essence, written off in history as mythical and ridiculous Christians, there is a new intrigue and interest in how they embraced Christian faith, a different way than assumed, and one that may inspire Christians today.

One can read all forty-six Gnostic books (fifty two were included, but six were duplicates) within the thirteen codices.[34] There are now various complete translations, and a host of books, particularly related to the *Gospel of Thomas*, which have been translated separately by several gnostic scholars. The first official edition after the discovery in 1945, edited by James M. Robinson, now with several revisions, is available in a collection titled *The Nag Hammadi Library in English*.[35] In spite of rumors and attacks that these gospels were about an imaginary Jesus, not the real Jesus, the gospels give testimony to a Jesus, who lived, died, and was resurrected. Some argue these early writings should be dismissed as trivial and are not worthy of respect, because they challenge some traditional beliefs, such as the virgin birth, a bodily resurrection, support women as priests, and give some different perspectives on Jesus. Others would say that is precisely why they should be read!

The Nag Hammadi Library, like the Bible, is not an easy read, but these books also give a message of God's love brought to this world by Jesus Christ. These texts, which had lain, silently, waiting to be discovered, speak volumes that the message of Jesus was more than establishing a new religion that would condemn and nullify all other religions as false. For the benefit of Christianity, their voice was that not all had to agree to be Christians followers of Jesus. Now, in spite of the early effort to make Christianity one voice with straightforward and unified beliefs, there is hard evidence that significant interpretations other than those approved by the church existed early in Christianity.

The gnostic voice was silenced, and ironically in its silence, became vilified as ridiculous and promoting a false set or systems of beliefs. Now that their secrets are out, instead of a mysterious, special knowledge hidden from others, there so-called secret faith encourages a perspective that may speak to Christians who want their faith to be beyond belief. Surprisingly, the intent of the Gnostics was more than joining in a battle for correct beliefs because their vision of Christ was beyond establishing dogmas, or a body of doctrines, to explain Christianity. These gospels witness that a deeper spiritual message of Jesus was almost lost forever — until now!

Several years after the discovery near Nag Hammadi, the Dutch professor, Gilles Quispel, sought out Muhammad Ali to inquire about the story he would tell about the books. As Tobias Churton reports in the book *The Gnostics*, Muhammad told Gilles:

> "When I got out from the jail (he was temporarily held), I found my mother had burned a lot of it and the only one which I really sold was for Mr. Raghib.
> I got eleven pounds (Egyptian) for it.
> "Gilles asked, 'Did Muhammad know where the books were now?'
> "'No, I have no idea,' Muhammad answered.
> "Did he have any regrets about the business?
> "Muhammad responded, 'I don't care about it at all.'"[36]

Surely, Jesus would have loved Muhammad! According to the Bible, Jesus honored humble and peasant people. Would not Jesus have been appreciative for him, and for the monks who hid the books and have allowed his voice and message to be heard in more than one narrow way or interpretation?

Notes: Chapter One: New Discoveries of Early Christian Gospels

[1] Elaine Pagels, *Beyond Belief: The Secret Gospel of Thomas*, (New York: Random House, 2003), 29.
[2] For "immoveable truth" see Roberts, Alexander and James Donaldson, Editors, *The Ante-Nicene Fathers*, Irenaeus, *Against Heresies,* Volumes 1-5, (New York: American Reprint of the Edinburgh Edition, Charles Scribners' Sons, 1905), 1:X. Irenaeus in Vol. 1: X writes that "the truth of the church is immoveable." *Against Heresies* will be quoted often. Hereafter, as does Dr. Pagels, Irenaeus' five Volumes of *Against Heresies,* will be noted as *AH.* "Ante-Nicene" means "pre" or before the Nicene Creed and writings; Irenaeus' work was believed to have been written c.a. 190 C.E. For the order to destroy gnostic books, which was issued in 367 C.E., see, Pagels, *Beyond Belief,* 176.
[3] The Gnostics (pronounced 'nos-tiks) were not one particular group, a specific denomination or church, but were a movement within the church much like the Protestants. Therefore, as explained in the Prologue, those labeled Gnostics *will* be capitalized. When used as an **adjective** the term *will not* be capitalized. As with the description, "orthodox Christians," so the description will be "gnostic" or "gnostic Christians."
[4] Marvin Meyer, *The Gnostic Discoveries*, (San Francisco: HarperSanFrancisco, 2005), 15. The Dead Sea Scrolls were found in caves, and there is debate whether the Gnostic Gospels were originally hidden in a cave or buried in an ancient cemetery. See Jean Doresse, *The Secret Books of the Egyptian Gnostics*, (New York: MJK Books, 1986), I, for the cemetery theory which is the least accepted theory.
[5] Elaine Pagels, *The Gnostic Gospels*, (New York: Random House, 1979), XI.
[6] Meyer, *The Gnostic Discoveries,* 36. Dating of when the originals were written is not firm as with the books in the New Testament, but some have argued that the Gospel of Thomas may have been written before the gospels in the New Testament. See, Pagels, *The Gnostic Gospels*, XV.
[7] For translations and discussions on various early manuscripts which are extant but non-canonical see, Bart D. Ehrman, *Lost Scriptures: Books that Did Not Make It into the New Testament*, (Oxford: Oxford University Press, 2003).
[8] Pagels, *The Gnostic Go*spels, XXXVIII.
[9] Although there are more theological writings and books than those called gospels, only five are named gospels, the collective name for all the books is commonly known as the Gnostic Gospels because of Elaine Pagel's first book, *The Gnostic Gospels.*

[10] Pagels, *Beyond Belief*, 97.
[11] Tobias Churton, *The Gnostics*, (New York: Barnes and Noble, 1987), 9.
[12] Churton, *The Gnostics*, 14.
[13] Stephen J. Patterson, Hans-Gebhard Bethge, James M. Robinson, *The Fifth Gospel*, (London, T&T Clark, 2011), 68.
[14] Churton, *The Gnostics*, 14.
[15] Ibid.
[16] Pagels, *The Gnostic Gospels*, XIII.
[17] Patterson, Bethge, Robinson, *The Fifth Gospel*, 73. Churton, *The Gnostics*, 15.
[18] Stephan A. Hoeller , *Jung and the Lost Gospels*, (Wheaton Illinois: Quest Books, 1989), 21.
[19] Churton, *The Gnostics*, 15.
[20] Martin Buber, the Jewish theologian, called Jung a Gnostic, which he personally refuted. Richard Smoley in *Forbidden Faith*, (San Francisco: Harper/San Francisco, 2006), 162, writes that in a letter to a friend Jung writes, "I will send you an offprint of my answer to Buber, who has called me a Gnostic. He does not understand psychic reality."
[21] Churton, *The Gnostics*, 14.
[22] Pagels, *The Gnostic Gospels*, XIII
[23] Bart Ehrman, *The New Testament*, (Oxford: Oxford University Press, 2008), 13.
[24] Ed M. van der Maas, Editor, *Halley's Bible Handbook*, (Grand Rapids, Michigan: Zondervan, Revised 2000), 1077.
[25] Ibid.
[26] Ibid.
[27] Herbert Krosney, *The Lost Gospel*, (Washington, D.C.: National Geographic Society, 2006), I.
[28] Krosney, *The Lost Gospel*, 273.
[29] Marvin Meyer, *The Gospel of Judas: On a Night with Judas Iscariot*, (Eugene, Oregon, Cascade Books, 2011), 4. Dr. Meyer points out that now some believe there were possibly five manuscripts within what is now known as Codex Tchacos. On the less technical side, this book ends with a delightful Readers' Theatre Epilogue, about this gospel and Judas.
[30] Irenaeus, *AH*, 2:20.
[31] Elaine Pagels and Karen King, *Reading Judas*, (New York: Viking, 2007), XXIV. With new pages of the *Gospel of Judas* discovered and translated by Marvin Meyer, his remarkable new *The Gospel of Judas* (2011) affirms further this nontraditional view of Judas.
[32] For information on "Q" or Quelle, see Bart D. Ehrman, *The New Testament*, 97.
[33] James M. Robinson, editor, (*The Nag Hammadi Library in English*, hereafter noted as *NHL*, the *Gospel of Mary*, San Francisco: HarperSanFrancisco, 1977), 525. The *Gospel of Mary* is a separate book within this important collection of all the manuscripts found

at Nag Hammadi. The reference here is an example where Mary refers to Jesus as both Lord and Savior, terms found in many of these gospels.

[34] Churton, *The Gnostics*, 12. Tobias Churton has a short, helpful summary of each of the books in the *NHL* and categorizes the books by which Codex they belong. See Churton's Appendix Two, Pg. 169.

[35] In *NHL*, different gnostic scholars give "Introductions" before the translation of each of the books in the collection. In the texts of this book, the reference will be stated most often as *The Nag Hammadi Library*, rather than the full title, *The Nag Hammadi Library in English*. 36.

[36] Churton, *The Gnostics*, 11.

Chapter Two

The Shock of Other Gospels

> It is not possible that there can be either more or fewer than four (gospels), for just as there are four regions of the universe, and four principal winds, the church itself requires only four pillars.[1]
>
> -Bishop Irenaeus of Gaul

Muhammad's innocent uncovering of these hidden gospels, which had been condemned by the church, brings evidence that early Christianity was not as unified in its beliefs as often assumed. Surprisingly, the Gnostic Gospels reveal that even the closest disciples and apostles of Jesus differed with each other over various beliefs.[2] The Gnostics, given this name by the church, were not disturbed over these differences, because their basic conviction was that the meaning of faith preached by Christ was beyond establishing unchallengeable beliefs. For sure, in spite of faith meaning more than blindly accepting doctrines, the Gnostics did have beliefs. Unexpectedly, many of these beliefs agreed with those held by the church, but certainly, there were beliefs that differed. However, the long standing impression that the Gnostics were those who wanted to establish their mythical beliefs as the true beliefs over and against the church is open to reinterpretation with the discovery of the Gnostic Gospels. This new understanding is possible because their gospels assert that all religious truth, even their own, was open to question. Because of this belief, the Gnostics challenged those in power in the church who claimed literally and boldly that they alone possessed the exclusive knowledge and truth of Jesus and God.[3]

Claiming superior knowledge over others about Christ, and insisting that there was only one true way to believe in him, began remarkably early in the development of the Christian Church in the Roman Empire. Priests of the new faith, particularly, those who would be elected bishops, were beginning to build a network of relationships that would bind them together collectively as being one church. This church had no tolerance for differing interpretations of Christ because it believed that it had received from Jesus the true beliefs of Christianity, which included the basic and fundamental doctrines of Christianity. Although there were some variations of beliefs among the bishops, to disagree with core doctrines, such as the virgin birth, a bodily resurrection for believers, and the risen Christ being in heaven judging the salvation for the quick (living) and the dead was unacceptable. All of these were literal facts and truths because these core beliefs came directly from Jesus to the twelve disciples. Especially, the primary beliefs, known as doctrines, had been passed on to those disciples who had been blessed as being apostles, meaning those called to spread his word, like St. Peter and St Paul.[4]

Therefore, the bishops were appalled that there were Christians who would challenge the authority of apostolic beliefs and the ecclesiastical structure of the church. Although the wisdom of there being only four true gospels was just being developed, exemplified in the introductory quotation, it was also alarming to certain bishops, like Bishop Irenaeus, that some Christians were reading gospels that they considered to be unworthy. The supposed danger was that these other gospels might lend support to false beliefs and doctrines not taught by the church.

Furthermore, bishops were disturbed that some would dare understand the creation accounts of the book of Genesis as possibly being allegorical stories. To develop myths from the details of these stories, which the Gnostics did, was unacceptable because what was reported in these ancient accounts was the literal truth. Indeed, they provided the exact details of how God created the earth and humankind. Consequently, the false beliefs and myths of the Gnostics, which were nonconforming to the truths of the church, were given a name by the bishops. The name of these collectively false beliefs and myths was "gnosis," to repeat, a term meaning "knowledge."Importantly, when this term was applied by the bishops to the Gnostics, this word meant their so-called "knowledge of God."[5]

What was the problem with the gnosis of these dissenting Christians? Well, theologically, their knowledge of God, or their gnosis, was erroneous and wrong, according to the church officials. These common folks just didn't understand the true knowledge of God. To add another caveat to the danger of their beliefs, their false gnosis was also mysterious, exclusive, and esoteric. Indeed, with great success, bishops, and those known as apostolic church fathers, eloquently named because of their second and third century theological writings, convinced the world that the gnosis of these so-called Christians meant mystical, special, and secret knowledge.[6] Therefore, these Christians could be classified as a group, and named Gnostics, because, in their challenges to the church's doctrines, they believed that they were the ones who "knew it all." Not so, said the church; they did not have true knowledge of God because of their false and secret gnosis.

With new documents from the Gnostics themselves, this labeling appears to have been a clever way to create the impression that they were a *cult* who believed that they, not the church, possessed the true teachings of Jesus. However, the Gnostic Gospels reveal that these "false" Christians were a movement *within* the church, which did not totally accept the wisdom and authority of bishops.[7] Because these believers went beyond the theological boundaries and doctrines being established by the bishops, they were portrayed as those who didn't believe in a real Jesus, and further, their Christianity was totally mythological. But, the primary reason why the Gnostics should be condemned and ignored was that they believed in their *gnosis* — secret mythical teachings — rather than in Christ, and they embraced a religion called Gnosticism![8] With the find at Nag Hammadi, such common judgments, images, and understandings that had formed about the Gnostics were about to change — radically.

The newly found works reveal that those now referred to as Gnostics believed in gnosis but in a quite different understanding than that of the bishops. With the Gnostics' secrets exposed in the Gnostic Gospels, made known to the world in their own words and works, the primary secret revealed is that gnosis meant something else than a set of doctrines or an exclusive magical path to the spiritual world. For the Gnostics, gnosis was a way of knowing, as the name or word implies, but not as a "knowing" in the sense that the church fathers explained gnosis — as being false beliefs based on mythological stories. In striking contrast to the fathers, in gnostic thinking, gnosis was a "knowing" as in a relationship or as one "knows" another person.[9] This difference may not seem that important, but in spiritual terms for the Gnostics, it was critical in developing one's faith. This gnostic meaning of gnosis will be more closely examined in Chapter Seven, for in spiritual terms, their understanding, especially, meant knowing or relating to the living Christ![10] This understanding of gnosis may appear to be subtle, but the meaning of faith changes dramatically from accepting doctrines "by faith" — to a dynamic spiritual relationship with Christ and God.

Consequently, faith for the Gnostics was foremost an intimate relationship, trusting in a spiritual power and not simply believing a system of beliefs. As Elaine Pagels expresses in the title of her book, the gnostic way of faith was "*Beyond Belief*."[11] Instead of being required to believe certain facts or doctrines about Jesus and God, faith was a not-knowing, in the sense that if we knew for sure, what was the need for faith? Knowledge in the form of beliefs was not the end of faith, but a tool in growing one's faith, or as they state, "to ripen faith."[12] Therefore, beliefs and myths were part of their process of seeking truth, but not final or absolute answers. Knowing God, or by their understanding of gnosis was seeking an honest relationship with not only the living Christ, but as noted in the first chapter, with the one Supreme God, whom they called both Mother and Father, and even more poetically at times, the All.[13]

According to the church hierarchy, this supposedly radical way of understanding Christianity as a spiritual and subjective journey of faith, which did not require one to hold true beliefs, was a misinterpretation of Jesus. Jesus' message was to believe in him and accept the doctrines that he had entrusted to the church through his disciples. There was no need to search for truth beyond the doctrines stated by the church, as faith was foremost "believing" — not "seeking." Now, with the Gnostic Gospels uncovered, rather than just believing another set of doctrines, being a gnostic Christian meant being on a journey of faith with Christ that was led by seeking, honestly and openly, for both truth and God.

To gain an understanding of the Gnostics as being seekers of truth, and being sincere Christians who had a deep faith in Christ, wasn't possible until the discovery at Nag Hammadi. Before then, most scholars and laypersons accepted the notion that they were demented heretics![14] Yes, but who made them so-called heretics? The Gnostics would now say, most likely, if able, not ourselves, but the ruling powers in *the* "church."[15]

"Church" did not mean a reference to various Christian churches in the world as being one or to an extension of the churches that had formed earlier in Asia Minor; church referred to a group of churches within the Roman Empire who were organizing themselves around the growing system of bishops. With Rome as the center of the Empire, these associated churches were not yet fully organized as an institution, but bishops of this church, and especially the Bishop of Rome, were becoming the center of authority and power for these churches. As their number of churches increased throughout the Empire, they were becoming a social and religious network that would describe themselves as the distinctive church body, which alone held the true teachings of Jesus. As this network grew, Elaine Pagels explains that a military style of hierarchy was being established for these churches. This allowed those in the network, by its strength of organization, to claim for themselves, not only the wisdom of Christ, but also the exclusive right and privilege to speak for him.[16]

Dr. Bart Ehrman in *Lost Christianities: The Battle for Scripture and the Faiths We Never Knew*, and in several of his books, argues that this church that was forming should be called "proto-orthodox."[17] Proto-orthodox meant that their beliefs and doctrines, which they were promoting, had not yet been accepted as the official, orthodox position of Christianity. His point of a church that was in the process of being developed is well taken and is an apt description. It is clear that they were presenting themselves as the distinct, orthodox, or true church, quite early in the development of Christianity. Certainly, this was so long before their church would receive the blessing of Constantine. Constantine, of course, in his time, would seal their church and its theology as being the orthodox voice of Christianity. Before Constantine, however, they made strong arguments, in their writings, that their church was the orthodox Christian church, which meant only their church held the true beliefs of Christianity. Why? Their church was the extension of that begun by Christ's apostles!

Because of this connection and relationship to the apostles, they insisted that only their church represented and preserved the true teaching and understanding of Christ and Christianity. They were the extension of the true church established by the apostles. Therefore, quite often, in their writings, the bishops and church fathers identify themselves as the "**apostolic church.**"

For example, the church father, Tertullian explains, "Therefore, the churches, although they are so many and so great, comprise but the one primitive church of the apostles — from which they all spring. In this way they are primitive. And all are apostolic."[18] In other words, the reason for their authority and exclusive truth was because this was the church that developed from the apostles of Jesus. No other church could avow to be truly Christian because the apostles established only one true church.

This claim to being the sole voice of Christianity was in full force by the early second century. Little doubt of their understanding themselves as the one true church is clear when Bishop Irenaeus near the end of the first century makes the remark, "It is a matter of necessity that every church agree with this church."[19] Why must they agree? The church father, Origen, writes, "We cling to the heavenly church of Jesus Christ according to the succession of the apostles."[20]

This succession allowed this church to claim that they held both the correct organization for a church and the true beliefs of Christianity. Why could they also make this claim? Because, as Irenaeus states, "True knowledge is the doctrine of the apostles and the ancient constitution of the church."[21] With this association of bishops and the belief that authority and truth had been granted exclusively to them, the conviction would only build that they were the one Church of Christ. The church father, Cyprian declares, "There is one God. Furthermore, Christ is one, and there is one church."[22] Therefore, the reason they were the one and true church was based on a unifying principle. As Tertullian explains these churches are "all are apostolic." [23]

As a matter of distinction, and to stress their influence on what would become normative or traditional Christianity, in this book, this early, developing church will be referred to as the "**apostolic church**." This is not to refute that they were the "proto-orthodox." Indeed, this church was the "proto" church in Bart Erhman's description. As stated, with Constantine's acceptance of their voice as the prominent form of Christianity, their primary beliefs and church structure would become the "orthodox" model both for the theology and organization of the church.[24] Before Constantine, with the deep conviction that they were the apostles' church, they would claim to be the exclusive voice for understanding the messages of Christ. This church was as aggressive and as bold as many churches today — there are still a few — who claim that only they represent Christ's truth.

Therefore, agreeing with Bart Ehrman about this church becoming the forerunner for establishing Christian beliefs, the adjective "apostolic" church makes it clear *why* they believed they were the orthodox and the distinct church. The term, apostolic church, expresses both the authority and emotion for their claiming ecclesiastical and theological superiority.[25] Adding to his statement above that "true knowledge was the doctrine of the apostles," Irenaeus states that since only their church possessed this knowledge, this made their church the "distinctive manifestation of the body of Christ."[26] Although both terms are descriptive of their church, the argument here is that "apostolic" better explains *why* they were the "proto-orthodox," and *why* they believed they were the distinctive, sole voice of Christian truth.

As innocently as it appears, this declaration of apostolic authority was a major watershed in the closure of other possible understandings and interpretations of Jesus. This argument gave them the right to condemn other forms of Christian interpretation, such as the Ebionites, Marcions, and Gnostics and to declare them all, heretical.[27] The beliefs of the apostolic church about Christ weren't interpretations but were *the* correct facts of Christianity. These facts needed no challenge, and their beliefs, even if questioned, were to be accepted by faith. Indeed, so successful were they in silencing any other possible interpretations, the result was that their beliefs would become the standard or normative way to understand faith and Christianity.

Often overlooked is that this apostolic church would have lasting influences, not solely on that which officially would become the Roman Catholic Church, which it did, but also many later forms of churches which would adopt their orthodoxy. As Bart Erhman accurately attests, "virtually all forms of modern Christianity, whether they acknowledge it or not, go back to one form of Christianity that emerged as victorious from the conflicts of the second and third centuries. This one form of Christianity decided what was the 'correct' Christian perspective."[28]

Referring to this early church simply as the "catholic church," as opposed to the Roman Catholic Church, would be fair, as well. Catholic, of course, is a word that means universal, but the precise reason they could claim they were the church for all, was their dependence on the apostles. Certainly, this apostolic church was to become the Roman Catholic Church. By its succession of Popes back to St. Peter, the Roman Church can claim its direct heritage to it, more than other Christian churches.[29] Of some significance, early in its formation of being the true church, it should be known that along with the word, "catholic," the words, "apostolic," and "orthodox" also were often used by early church bishop to describe their church.[30]

Clearly, catholic with a capital "C" would win out as its official name. Before the word "catholic" became a noun, it was an adjective meaning universal. For example, an early apostolic father, Ignatius, wrote, "Wherever the bishop appears, let the congregations be there also. Just as, wherever Jesus Christ is, there is the catholic church."[31] In a manuscript named the *Martyrdom of Polycarp*, it reports, "Our Lord Jesus Christ is the Savior of our souls, the Governor of our bodies, and the Shepherd of the holy, and the catholic church in every place."[32] Slowly, the word catholic, meaning universal, was becoming a noun, as illustrated when Bishop Irenaeus stated this about his church, "The Truth is to be Found Nowhere but in the Catholic Church, the sole Depository of Apostolic Doctrine."[33] Therefore, this apostolic church also could be known as the *early* Roman Catholic Church, but as will be seen, its influence was not limited to the Roman Church alone. Many other churches would accept the beliefs of this apostolic church as their own.

Therefore, this early church then could be referred to as "catholic," or "primitive," or "proto-orthodox," or even as the early "Roman Catholic Church," but that wasn't its official name yet. Whichever description one prefers, the true power of this church, which was calling itself the distinctive body of Christ, rested in its conviction that it alone held the beliefs of Jesus and his apostles. Without an official name, but because their church was that of the apostles, they then had the right to correct all other Christian perspectives like those of the Gnostics. As Tertullian perhaps best expresses it, "let all the heresies offer their proof as how they consider themselves to be apostolic."[34]

Supposedly, because the Gnostics couldn't prove they were apostolic, although they revered gospels by the apostles, Thomas, Philip, and Mary Magdalene, it would appear that there was a real division between those in the apostolic church and those deemed Gnostics. Beyond the shock of gospels by other disciples of Jesus, another new understanding related to these gospels is that they were not the teachings of a private or secret cult or church that believed in a religion called Gnosticism. Because the fathers taught the Gnostics were against the church, and even promoted a false religion, their assumed division could appear to be obvious. Now, with further research, the landscape for the division of the Gnostics and the apostolic church becomes gray. In this case, "gray" means that their divide was not as distinct as has been assumed. Gnostics, at least at first, were a part of the apostolic church.

If one has been under the impression that the Gnostics and apostolic church were two groups vying for power, don't feel alone. Indeed, without the new information from Nag Hammadi, this indictment that the Gnostics were a cult and a dangerous threat to Christianity was a fairly common assessment, particularly, in the past, but remains so even in modern times.

One of the best examples of the Gnostics being eccentric, and even against Christianity, is in a description by Paul Johnson in his 1976 book *A History of Christianity*. He explains:

> Certainly gnostic sects were spreading at the same time as Christian ones. Gnostics had two central preoccupations: belief in a dual world of good and evil and belief in the existence of a secret code of truth. Gnosticism is a 'knowledge' religion — that is what the word means — which claims to have an explanation of life. Thus it was, and indeed still is a spiritual parasite.... Then he adds, Paul fought against Gnosticism, recognizing that it might cannibalize Christianity and destroy it. [35]

No wonder that the Gnostics and the apostolic church would be understood as two distinct groups or churches in the early Christian community. Now, there are formidable challenges to the judgment that the Gnostics were just another sect that wanted to destroy Christianity. In fact, an entirely different view is emerging.

As noted in the Prologue, several gnostic scholars including Elaine Pagels and Marvin Meyer do not capitalize the word "gnostic" as a noun. Why? To do so tends to extend the impression that they were one church against another. J. Michael Matkin in *The Gnostic Gospels: A Layperson's Guide* makes it clear why in his book he does not capitalize the words, "gnostic" or "orthodox." He explains, "This is to prevent us from simply seeing these two sides as two distinct camps in the early Christian community."[36]

The common assumption has been that the Gnostics were separatists or a distinct group who rallied against the church. The relationship was much more complex. Therefore, referring to the early church as the apostolic church also comes with the new understanding that they and the Gnostics were not two different churches or groups vying for power. As Karen King of Harvard remarks,

> Early Christian literature does not divide neatly into orthodox and heretical camps; there are unexpected overlaps and surprising similarities, and crucial points of difference are not always where we expect them to be. As a result, scholars have come to realize that the diverse forms of early Christianity were much more entangled than previously thought.[37]

This entanglement is verified, as mentioned earlier, in a rather startling realization that at least some Gnostics, if not most, were members or participants in the church.[38] Rather than a separate organization, the church father Irenaeus writes about the Gnostics, underlining their participation in the church, "They ask, when they confess the same things, and participate in the same worship...."[39] What the Gnostics were asking is not made clear by Irenaeus, but it seems that whatever they asked was not pleasing, as he writes in the same passage, "we call them heretics." [40]

Heretics — being a part of the Church? Oh no! Of course, they must be weeded out. Those who would separate truth from falsehood were the bishops who were supposedly more informed and closer to God. Therefore, another name that could be used to identify this church could be as Tertullian, a layman, once described it as the "Church of the Bishops."[41] Certainly, whether fully formed or not as an institutional church, the right to call those who disagreed with them as "heretics" began quite early and in earnest.[42] Although there were various dissenting voices to their insistence on exclusive truth, in the early development of the church, the Gnostics were considered by the fathers to be the most *vile* heretics.[43]

Vile heretics? Yes! Beyond the Gnostics being closely associated with the church, a threat within, and not just a fringe group, a primary reason for their classification as misinformed heretics was that these Christians were accepting gospels other than the four favored by the Church. In addition to his so called "scientific" reason that there were four regions and four winds in the universe, which was the basis for their being four pillars for the church, Bishop Irenaeus also would declare, emphatically, in *Against Heresies*, "The Gospels are Four in Number, neither More nor Less."[44] What is now known is that the condemnation of gospels than those chosen as holy by early church bishops was so thorough that other early gospels became not only lost, but, essentially, unknown. Because the truth was established by the apostolic church that all other gospels were worthless and were written by heretical, false Christians, any conception that they could contain any truth about Jesus, or the Christian faith, was considered all but a closed case in the history of Christianity.

Of importance, the Nag Hammadi discovery was not the first indication that there might be gospels, other than those chosen as holy by the Church, which were respected by early Christians. At first, as fragments of some of these other gospels were being discovery, one might think that these clues of other gospels might be seen as exciting or helpful in illuminating the story of Christ. However, with the entrenched truth that there were only four gospels that were authentic, such a possibility was a threat to a basic foundation of Christianity — that only the gospels of Matthew, Mark, Luke, and John told the true story of Jesus. In addition, some of the early findings seemed to give support to the classical perception that these gospels did not present Jesus as a real person and that the Gnostics were totally mythical and imaginative. The assumption was that these false and ridiculous Gnostic Gospels need not be taken seriously.[45]

Slowly, however, some of the manuscripts began to reveal that there was more to the story of Jesus and his messages than what had been assumed. Beneath the rubble of so-called absolute truths, hints of a wider message of Jesus were beginning to rise with translations of partial pieces of Greek, Latin, and Egyptian Christian texts. Then, there came the discovery of not just fragments or sections of these gospels, but a library of books with the find at Nag Hammadi. The first shock was that the existence of other gospels was not only a possibility, but, now there was hard evidence of these being the so-called heretical gospels that had been ordered destroyed by the church in the Fourth Century.[46] The second shock was that when these gospels were translated, their contents would reopen the closed case that the apostolic church, and only their favored gospels, possessed the exclusive truths of Christ and Christianity.

Shock is the first stage of disbelief, but as reality settles in and is enforced with solid evidence, truth becomes more than authority. As Aristotle once said about his teacher/mentor, "Plato is my friend, but truth my greater friend."[47] Likewise with Christianity, the newly known gospels do not dismiss Christian truths or the truth of Christ but do support a wider meaning of Christian truth. More than just allowing one to be Christian, while rejecting such traditional doctrines as the virgin birth or bodily resurrection, the Gnostic Gospels recapture that faith is not about believing certain doctrines. Rather, faith is about seeking and loving God through Christ, and as the Gospel of Matthew teaches, with our hearts, souls, and minds.[48]

Beyond the shock of other gospels and realizing that they are not a threat to the foundation of Christianity, there are emotional, logical, and religious obstacles that will be encountered as some traditions are questioned. Professors of Religious Studies, Tom and Barbara Boyd of the University of Oklahoma, have expressed these challenges as being "hurdles" that these new gospels face in order for them to be accepted as instructive and helpful for Christianity. There are several hurdles.

For example, many have hardly heard of these gospels. Others are reluctant to accept that gospels beyond those in the Bible could have existed. Some want to believe that they have nothing to do with Christianity, and even before reading them, accept the earlier churches' judgment that they are false. Many on the basis of historical rumors will assume that they are totally mythical tales. A common mistake is to confuse them with the Dead Sea Scrolls and not realize that these gospels are as significant, if not more to Christianity. Emotionally, bound by certain beliefs and doctrines, some aren't open to change and don't believe anything new could be added to Christianity. Others are reluctant because they think that these gospels are about encouraging persons to leave their current churches and joining another. Some will say these gospels have nothing to say simply because they are not in the Bible. Therefore, they are not relevant for today's Christianity. These "hurdles" are understandably part of the old story of the Gnostic Gospels, which were ordered destroyed in order to silence Christian' voices, that said there was more than one way to believe and be authentic Christians. Now, with actuality of the new gospels being able to speak for themselves, there is a new story.

Instead of impairing the foundations of Christianity, as the first responses to the Gnostics and their gospels assumed, the Gnostic Gospels bring new light upon the reasons of prejudice and misinformation for the Gnostics. More importantly, they reveal why many celebrate these new gospels because they change some beliefs and perspectives that just don't make sense today. As they amplify the messages and meaning of Christ, and expand on many of the themes and beliefs in the Bible, they bring fresh air and a wider message to the truth of Christianity. Many new positive understandings of Christ, unexpected from these so-called radically minded heretics, will be presented in subsequent chapters as they bring new perspectives on the meaning of faith. Such a positive response is now growing; yet, understanding the history before Nag Hammadi is helpful and insightful in understanding why the Gnostics and their gospels were long considered heretical and mythical Christians.

With the amazing discovery at Nag Hammadi, now, whether they are appreciated or not, the fact is that there are other gospels, not only the foundational ones in the Bible, which sing praise to the Lord. Their song is new to modern ears, but their ancient voice brings a hymn of freedom. Messages of Christ, long hidden in the sands of Egypt, expound his love for all; they encourage all to awaken to the Spirit of God both within and around them. They teach not a hidden and mysterious secret but encourage persons to know (gnosis) Jesus as a friend. By seeking honestly and openly, not declaring full knowledge of everything, faith grows and is ripen by all the knowledge in the world. Christians become those who do not have the corner on truth but seek and worship God because of Christ. Able to speak and sing for themselves, these Gnostic Gospels add to the depth and love of God found in the Bible.

Notes: Chapter Two: The Shock of Other Gospels

[1] Irenaeus, *Against Heresies*, (See details in Chapter One Notes) hereafter noted as *AH*, Vol. 1: IX. Also can be found on the internet at The Gnostic Society Library or Early Church Documents.

[2] Elaine Pagels and Karen L. King, *Reading Judas*, (New York: Viking, 2007), 22

[3] Irenaeus, *AH*, Preface and Vol. 3: XXIV.

[4] Irenaeus, *AH*, Vol. 3: III.

[5] J. Michael Matkin, *The Gnostic Gospels,* (New York: Alpha Books, 2005), 13.
[6] Elaine Pagels, *Beyond Belief,* (New York: Random House: 2003),32.
[7] Pagels, *The Gnostic Gospels*, (New York: Random House, 1979), XIX. The Gnostics being a part of the church will be documented further as the book develops.
[8] Pagels, *Beyond Belief,* 32.
[9] Matkin, *The Gnostic Gospels*, 13.
[10] Pagels, *Beyond Belief,* 32.
[11] Pagels, *Beyond Belief,* title of the book.
[12] James M. Robinson, Editor, *The Nag Hammadi Library In English*, hereafter referred to as *NHL*, HarperSanFrancisco: 1978), *Gospel of Philip*, 156.
[13] Robinson, *NHL*, *Gospel of Thomas*, 135.
[14] Marvin Meyer, *The Gnostic Discoveries*, (HarperSanFrancisco: 2005), 2.
[15] Irenaeus, *NHL*, Vol. 3:XXIV where he refers to the "Uniform Teaching of the Church," but also the terminology the church is often used.
[16] Pagels, *The Gnostic Gospels*, 179. Also, Tape Interview by Future Primitive, Oct. 2009.
[17] Bart D. Ehrman, *Lost Christianities,* (Oxford: Oxford University Press, 2003), 13. I have chosen to use the term, "apostolic church" to clearly identify this early church which set itself apart as being the one form of church which Jesus wanted and would bless. At some point, but without an exact time table, the proto-orthodox did become the Orthodox and were the major forerunner of what would be known as the Roman Catholic Church.
[18] David W. Bercot, Editor, *A Dictionary of Early Christian Beliefs*, (Peabody, Massachusetts: Hendrickson Publishers, Inc., 2008), 148.
[19] Irenaeus, *NHL*, Vol. 3: III.
[20] Bercot, *A Dictionary of Early Christian Beliefs*, 32.
[21] Bercot, *A Dictionary of Early Christian Beliefs*, 31.
[22] Bercot, *A Dictionary of Early Christian Beliefs*, 149.
[23] Bercot, *A Dictionary of Early Christian Beliefs*, 148.
[24] Ehrman, *Lost Christianities*, 250.
[25] Bercot, *Dictionary of Early Christian Beliefs*, 29. Tertullian states, "the doctrine which comes down from the apostles is that which has been kept as a sacred deposit in the churches of the apostles."
[26] Bercot, *A Dictionary of Early Christian Beliefs*, 31.
[27] Bart D. Ehrman, *The New Testament*, (New York: Oxford University Press, 2008), see the Glossary of Terms for descriptions of these groups, 501.
[28] Ehrman, *Lost Christianities*, 4.
[29] Irenaeus, *NHL*, Vol. 3:III.
[30] Williston Walker, *A History of the Christian Church*, (New York: Charles Scribner's and Sons, 1959), 57.
[31] Bercot, *Dictionary of Early Christian Beliefs*, 146.
[32] Ibid.

[33] Irenaeus, *NHL*, Vol. 3: XXIV.
[34] Ehrman, *Lost Christianities*, 4.
[35] Paul Johnson, *A History of Christianity*, (New York: Simon & Schuster, 1976, 45.
[36] Matkin, *The Gnostic Gospels*, 10. Despite this book's full title, *The Complete Idiots Guide to The Gnostic Gospels*, it is a helpful resource!
[37] Karen King, *What is Gnosticism*, (Cambridge, Massachusetts: Harvard University Press, 2000), 152.
[38] Pagels, *The Gnostic Gospels*, 39.
[39] Irenaeus, *AH*, Vol. 3: II:15.
[40] Ibid.
[41] Pagels, *The Gnostic Gospels*, 132. (Tertullian, De Pudicitia, 21)
[42] Irenaeus, *AH*, Vol. 2: XXXII.
[43] Meyer, *The Gnostic Discoveries*, 2.
[44] Irenaeus, *AH*, Vol. 3: IX.
[45] Pagels, *Beyond Belief*, 32.
[46] Pagels, *The Gnostic Gospels*, 145.
[47] Quoted by James Cleick, *Isaac Newton*, (New York: Vintage Books, 2003), 26.
[48] Bible, R.S.V., Matthew 22:37.

Chapter Three

The Rise of the Gnostic Gospels

> It's the same with the Christians (so called). They are so busy condemning themselves and others, or preaching at people, or worse, killing for Christ. None of them (sic) understanding, or trying in the least to behave like a Christ. It seems to me the only true Christians were (are) the Gnostics, who believe in self-knowledge, i.e., becoming Christ themselves, reaching the Christ within. The light is the Truth. All any of us are trying to do is precisely that: Turn on the Light.[1]
>
> -John Lennon, *Skywriting by Word of Mouth*

The rise of the Gnostic Gospels continues to intrigue not only those who have left or dismissed their particular church's improbable beliefs and strict teachings, but those who believe Christianity can find a less self-righteous stance and a more ecumenical style of faith. Many have now heard of these different gospels, and in spite of many books on the subject, and particularly, the *Gospel of Thomas,* most only have a cursory knowledge of the Gnostics.

Although made rather innocently, John Lennon's remarks in the introductory quotation describing the Gnostics as those "…who believe in self-knowledge, ie., becoming Christ themselves, reaching the Christ within" are quite on target in summarizing some of the new perspectives that were unknown before Nag Hammadi.[2] His remarks to his wife, Yoko, in *Skywriting by Word of Mouth,* written in 1978, give strong support for the Gnostics and may add some reason for a renewed interest. Lennon's view of Christianity is a bit harsh, but it reflects how a fair number of people are upset with some forms of Christianity, and also other religions, that have aided hatred, killing, and violence. To see Jesus condoning any of these acts or attitudes grates against what he taught. However, as Lennon suggests, Christianity has been a participant in this madness, contrary to the one whom some have called the Prince of Peace. In spite of this insight, John Lennon's opinion, "It seems to me the only true Christians were (are) the Gnostics," this sort of special status for these folks won't help either.[3] Insisting on one's way as the only true way has been a factor leading to religious violence. For everyone to become Gnostics isn't an answer, in spite of Lennon's comments. As Karen Armstrong documents in her book *The Battle for God*, for any group or church to claim that they are the only true Christians only will cause harsh religious conflict to continue.[4]

In this light, the new knowledge from the Gnostic Gospels is that the Gnostics were, contrary to previous images, a movement that stood against religious arrogance and exclusive authority. Indeed, one reason their voice is drawing serious attention is because faith for them, as revealed in their writings, was more of a spiritual journey than a battle of beliefs. Of course, the impression was successfully established that the Gnostics were a group who thought their knowledge of God was greater than others because of their strange beliefs. However, both the review of history, and particularly, the Gnostic Gospels, bring information that this claim of superiority was not true as a whole. Some Gnostics did believe they were the "chosen," a term also claimed at times by Jews, and later by some Christians, and many other groups who have been convinced that they possess the corner on religious truth. Particularly, the Sethians, one school or branch of the Gnostics, claimed to be the exclusive seed or race chosen by God, interestingly, allowing Jews and Christians to obtain salvation because both were descendants of Seth.[5] Thankfully, such privileged status was not claimed exclusively by all the Gnostics, and in spite of the apostolic fathers portraying gnostic theology as totally elitist, false, and heretical, a new perception and understanding is emerging.

This revised understanding is because these new gospels clarify gnostic positions. They correct many misconceptions long embedded before these hidden gospels could speak above rumors, inaccurate historical accusations, and hearsay. Helping to understand why and how the Gnostics were assumed to be irrelevant and totally mythical Christians comes to light by reviewing some of the historical literature associated with them. In light of the Gnostic Gospels, ironically, these literary resources now, significantly, help to alter the preconceived story of the Gnostics.

Because the church fathers had mentioned several gospels as being false, their existence in antiquity was thought possible, but the first modern clue that writings considered gnostic could be extant began with discoveries of books in the Eighteenth Century. These manuscripts are now known to have been written much later than those found in the *Nag Hammadi Library*, but at the time that they were translated, they were considered to be not only gnostic but also represented Gnosticism's mythical essence.[6] These discoveries were not encouraging, nor helpful in supporting the image and understanding of the Gnostics, nor any of their possible gospels, as they are quite mythical and outlandish in the stories they tell. Therefore, not all the blame for a misunderstanding of the Gnostics can be on the early bishops. The claims of apostasy by the bishops were extended and exaggerated after their time in these later manuscripts. Clearly, they have some relationship to the earlier gnostic myths, yet, at the time of their translation, they reinforced the perception of the Gnostics as not having any truth for the understanding of Christ and Christianity.

The first known fragment, of what was considered to be gnostic literature, is attributed to a Scotsman named, James Bruce.[7] In 1769, while traveling in Egypt, he purchased an ancient Coptic manuscript. Not published until 1892, or one hundred twenty three years later, the *Bruce Codex* as it is known, is closely related to Sethian mythology. However, it is now believed to have been written in the fifth century C.E., or a century later than the books of *The Nag Hammadi Library.*[8] This codex of seventy-eight pages contains a section called "Great Treatise according to the Mystery." The book begins with a conversation that Jesus has with his disciples. As the story progresses, Jesus travels with the disciples who possess sixty treasures. Hymns and prayers are included, and Jesus teaches revelations that are called the "Treasury of the Light."[9] One of the teachings describes how sins are released from a man turning his soul into pure light. This purity brings forth the Three Amens, the Triple-Powers, the Five Trees, and the Seven Voices.[10] Was this mythology or what? An important aspect was that these revelations from Jesus were also called secret teachings! From the wild tales within the *Bruce Codex*, one can understand what was to be called Gnosticism was believed to have been a secret and strange religion. Unfortunately, this was only the beginning of so-called gnostic sources, and why the Gnostics were not just considered heretics, but extremists!

The next important find, supposedly, giving evidence of the Gnostics being left of center, was a popular manuscript, eventually banned by the Church, named *Pistis Sophia* or in translation as *Faith Wisdom.*[11] Much more widely known than the *Bruce Codex*, this document was purchased in London, in 1772, by a physician, Dr. A. Askew, who was a collector of old manuscripts.[12] *Pistis Sophia*, containing three hundred fifty six pages, was catalogued officially as the *Codex Askewianus* by the British Museum, where it is still housed today.[13]

Considered to have been written around the same time as the *Bruce Codex*, the book tells how the aeon, Pistis Sophia, fell from her high position in the heavens and was redeemed by her repentance. Jesus returns to earth, stated as being sometime during the first eleven years after his resurrection, and instructs his disciples in the "Treasury of Light" and other secret mysteries.[14] Perhaps, these writers knew or had heard of the *Gospel of Mary;* the book raises the status of Mary Magdalene because she has several serious, personal conversations with Jesus.[15]

Pistis Sophia was not published in English until 1896, or one hundred twenty four years after its discovery by a notable British scholar, G. R. S. Mead. Of some significance, he was later was to have a friendship with the psychiatrist, Dr. Carl Jung.[16] This intriguing manuscript clearly extends beyond the tales of some of the books of the *Nag Hammadi Library*. Because the enhanced stories of Jesus are clearly fictional and mythical within *Pistis Sophia*, it is no wonder the Gnostics were considered by those of this century as ridiculous Christians. Up to this point with these two documents, the *Bruce Codex* and *Pistis Sophia* considered gnostic discoveries, there was little reason to believe otherwise.

A milestone, not truly at the time of the discovery, but an indication that maybe there be more to the Gnostics than mythology, began in the 1890's when pieces of a *Gospel of Thomas* were found.[17] The pieces were written in Greek, and that was significant, because it is believed that the earliest gospels in the Bible were written in this language. Unfortunately, there were just three differing pages of Thomas' gospel, and they were fragmentary. The fragments were found in an old rubbish dump in an Egyptian town named Oxyrhynchus (modern day Bahnasa), where fragments of some of the Nag Hammadi books have been discovered, as well.[18] Before Nag Hammadi, these fragments could not be confirmed as belonging to the *Gospel of Thomas*, but when compared, although there were some variations, there would be startling evidence that these very early pieces were extant excerpts from Thomas's gospel. The opening line of the Greek, *Gospel of Thomas*, has been translated and was nearly identical with the first line in the Nag Hammadi's *Gospel of Thomas.*[19] The Greek Gospel is dated around 200 C.E., making it much older than the Gospel found at Nag Hammadi, helping to affirm the Thomas gospel's early circulation. The Coptic *Gospel of Thomas* is now, of course, at the Coptic Museum in Cairo. The pages of the Greek Thomas gospel are catalogued as Oxyrhynchus 645 and housed at the British Library in London.[20]

In 1896, another major step was taken in understanding the earlier Gnostics by their own writings. A German scholar, Dr. Carl Reinhardt, purchased a Coptic manuscript that contained parts of the *Gospel of Mary Magdalene.*[21] This had to be a shock! Taken to a museum in Berlin, this manuscript became known as *Berlin Gnostic Codex 8502.* As it turned out, this codex also contained parts or segments of four of the books found at Nag Hammadi. For some unknown reason, only the *Act of Peter* was translated and published in German in 1903.[22] Not until 1955 were the other three books published — also in German. These published books were the *Gospel of Mary* (Magdalene), *The Secret Book of John*, and *The Wisdom of Jesus Christ.*[23] What's the significance? As with the three books, found along with the *Gospel of Judas*, they were duplicates of Nag Hammadi books. These additional four books give further evidence that the newly found books were not singular creations and were more widely distributed than most had assumed.

Slowly, something was beginning to change the gnostic landscape. Original gnostic sources were being discovered, and from these little known manuscripts, scholars were beginning to wonder if there might be more information and knowledge about these heretics beyond hearsay and their negative tradition. Once again, in front of a more positive understanding of the Gnostics, there would be another major maze.

An assumption was developing that the Gnostics were those who embraced a false "religion" called Gnosticism, which seemed pretty straightforward. However, now, there is a serious question whether at the time of the earliest Gnostics that their so called religion existed at all. Certainly understandable is why the Gnostics were seen as embracing a different religion, or at best, a corrupt form of Christianity, but Karen King in her book *What is Gnosticism?* argues that the term is a *later* creation imposed on the Gnostics. As will be expanded upon in Chapter Five, King's research indicates that the first use of the term, Gnosticism, was by a Protestant in 1669 C.E. to condemn and vilify Catholics as being idolatrous Gnostics.[24] Wow! Now the Catholics were heretics! Gnosticism and Gnostics were not very pretty terms, and Karen proposes that these labels were placed on them in order to categorize and characterize them, and particularly, to set them apart from normative Christianity.[25] She leaves little unturned when she states that Gnosticism has been used to mark "the erroneous, the heretical, the schismatic, as well as all things threatening, anomalous, esoteric, and arcane."[26] Karen's position is also argued in Michael Allen Williams *Rethinking Gnosticism; An Argument for Dismantling a Dubious Category*.[27] Both scholars argue that there was *not* an early religion called Gnosticism. Rather, by classifying some of their beliefs as a religion, and classifying it as false, allowed gnostic thoughts to be written off and unworthy of serious consideration.

In addition, there developed another tradition of identifying gnostic beliefs with other religions and philosophies, which has confused the issue of Gnosticism even further. For example, as interest in the Gnostics has risen, some have tried to identify the Gnostics with ancient Greek philosophies, Jewish mysticism – particularly the doctrine of Kabbalah, the Manichaeans or followers of Mani in Iran, the Cathers of France, the Rosicrucians of Germany, Zoroasterism of ancient Persia, and now those known as Parsis in India.[28] With such a plethora of connections, one might say most anything that appeared as an offbeat religion and had an "ism" connected to its name was gnostic or related to Gnosticism!

However, the best that can be said is that all these religions or movements may have been influenced by some of the themes of the Gnostics, indirectly, but not with a direct link, with possibly the exception of the Mani's of Iran.[29] Perhaps inspired by the Gnostics' rebellion against mainstream orthodox thought, it needs to be emphasized that these groups were not the Gnostics of early Christianity. Most of the connections have been to concepts in their myths and to their spirituality. Although these connections have been helpful to popularize the Gnostics, they also, as Karen King suggests, have aided in a tendency to objectify their beliefs as static and final, often not disclosing their dynamic intent.[30] Now, the discovery is being made that more than a set of alternative beliefs that the Gnostics embraced Christian faith as a spiritual journey not bound by rules and unquestionable doctrines.

Sensing that there was a dynamic dimension to the Gnostics, with very limited knowledge, two important scholars in 1934 wrote differing, but unusually popular books on Gnosticism. Eleven years before the Nag Hammadi discovery, Hans Jonas depicted in his book *Gnosis und Spatantiker Geist*, translated later in English, as *The Gnostic Religion*, that Gnosticism was a parallel philosophy to the rising popular philosophy, existentialism.[31] In essence, Jonas depicted Gnosticism as a pessimistic Christian philosophy, or as the existentialists were beginning to assert, that life was absurd, and his position was that the Gnostics understood this. Here, yet again, was an example of trying to impose or imply the tenants of Gnosticism not as religion but as a modern, popular philosophy — or ism.

In contrast, Walter Bauer, in his 1934 book, *Orthodoxy and Heresy in Earliest Christianity* argued that Gnosticism had to be far more diverse in its heresies than the orthodox had presented, and the Gnostics were a part of different forms of Christianity.[32] Not a bad guess! However, the point is that these two books are noted as classics in the rise of the interest in the Gnostics and Gnosticism, but the drawback was the fact that had very little solid information on which to rely.

Then in 1945, the primary sources of the Gnostics ascended, not as a bomb, but as a fissure from the earth, to retell the story of the Gnostics. After the books were collected, an international team of scholars, which included the fore-mentioned Gilles Quispel, began translating the manuscripts.[33] The first book published from the manuscripts was by Jean Doresse in 1958, *The Secret Books of the Egyptian Gnostics.*[34] This book's importance was that it contained a translation of the *Gospel of Thomas*, but it was in French![35] In 1959, a collaboration of scholars published in English *The Gospel of Thomas.*[36] This new gospel did not make an overwhelming impression, and perhaps a reason was the controversy over the Revised Standard Version (RSV) of the Bible, published in 1949, which was still in 1959 in the eye of a Christian storm. How could any Bible replace the King James Version? Of course, for some, it was the only Bible that Jesus would have blessed and that St. Paul would have read! To add another gospel to this mix, particularly from the disciple who was well known as the "doubting Thomas," was too much.[37]

To overlook the Apostle Thomas and the other gnostic writings as superfluous was not the case for Dr. Carl Jung. His lasting contribution to psychology is well known, and his serious interest in the Gnostics is becoming better known. His attraction to the Gnostics, and how he obtained Codex 1, has already been noted, but the "why" of his interest is also an important part of the story in the rise of these gospels' popularity and credibility.

Jung was to be Freud's self appointed, heir apparent, but in 1912 the two parted company because Jung was becoming interested in art, religious symbols, and myths. After this, in 1916, Jung had a significant visionary experience in which he wrote that it was on a Sunday that he heard his doorbell ring, but no one was there; then his whole house became filled with spirits. In unison, as told in a biography, they reported to Jung, "We have come back from Jerusalem where we found not what we sought."[38] The relevance of this statement is that it is the first line in Jung's book *Seven Sermons to the Dead,* which he says was influenced by the Gnostics.[39]

In this book, the story is told by a man named Basilides of Alexandria. Of some interest, Basilides was known as one of the earliest of the gnostic teachers.[40] In his book *Forbidden Faith: The Secret History of Gnosticism*, Richard Smoley gives an explanation to the question, what did the dead fail to find in Jerusalem? Smoley writes, "Maybe it was spiritual experience. Mainstream Christianity has provided much doctrine and ethical guidance, but in offering genuine inner experience to the spiritually dead, it has fallen short."[41]

Of course, this isn't the only way to interpret Jung's vision, but another part of the puzzle of Jung's involvement with the Gnostics is that two books written by Helena Blavatsky (l831-1891), the founder of the Theosophical Society, indirectly aided in Jung's interest.[42] Blavatsky wrote *Isis Unveiled* in 1877.[43] Then in 1888, she wrote, *The Secret Doctrine.*[44] In both of these popular books, she spoke directly about the Gnostics whom she associated with the Jewish Kabbalists.[45] In her first book, referring to the eternal nature of wisdom, she wrote, "If the Gnostics were destroyed, the Gnosis, based on the science of sciences, still lives."[46] In her second book, she stated that "to the disgust of the Church Fathers" followers of gnosis were "taught to think."[47] Now that was a switch!

Related to these theosophical works, the most direct influence on Jung was the scholar mentioned earlier, G. R. S. Mead, who had translated *Pistis*

Sophia into English in 1896. Dr. Mead was an associate of Helena Blavatsky and became the editor of "The Theosophical Review."[48] Why is this significant? Jung had traveled to London to meet personally with Dr. Mead, and in Jung's personal library at the time of his death, there were eighteen books written by Mead, all published by the Theosophical Society.[49]

Jung did not identify himself either as a Theosophist or a Gnostic. However, just his association and interest in them made him open to the charge, particularly, of being a Gnostic. When the highly respected theologian Martin Buber stated that Jung was a Gnostic, Jung sent a strong reply denying it and wrote that Buber simply did not understand psychic reality.[50] The message was straightforward to Buber, and in this sense, Jung is helpful to the purpose of this book, which is not to have people become Gnostics, but as with Jung, to be inspired by the Gnostics' openness to new and different knowledge. For sure, Jung's interest in the Gnostics was far more in their mythology than their Christian witness. Of course, his knowledge of the other codices, beyond his own, was limited. However, Jung's interest and direct relationship to the Gnostics may also be a considerable factor for today's renewed interest. Indeed, now, as the first Nag Hammadi codex is commonly referred to as the Jungian Codex, this only underlies his scholastic and personal interest.

Although Jung was one of the first well known scholars to give the Gnostics serious or positive respect, the interest in the Gnostics has began to reach far beyond Jung's intrigue. This new interest has come like an unexpected storm, in spite of the complicated history. With the firsthand knowledge of their writings, a growing openness to other gospels, and a desire for Christianity to regain its spiritual and inner faith experience, the Gnostics are attracting both academic and popular attention.

This attention, after the discovery at Nag Hammadi, did not happen overnight as storm clouds were present in the genesis of the Gnostic Gospels' revelation to the public. The translation process did not begin in earnest until the 1950's, and like the Dead Sea Scrolls, there were numerous controversies as to the process and ownership of translations. Only after their publication in several languages did the common person have a chance to attempt some understanding of their content and meaning. As the gospels are so new to many, the surprise of their power and implications for Christianity are only beginning to be understood by the common person in the pew. Interestingly, serious study and creation of books about the

Gnostics first came from religious studies programs at leading universities such as Princeton, Harvard, Yale, North Carolina, Claremont, and Chapman – to name a few. Dr. Pagels' *The Gnostic Gospels*, published in 1979, was the first book to attract more than academic interest, and then, particularly, with Dr. Pagel's second book in 2003, *Beyond Belief, the Secret Gospel of Thomas*, which became a national best seller, many churches and study groups became interested.[51]

This interest further widen with the advent of Dan Brown's popular book also published in 2003, *The Da Vinci Code*, in which he quoted several passages from the Gnostic Gospels to support his argument that Mary Magdalene and Jesus were married.[52] Although the passages he quoted don't give definitive proof of that possibility, they have made clear that Mary Magdalene had a gospel attributed to her and was highly respected by Jesus, giving support for women being priests and leaders of the church. Again, the publication of *The Gospel of Judas* by the National Geographic Society in 2006 also caused the creation of a number of books about this controversial gospel and stirred interest in the reality of other gospels.[53]

In a time when many Christians want Christianity to mature beyond simply being a system of beliefs, the excitement of other Christian gospels and gnostic influences are beginning to be felt and appreciated. Gnostic elements have been depicted in works of several well known writers such as William Blake (*The Ancient of Days*), Herman Melville (*Moby Dick*), and other classical writers.[54] More directly, modern authors such as Herman Hesse (*Steppenwolf*), and Harold Bloom *(The Flight to Lucifer: a Gnostic Fantasy*) have created interest in gnostic motifs.[55] Dr. Bloom of Yale has written a chapter titled "A Reading," which is included in *The Gospel of Thomas* by Marvin Meyer of Chapman University.[56] This same commentary on Thomas' Gospel is also found in Bloom's book *Where Shall Wisdom be Found?*[57] Bloom's book begins with the statement, "The popularity of the Gospel of Thomas among Americans is another indication there is indeed the American Religion: creedless, Orphic, enthusiastic, proto-gnostic, post-Christian." [58]

A Jungian analyst, Dr June Singer, has written several books on Gnosticism, a popular example being *A Gnostic Book of Hours.* She is highly respected by The Church of Gnosis and the Theosophical Society.[59] One of their leaders, Dr. Stephen Hoeller, also director of the Gnostic Society of

Los Angeles, has written several books promoting the religion of Gnosticism and Gnostic Churches.[60] Taking an entirely different approach than the Gnostic Society, questioning many aspects of Christianity, are the books, which contain many gnostic references, by Timothy Freke and Peter Gandy, such as their popular *The Jesus Mysteries*.[61]

Other gnostic relationships have been detected in modern media sources. A frequent example is the Matrix Movie Series, inspired by the writings of Philip K. Dick.[62] J. Michael Matkin writes about the Matrix movies, "broadly speaking, gnostic ideas are at the core of the trilogy's view of reality."[63] Matkin adds that Dick's gnostic views have left their marks on movies like *The Truman Show*, *Dark City*, *Vanilla Sky*, and *Pleasantville*.[64] The list of gnostic inspired movies, television shows, comics, cartoons, and music is quite extensive in Meera Lester's book *The Everything Gnostic Gospels*, in the chapter titled "Gnostic Themes and Images in Pop Culture."[65] However, all these so-called gnostic sources from the movies from *Hedwig and the Angry Inch* to Bill Nelson's music album *Chance Encounters in the Garden of Lights* seem more like finding something otherworldliness in them and calling their inspiration, "Gnostic."[66]

More on target than most, one interpreter of such films, and particularly the Matrix series, suggested that the basic gnostic theme implied in these works is "that the world we're living in is not the ultimate reality."[67] Indeed, that is a primary message of the Gnostics, but more than saying that reality is a simple divide between heaven and hell, the gnostic voice is that there is more to reality than a choice between these two future worlds. What is essential is that a spiritual reality can be missed in the world in which we live. As Richard Smolley suggests in his book *Forbidden Faith*, something even in conventional Christianity is missing. He states, "What is missing in Christianity as we know it now is not merely a collection of facts but a connection to some vital inner experience.... And this is what the Gnostic vision holds out to us."[68]

The Gnostics, their gospels, and Gnosticism have become popular subjects, as indicated by thousands of web sites concerning the Gnostics on the internet.[69] Many perspectives can be found in these sites as well, and the good news is that such a tide of interest lifts all ships. In the gnostic perspective, at least in the spirit of the Gnostic Gospels, truth has room for different beliefs and viewpoints.[70] Although the early apostolic church's stance of declaring that only it knew the truth of Christ is challenged in this book, there is room at the table of belief for them. In several of the Nag Hammadi books, as will be seen, some of the basic beliefs of the proto-orthodox and gnostic Christians do overlap and are built from interpretations from common ground. For example, the Gnostics definitely believed in the life, death, and resurrection of Jesus, and, for sure, they had variations on these beliefs, which many will find interesting and agree with their perspectives. More importantly than agreeing or disagreeing over doctrines, such as the virgin birth or bodily resurrection, or other beliefs, the greater reason for the acceptance and popularity of the Gnostics will be because of the way they understood the term "faith."

Somehow or someway, faith has more often than not come to mean what one believes. With the Gnostics the meaning of faith gets a new emphasis and direction. More than an agenda of doctrines and beliefs that must be held, defended, proven, explained, or believed, faith becomes an inner experience that does not have to be the same for all Christians. With the focus on faith being a vital inner spiritual experience, two major elements arise in the gnostic perspective in regards to faith in Christ.

First, faith, both in its subjective and objective nature, can change and should be open to change. Gnosis in the form of new knowledge demands it, and in the form of insight can help our faith to ripen and mature.[71] Secondly, faith is not a set of answers, but by its very nature, a seeking, a continuous process of trust and hope, knowing that our belief is never complete. Faith is seeking the truth, not declaring it!

The lure of the Gnostics is not simply an alternative answer to traditional Christianity, but a confirmation of what many accept today that the message of Jesus was a call to seek honestly, lovingly, and openly the love of God through a relationship with the living and present Christ. As Elaine Pagels writes, "The gnostic understands Christ's message not as offering a set of answers, but as encouragement to engage in the process of searching...."[72]

Had Muhammad Ali-al-Samman not broken open the clay vase, we most likely would not have heard or known about the reality of these gospels. Nor would be known the fact that some early Christians heard the message of Jesus with a depth wider than just believing was the meaning of faith. As Marvin Meyer states, "The gnostic gospels and texts...are providing remarkable ways of understanding Jesus and the beginnings of Christianity, but none would be possible were it not for recent discoveries of papyrus manuscripts buried in the sands of Egypt."[73] Beneath the sand, unknown to the world, these gospels which had been denounced as bogus, heretical, and un-Christian, laid silent, waiting to tell their story. Rising from their Egyptian tomb, and now translated for all to read, these gospels open with a new key, greater insight into the dynamic message of Jesus. Gnosis isn't a new set of beliefs, but a knowing that points to a power within us all, which is hidden until we bring that forth. As Jesus implies in saying #108 in the *Gospel of Thomas*, "those who drink from his mouth will be like him, and he will be one with them, and they will understand what is hidden."[74] What is hidden is not a deep, dark secret but the power of a spiritual relationship with the living Christ.

Thanks to the fourth century monks of Nag Hammadi, whose story will be told, this message of Jesus, which is both old and new, was not suppressed or destroyed. The Gnostics have the power to refresh the way we believe in many Christian doctrines, the Bible, and Jesus. Once the shock of new gospels being a threat to Christianity is surpassed, the radical realization will not be fear, but as one of its gospels teaches, will bring to the Christian faith, joy![75] The Gnostic Gospels and their other books raise questions that have the potential to free Christianity from centuries of simple answers, and for many, unacceptable beliefs. As faith becomes a journey, a process rather than a product, not promoting certain churches or beliefs, the rise of the Gnostic Gospels will continue to gain strength as a way to understand and respond to the message of Jesus.

Notes: Chapter Three: The Rise of the Gnostic Gospels

[1] John Lennon, *Skywriting by Word of Mouth*, (New York: Harper & Row, 1986), 35
[2] Ibid.
[3] Ibid.
[4] Karen Armstrong, *The Battle for God*, (New York: Random House, 2000), X.
[5] A review of Sethian Mythology will be presented in Chapter Seventeen. They believed faith descended from Seth, the third son of Adam and Eve, blessing both Jews and Christians.
[6] Karen King, *What is Gnosticism,* (Cambridge, Massachusetts: Harvard University Press, 2003), 157.
[7] Elaine Pagels and Karen L. King, *Reading Judas*, (New York: Viking, 2007), 2.
[8] Pagels, *The Gnostic Gospels*, (New York: Random House, 1979), XXIV.

[9] Jean Doresse, *The Secret Books of the Egyptian Gnostics*, (New York: MJF Books, 1986, English), 76.
[10] Doresse, *The Secret Books of the Egyptian Gnostics*, 77.
[11] Ibid.
[12] Richard Smoley, *Forbidden Faith*, (San Francisco: HarperSanFrancisco, 2007), 151.
[13] Ibid.
[14] Doresse, *The Secret Books of the Egyptian Gnostics*, 65.
[15] Meera Lester, *The Everything Gnostic Gospels Book*, (Avon, MA: Adams Media, 2007), 87.
[16] Smoley, *Forbidden Faith*, 159.
[17] Marvin Meyer, *The Gospel of Thomas: The Hidden Sayings of Jesus*, (New York: HarperOne, 1992), 4. Also see Stephen J. Patterson, Hans-Gebhard Bethge, James M. Robinson, *The Fifth Gospel*, (London, T & T Clark International, 2011, 26).
[18] Marvin Meyer, *Gnostic Discoveries: The Impact of the Nag Hammadi Library*, (San Francisco: HarperSanFrancisco, 2005), 21.
[19] Meyer, *The Gospel of Thomas*, 4.
[20] Meyer, *The Gospel of Thomas*, 6.
[21] Meyer, *Gnostic Discoveries*, 20.
[22] Ibid.
[23] Ibid.
[24] King, *What is Gnosticism?*, 7.
[25] King, *What is Gnosticism?*, 11.
[26] King, *What is Gnosticism?*, 18.
[27] J. Michael Matkin, *The Gnostic Gospels*, (New York: Alpha Books, 2005), 260. Also, Michael Williams, *Rethinking Gnosticism: An Argument for Dismantling a Dubious Category*, Princeton, NJ: Princeton Press, 1996).
[28] Smoley, *Forbidden Faith*, 53.
[29] King, *What is Gnosticism?*, 5.
[30] King, *What is Gnosticism?*, 16.
[31] Smoley, *Forbidden Faith*, 163.
[32] Pagels, *The Gnostic Gospels*, XXXIII.
[33] Churton, *The Gnostics*, 14.
[34] Dorsee, *The Secret Books of the Egyptian Gnostics*, 65.
[35] Dorsee, Ibid., *Les livres secrets des Gnostiques d'Egypt,* (Paris: Librairies Plon,1958).
[36] Churton, *The Gnostics*, 16
[37] John 20:24
[38] C. G. Jung, *Memories, Dreams, Reflections*, trans. Richard and Clara Winston, (New York, Vintage, 1989), 190-191.
[39] Smoley, Forbidden Faith, 160.
[40] Matkin, *The Gnostic Gospels,* 38.
[41] Smoley, *Forbidden Faith*, 153.
[42] Ibid.

[43] H. P. Blavatsky, *Isis Unveiled: Secrets of the Ancient Wisdom*, ed. Michael Gomes, (Wheaton, IL: Quest, 1925) 136.
[44] H. P. Blavatsky, *The Secret Doctrine,* (Point Loma, CA : Aryan Theosophical Press, 1926), 389.
[45] Smoley, *Forbidden Faith*, 155.
[46] Ibid.
[47] Smoley, *Forbidden Faith*, 156.
[48] Smoley, *Forbidden Faith*, 158.
[49] Smoley, *Forbidden Faith*, 159.
[50] Smoley, *Forbidden Faith*, 162.
[51] David Van Biema, "The Lost Gospels," Time Magazine, December 22, 2003, Pg. 54. The subtitle of this excellent article is "Early texts that never made it into the Bible are suddenly popular. What do they tell us about Christianity today?"
[52] For an excellent discussion of the details and Dan Brown's accuracy see: Barth Ehrman, *Truth and Fiction in The Da Vinci Code*, (Oxford, Oxford University Press, 2004), 95.
[53] Hebert Krosney, *The Lost Gospel: The Quest for the Gospel of Judas Iscariot,* Washington, DC: National Geographic, 2006), 206.
[54] King, Ibid., Pg. 5.
[55] Meera Lester, *The Everything Gnostic Gospels Book,* (Avon, Massachusetts: Adams Media, 2007), 261.
[56] Meyer, *The Gospel of Thomas*, 125.
[57] Harold Bloom, *Where Shall Wisdom Be Found*, (New York: Riverhead Books, 2004), 259.
[58] Ibid.
[59] June Singer, *Gnostic Book of Hours*, (New York: HarperCollins, 1992).
[60] For example, Stephan A. Hoeller, *Jung and the Lost Gospels*, (Wheaton, IL: Quest Books, Theosophical Publishing House, 1989).
[61] Timothy Freke and Peter Gandy, *The Jesus Mysteries: Was the 'Original Jesus" a Pagan God?*, (New York: Three Rivers Press), 1999.
[62] Smoley, *Forbidden Faith*, 187.
[63] Matkin, *The Gnostic Gospels*, 267.
[64] Matkin, *The Gnostic Gospels*, 266.
[65] Lester, *The Everything Gnostic Gospels Book*, 259.
[66] Lester, *The Everything Gnostic Gospels Book*, 260.
[67] National Public Radio Program, Morning Addition, printed report, "The Spiritual Message of The Matrix," May 16, 2003.
[68] Smoley, *Forbidden Faith*, 9.
[69] Google: gnosticschristians.com, or gnosticschristians, for author's web site, which will lead to a host of others. Normally near the top of searches for gnostics, look for / A Different Way to be a Christian.
[70] King, *What is Gnosticism?*, 246.

---

[71] Pagels, *The Gnostic Gospels*, XVIII.
[72] Pagels, *The Gnostic Gospels*, 135.
[73] Meyer, *The Gnostic Gospels of Jesus*, (San Francisco: HarperSanFrancisco, 2005), VII.
[74] Meyer, *The Gnostic Gospels of Jesus*, Pg. 5.
[75] James M. Robinson, *The Nag Hammadi Library*, San Francisco: Harper SanFrancisco, *Gospel of Truth*, 40:1.

Chapter Four

The Gnostic Understanding of Jesus — a Surprise!

> The recent discoveries help us see how hard countless church leaders had to work to create the impression that many of us used to take for granted — that Christianity actually was a single, static, universal system of beliefs. Creating this impression was itself a remarkable achievement — one to which certain fathers of the church were dedicated. [1]
>
> -*Reading Judas* by Elaine Pagels and Karen King

The books that Muhammad and his brothers found beneath the blanket of large stones and soft soil bring a pivotal change in the understanding of early Christianity. Beyond the misconception that Christianity was a straightforward system of beliefs on which nearly everyone agreed, the Gnostic Gospels also have brought new information about the gnostic beliefs about Jesus. Because the primary focus historically had been on the gnostic myths, the expectation from the Gnostic Gospels was that these Christians would have believed that Jesus was only a mythical character. This mythical view enforced the reasoning that any gnostic interpretations of Jesus would not have validity. Their beliefs about Jesus would be simply imaginative, and their Christianity would be just another system of beliefs and clearly heretical.

However, a surprise was in store. These lost gospels bring firsthand information that Gnostics believed in a real Jesus who lived and died on a cross. They also bring new knowledge that they took the wisdom of Thomas, Philip, and Mary as being as valuable as the other disciples for understanding Jesus. They did not dismiss the teachings of Matthew, Mark, Luke, John, and even Paul, but they understood them in a wider vision than the bishops of the apostolic church. Therefore, the Gnostics had some differing beliefs, but they did not have a united system of beliefs, nor myths, as often presented in scenarios of "what the Gnostics believed." They created mythical stories, but their belief in Christ was more than their myths. Even though one would think they would have radically different beliefs than traditional Christianity, surprisingly, their understanding of Christ and the messages they heard from him were in many ways similar, but not as narrow and insistent as the church. The newly found gospels bring indisputable evidence that the Gnostics believed in Christ, and even the church, but not in the way certain leaders of the church said they were supposed to believe!

According to the church fathers, whose writings are dated generally from 100 C.E. to 250 C.E., the beliefs of the apostolic church should be accepted as the literal truth, meaning — they said what they meant and meant what they said — without any room for interpretation. Especially, any metaphorical or allegorical meanings should not be added. The beliefs expounded by the church represented historical actuality and theological reality. Their beliefs were undisputedly the literal truth. With this matter-of-fact approach, their theology has been categorized as literalism, and in this book, these early interpreters of Christianity, which included both bishops and church fathers, will be referred to as literalists.[2]

Most people associate literalism with accepting the words of the Bible as literal truth, but in this period, the age of the church fathers, there was no Bible![3] The books, which were to become the canon of the Bible, had not yet been chosen or formalized. Therefore, this early literalism should be recognized as a literalism of beliefs and doctrines, and not that of the Bible.[4] Interestingly, this literalist theology was expressed first in the apostolic church's early ritual of baptism which included beliefs that should be accepted as facts.

During baptism, according to early records of this young church, converts were asked to confess faith in Jesus, and then to affirm beliefs, including a virgin birth and a bodily resurrection for Jesus and his believers.[5] To be clear, the Gnostics did not have a problem confessing faith in Christ in baptism. However, they had a serious difference regarding the inclusion of several beliefs deemed by the church as necessary to be a

Christian, and particularly, that these beliefs had to be accepted, literally. For example, as far as the virgin birth, they believed that it could be interpreted beyond it being a historical event, but they questioned it as being a doctrine that needed to be believed literally to gain salvation.[6] The Gnostics believed in resurrection, but their opinion was that it would not be a physical, bodily resurrection, but rather a spiritual resurrection.[7] How dangerous, the fathers exclaimed! These Christians were rejecting their baptismal beliefs and the church's theology. To do so would threaten not just the authority and wisdom of the bishops, but the Gnostics' salvation and gift of eternal life.

These two beliefs, concerning the virgin birth and bodily resurrection as unquestionable facts, only scratched the surface of many differences the Gnostics would have with those claiming the exclusive right to explain the details of both Christ and Christianity. Yes, the Gnostics believed in Christ and accepted some of the basic tenants of what is known today as normative or orthodox Christianity, but they also believed that faith was not limited to the literalist interpretation of beliefs. Disagreeing that accepting certain beliefs of the church were necessary to be a Christian, a Gnostic's response to a church father has been stated as, "We too, have accepted the faith you describe, and we have confessed the same things — faith in God, in Jesus Christ, in the virgin birth and the resurrection — when we were baptized. But since that time, following Jesus' injunction to 'seek, and you shall find,' we have been striving to go beyond the church's elementary precepts, hoping to obtain spiritual maturity."[8]

Gnostics were baptized Christians, but baptism for them did not mean as the fathers would teach, accepting on faith the church's beliefs, and in doing so, forever sealing one's salvation.[9] Baptism confirmed their belief in Jesus, but more importantly, this ritual meant the beginning of a journey of faith. Thus, their emphasis after baptism was on one's subjective and spiritual relationship with Christ. Because of this relationship, which was dynamic and not static, beliefs and myths were subject to change, particularly with new knowledge.

Change in one's beliefs? How could that be when certain scriptures and the teachings of the apostles made firm the truth of God? Well, change in beliefs could happen because Christianity was about a relationship with the living Christ and truth. Faith in Christ should be firm and strong, but truth was open to new knowledge. Oh no, said the bishops, truth was unchangeable, and beliefs beyond their teachings were myths.

Certainly, the Gnostics would argue for their myths as expressing truths. Unlike the bishops, whose stories and beliefs were not mythical in any way, according to them, the Gnostics accepted that their mythical stories were open to variations. Their myths were not one story, and they were not presented as the last word of eternal and unchanging truth. Certainly, with today's knowledge, their myths can be questioned, if not dismissed as the literal truth of creation, well when read, not even "if." Of course, this does not exclude the insight that there are deeper messages of wisdom within their myths that may or may not have merit. However, the problem became that these intriguing and imaginative myths of the Gnostics dominated and clouded the understanding of their belief in Jesus. Surely, the Gnostics, if they had any belief in Jesus would be that he was mythical and not real. Therefore, shocking to some, the Nag Hammadi texts brought evidence that they believed Jesus was not only a real person but also a true Savior![10]

When the suppressed gospels were translated, these writings affirm a different story than expected. It was a surprise that that the Gnostics believed Jesus was an actual person of flesh and blood. For example, a book within the Gnostic Gospels called *The Tripartite Tractate* relates, "Not only did he take upon himself the death of those he thought to save... He did so because he had let himself be conceived and born an infant, in body and soul."[11] In the *Gospel of Truth*, the author reports about Jesus' death, that he was "nailed to a tree and slain."[12] Then it says in more poetic terms, "Having stripped himself of the perishable rags, he put on imperishability."[13] As to his being both human and divine, *The Treatise on the Resurrection* asks, "How did the Lord proclaim things while he existed in flesh and after he revealed himself as the Son of God?"[14] The answer is, "He embraced them both, possessing the humanity and the divinity."[15] Contrary to early critics, Jesus' being human and being also the Christ were both very real understandings for the Gnostics!

Because the Gnostic Gospels do not give a history of Jesus' life on earth, as in the Biblical gospels, one could argue that they did not see Jesus as a real person because they don't report the details of his life. As they did not reject the four gospels in the Bible, it also can be argued that the stories of Jesus were sufficiently told and that the basic story line of Jesus was given in them. Perhaps, the Gnostics didn't want to get into the argument about the details of his life, because even within the four gospels in the Bible, there are many conflicting differences, which Bart Ehrman explicitly details in his book *Misquoting Jesus.*"[16] A good example of arguing over details as necessary for belief in Jesus might be the assertion that the virgin birth had to be accepted as a literal event. Was that detail necessary for eternal life? Not that concerned about whether that belief was essential for faith somehow conveys that there was more on the Gnostics' minds. Much like the Gospel of John, with its theological emphasis, their greater interest was in the message and meaning of his life as Lord and Savior.[17]

Lord and Savior? Yes, this is a description of Jesus that the Gnostics use often. As stated, many of the messages that the Gnostics believed were not dissimilar to the literalists. Often, the Gnostics, however, are charged with seeing Jesus as only being a teacher of wisdom. The charge is a terrific argument for those who insist that their way is the only to believe in Jesus. In doing so, the critics dismiss and then don't understand that being a Christian was far more than accepting beliefs and doctrines, for the Gnostics. What the Gnostic Gospels reveal is that the Gnostics indeed did have a sincere belief in Jesus, but they also took the wisdom teachings of Jesus much more seriously than the literalists.

For example, in the *Gospel of Thomas*, the sayings and teachings of Jesus are central. As they tell the story of Jesus, they don't dismiss all beliefs, but the most striking difference about their understanding of Jesus' teachings is that they are personal and spiritual. Jesus' teachings are complex and profound; they are not easy answers. What the new gospels show is that the Gnostics take many of the same teachings that the literalists like to highlight, but the intriguing insight is that they bring a whole new emphasis and variation of interpretations to Jesus' teaching and wisdom. What follows is not meant to be the pure and exact way the Gnostics interpreted Jesus' teachings. Their way of belief allowed for variations, but they did have some significant differences with the literalists that need to be highlighted.

The Gnostics' understanding of Jesus was that he brought a powerful message in that he revealed that life was more than a material existence. Life was not whole until persons awaken to the spirit of God, which was both within and without.[18] Gnostics believed all persons had the capability of knowing God and that was achieved by seeking his Spirit.[19] God was not a judge ready to condemn those who did not believe in him correctly, nor was he a wrathful and uncaring power, but God was a caring Spirit. God sent Jesus to let persons know he was a loving God who understood human sufferings and challenges.[20] Neither seeing humankind as all good or all bad, believing in Jesus was a way of opening a door to a positive relationship with God's spirit, to accept forgiveness of sins, and open oneself to new and eternal life.[21]

These teachings could be affirmed by their belief in the positive power of the cross. For example, the *Gospel of Philip* says, "Truth did not come into the world naked, but it came in types and images. But one receives the unction of the power of the cross. This power the apostles called the right and the left. For a person is no longer a Christian but a Christ."[22] The power of the cross was to lead persons, not just to be Christians in name, but to be Christ-like! This spiritual understanding of God and Jesus then led one to ask, not whether one was a Christian by their beliefs, but how they lived and loved.

Jesus' call to believe in him was only the beginning of faith for the Gnostics. Christianity wasn't conceived as a religion possessing all the answers but was a way to live by following his lead and teachings. Therefore, as with traditional teaching, Jesus taught that his followers were to live in his love and in so doing to love others. However, for the Gnostics, the crucial question was not whether one simply *said* they believed in loving others, but *how* one loved? How one loved others is always open to review and question.

The distinction of how one loved was based, not on a certain set of rules, and certainly not on one's theological beliefs, but on the crucial concepts of questioning and self examination. This was based on a central but often misunderstood concept of the Gnostics called "*self knowledge.*" The apostolic church believed this concept was heresy. Why? It implied that persons believed in their own knowledge rather than the knowledge of the church and God. How could a person have better knowledge than the collective wisdom of the church when the church knew more than the common person, not only about God, but also ethics and morality? Therefore, to live and love others was to do as the church taught rather than the chaotic notion of everyone deciding for themselves. The Gnostics didn't totally disagree with the wisdom of the church, but they took knowledge a step deeper by questioning what was true rather than blindly accepting the dictates of the church.

Applying their belief of self knowledge, along with the question, how one loved others, was also the question, how one loved *oneself*? The Gnostics believed both of these questions were implied in Jesus' new commandment. Expanding the Hebrew teachings of Deuteronomy 6:4-5 about loving God whole heartedly, and Leviticus 19:18 about loving one's neighbor, Jesus in Mark 12: 28-31 responds to a scribes question about the commandments. Jesus replies, "The first is, 'Hear, O Israel: the Lord our God, the Lord is one; you shall love the Lord your God with all your heart, and with all your soul, and with all your mind, and with all your strength. The second is this: You shall love your neighbor as yourself. There is no other greater commandment than these."[23] Normally, taken as a theological statement, the Gnostics believed, because of their special belief in self knowledge or knowing oneself, that this commandment was more a challenge of Jesus rather than a statement of faith.

Often called the great commandment, this central and traditional teaching of Jesus was honored and held high by the literalists, but a subtle difference was that the literalists would understand it as a description of Christians. Indeed, the literalists would say they were called by Jesus to love others, and Christians were those who loved. However, loving others developed a strange twist or assumption for them that made the commandment a statement of faith. Love became quite closely associated with what one believed. The Christian way to love others was by teaching those, who did not believe like them, that they were on the way to hell. This was "loving," because they were warning them of the awful fate ahead, if they were not judged favorably by Jesus. Didn't the Gnostics and other heretics understand that in saving them from the torture of hell, they were being loved?

Of course, these heretics got the message — as many still receive this gracious, compassionate, "loving" message today. In spite of this dire warning, the Gnostics also heard an additional message in Jesus' commandment that would get them in deeper trouble with both the judgment of Jesus and God — according to the literalists. By the Gnostics believing in self knowledge, and relying on that more than the church, the bishops would charge that they made the mortal sin of believing in themselves — *instead of Jesus.* Indeed, gnostic Christians would claim they believed in themselves, but what the bishops failed to understand was that they believed both in Jesus and themselves. They did so because of their deeper understanding of Jesus' commandment.

Within the question of self knowledge, and the teaching to love others, was a *preliminary* question in Jesus' commandment. Not to be overlooked, in his teaching was the question of how one loved oneself. Jesus said, "You shall love your neighbor as yourself." Certainly stated as a directive, the words also imply that loving oneself was necessary. Therefore, how one loved oneself was open also to self examination, or knowing oneself.[24] If one was to love others, in essence, one should get their own house in order, as implied in Jesus' commandment, and this included asking if one loved oneself, honestly.

As Elaine Pagels expresses in her book *The Gnostic Gospels*, the question to be asked was, did one love what is loving and helping oneself, or did one love what they hated? If one was loving what they hated that could lead to depression and demise? In contrast, there was a real upside of loving what one loved. In loving oneself, not in the sense of total selfishness, but in the sense of self respect and worthiness, doing so led to a crucial realization or discovery. This discovery was the knowledge that Jesus taught: God's spirit was within! Disagreeing with the theology that there we are all bad, and there is no good in us, which the church would eventually say included all babies, the Gnostics take another approach. God's spirit is within; it is our responsibility to recognize this and awaken to its presence within us.

No, the Gnostics did not believe everything was totally good or bad. From their myths, some want to say the world was all bad and the spiritual all good. As will be learned in understanding their myths, it wasn't that simple. Indeed, the spiritual is more important than the material, but in the midst of the world, something positive and good could be elevated. Certainly all sin and come short of the glory of God, as Paul, expressed it, and in spite of God's spirit being within, this didn't mean one was without sin and didn't need Christ's forgiveness. Indeed, self examination was a tool in recognizing one's sin, but it was also a way to come to another realization about oneself. Knowing oneself, which was more a concept than a doctrine, led to a more fundamental belief they believed Jesus taught. Particularly, in the *Gospel of Thomas,* is this teaching highlighted: we are *children of God.* This may sound trite, but it is central in how the Gnostics believed in Jesus in a different way than the literalists.[25]

Within this belief lies a primary difference in the interpretation of Jesus than presented in the Gospel of John. John argues in his gospel that God's spirit resided only in Jesus and the only way to access the spirit of God was to believe in him.[26] Elaine Pagels explains the dramatic difference, "Thomas's gospel encourages the hearer not so much to believe in Jesus, as John requires, as to 'seek to know' God through one's own, divinely given capacity, since all are created in the image of God."[27] Pagels adds the observation, "Thus, Thomas expresses what would become a central theme of Jewish — and later Christian mysticism — a thousand years later; that the 'image of God' is hidden within everyone, although most people remain unaware of it presence."[28] This understanding of the image of God, or as gnostic Christians would say, the spirit of God that dwells within, then leads to another teaching of Jesus in the *Gospel of Thomas,* "It is our responsibility to bring this spirit forth." [29]

For the Gnostics, bringing forth this light and understanding that we are children of God was more a spiritual process than accepting that the only way to be saved was to believe in Jesus, and only in Jesus. In contrast, the literalists stressed that the only way to God was to believe in Jesus and that was the only way to become a child of God. This is not to say that John's gospel does not contain truth and beauty, but it illustrates that the understanding of Jesus' message was heard differently by two close disciples. Certainly, Thomas believed in Jesus, but Thomas' gospel, which will be the subject of Chapter Nine, makes clear that Christianity was more than just simply believing in Jesus in order to gain salvation.

Surely, John would say the same that Christianity was more than a belief in Jesus, but for John, if one did not believe in Jesus, there was no way to God or to relate to God. Thomas's gospel suggests there are other ways to believe in Jesus, and one of those ways is by continually awakening to God's spirit within us. Thus self knowledge, when properly understood, was not a path to despair, but it was a way to relate to God at a deeper moral, spiritual, and dynamic level than just saying one believed in Jesus.

Christianity, in this light, was more a spiritual awakening than a religion defined by a set of beliefs. Beliefs were a natural part of the quest, but Jesus made clear that more than one interpretation of faith was not only acceptable but a valid part of the search for truth. For example, Jesus, himself, did not put his teachings and doctrines in written form, but trusted all his disciples to do so. Although, all had a strong belief in him, even in the Biblical Gospels, there are variations of emphasis and interpretations of his messages and beliefs. Regarding beliefs, Jesus left open the door of interpretation, and this did not belittle faith.[30] By their acceptance and reverence of more than four gospels, the Gnostics showed that they did not believe Jesus had blessed only a certain four, or even a special few, of his disciples with his true and correct interpretation. Nor did they believe that he had honored any one disciple's understanding of him as definitive and superior to others. In fact, it is recorded in the Biblical Gospels that Jesus directly challenged those in his own religion who assumed only they had the correct way to believe in or worship God.

For example, Jesus argued with the Pharisees, who were quite legalistic and narrow in their interpretation of Jewish law, and argued also with the Sadducees, who were the scribes and priests of the Jewish temple.[31] Jesus did not condemn their religion and belief in God, but he was critical in their *way* of belief. Interestingly, his challenge wasn't only to those of his own religion. In supporting self examination, the Gnostics observed Jesus challenging persons and groups to examine their ways of belief, particularly, for those whose style was arrogant and overbearing, as with the rich man whom encountered Jesus.[32] They heard Jesus teach that when one believed that they knew all the answers to life and possessed the true religion, this only shut the door to truth and change. An openness to change, after self examination or self knowledge, was a vital aspect in the gnostic process of spiritual growth and faith.

As will be illustrated in Jesus' sayings in the *Gospel of Thomas,* which require deep thinking, instead of simple answers, the Gnostics recognized that Jesus' style was to teach profound, complex, and thoughtful lessons for life. Using one's mind in deciding how one followed him was essential in all his teachings, including those in the New Testament. For example, in what is called his Sermon on the Mount in the Gospel of Matthew, Jesus taught, "Do not judge so that you may not be judged," and "Love your enemies."[33] These verses seem straightforward, but even these verses in light of the *Gospel of Thomas* may have deeper questions and complexities than often applied. Particularly, another verse in Jesus' sermon, which says, "You must be perfect," would mean more than a given answer, and in Thomas' context, would mean to be a continuing question of oneself.[34] To put that another way, Jesus didn't just give simple answers. The *Gospel of Thomas* implies that Jesus was more than a teacher of idealistic wisdom, but a teacher/preacher who raised questions about both life and how one lived life.

Further, in his teaching, Jesus used parables without precise conclusions, urging persons to think for themselves and resolve meanings for their own circumstances. When asked questions, he often turned the answer back on the inquirer.[35] For the Gnostics, Jesus didn't give straightforward doctrines or beliefs to be set in stone, but his teachings, foremost, gave directions for developing a loving and spiritual life. The Gnostics believed both one's moral and spiritual life was to be developed continually. Morality was not simply accepting blindly a viewpoint or moral position dictated by the church.

As regards beliefs, Jesus never refers to his virgin birth or makes that an issue. Often after his miracles, he gave his disciples the rather curious and baffling instructions, "tell no one."[36] Even after his resurrection, Jesus did not dictate a single meaning to that powerful event. As to the form of resurrection, bodily or spiritual, he makes no statement. In his post-resurrection appearances, he did not state in a creed the correct or precise way to believe in him. Therefore, developing what one believed was an extraordinary trust that he embedded in all his disciples. His message, beyond beliefs, was in its core about trusting and always seeking a spiritual relationship with God. This was possible through him because Jesus was the truth, as their *Gospel of Truth* attests. The way of truth was trusting and building one's relationship with him — not indisputable rules and theological positions.

For the Gnostics, because Jesus' preaching, teaching, and life encouraged his followers to seek humility, they did not embrace a judgmental, arrogant Jesus, whose message and mission was to get everyone to believe in him or be doomed to hell. Forgiveness, understanding, and love were not only up to God, but our challenge, as well. His resurrection, far more than guaranteeing a bodily resurrection, was about embracing new life and hope in one's present life.[37]

Not preaching any collection of beliefs, his message was that his believers were to seek the knowledge of God using their God given emotions and brains. More than a liberty to believe anything or whatever without thought, it was a call to use all kinds of knowledge as honestly as possible, in order to live, to love, and to grow in faith. In other words, Jesus gave us a freedom in our belief in God, but that freedom should be limited, not by laws or beliefs, but by our honest effort to love God and others, using our hearts, minds, souls and strengths.

In many ways, these views of Jesus are surprising because they were not expected from the Gnostics. Interestingly, they affirm the way many modern Christians now believe and allow Jesus to move beyond the narrow stereotypes of some forms of Christianity.

When one compares the gnostic way of believing in Jesus, their faith was not radically different from many aspects of normative Christianity. However, it was different enough to be seen as heretical by those whose voice would prevail. There are many elements of common ground with traditional Christianity, but the gnostic interpretation of Jesus has both some subtle and not so subtle differences. These differences were enough so that were unacceptable to those who charged that the Gnostics were the ones who just thought they knew it all. Bottom line, the Gnostics didn't agree with those Christians who said they were the true ones in the know!

Of course, to reiterate, not all Gnostics agreed exactly with these perceptions or ways to understand Jesus, as presented above, as they had various versions and differences of the Christ story. That is the beauty of the gnostic way of faith. As there were different responses to Jesus by his closest disciples, indeed as so today, the lesson is that Christianity should not be a battle, insisting that one's views or beliefs about Christ is the only true ways to believe. Rather, Christian truth has more than one way to believe in Christ, more than one way to relate to God; there are various paths to the mountain top of faith. Therefore, the question is not whether one accepts or believes gnostic beliefs or myths, but rather the challenge is to be inspired by their focusing on faith as a process of seeking. Certainly, there will be those who argue that these new Gnostic Gospels are about rejecting true Christianity and accepting gnostic beliefs, such as a spiritual resurrection. Even that is to miss the gift of these gospels, as they are not about having a battle about that, or even about the virgin birth, or a battle about the correct way to believe in Jesus, but are a call to us to expand our view of faith and Jesus' message.

The impression that Christianity was one voice with a basic, clear, and concise understanding, of course with some variations, was the legacy of Christianity before the Gnostic Gospels were made public. These gospels underline the important statement by Elaine Pagels and Karen King that the ordered destruction of these other gospels of Jesus happened in order that the message of Christianity could be taken for granted as "a single, static, universal system of beliefs."[38] This one united voice echoed the chosen beliefs and doctrines that the apostolic church supposedly had inherited directly from Jesus and his disciples. With the ascent of the Gnostic Gospels, a primary question that is raised is whether Jesus' message was more than establishing a particular system of beliefs, literalist, gnostic, or any other?

With the Nag Hammadi books, there is a significant change in understanding who the Gnostics were. What is being learned is that they heard the message of Jesus in a different key, or light, than those of many church fathers. Not as heretical as portrayed, their Gospels witness to a different but ancient interpretation of Jesus, which is attracting respect and interest because they open the door to a less judgmental and more loving Christ. For the Gnostics, faith in Jesus isn't about believing all the details of his life — or else! More substantial is to appreciate and to believe in his spiritual presence as the living Christ.

To summarize, without being dogmatic, or insisting that their way is the only way to believe in him, these gospels teach, in their essence, that Jesus brought a liberating gospel of good news from God — as most Christian traditions preach and affirm. However, more than bringing a static set of beliefs, Jesus' message was that we all have the innate capacity to know God and need to awaken to his spirit within us, recognizing that we are children of God. When awakened to that reality, we have the responsibility to bring forth our own positive relationship with ourselves, others, and God. Faith is seeking that relationship with our hearts, minds, souls, and most importantly, with love. To be a Christian is not to know everything about God and the world, nor is faith a consent to doctrines. Faith is to be on a journey of love with the living and spiritual Christ. The newly found gospels allow that the meaning of Christ can be more widely understood, and as do the gospels in the Bible, lift up the power and love of Christ.

Notes: Chapter Four: The Gnostic Understanding of Jesus—a Surprise!

[1] Elaine Pagels and Karen King, *Reading Judas*, (New York: Viking, 2007), 102.

[2] Literalism is often associated with taking the Bible literally. Christian Scriptures had not been collected into a Canon. Early literalism meant taking stories about Jesus such

as his virgin birth, miracles, and bodily resurrection as historical events. The beliefs of their church were the literal truth of Christ and Christianity. The early apostolic church was a precursor of Biblical literalists and the theological position of what is commonly called fundamentalism today. Literalism in this book refers primarily to the theological interpretation of most early Bishops claiming that all they taught about Jesus was "immoveable truth." See Irenaeus, *Against Heresies*, referred hereafter as *AH*, Vol. 1:X.

[3] For a excellent overview of church fathers see, Bart D. Ehrman, *After the New Testament: The Writings of the Apostolic Fathers*, 24 lectures, Chantilly, VA: The Teaching Company, 2004) For male priest only, see Pagels, The Gnostic Gospels, New York: Random House, 1989), 72.

[4] Although the books in the Bible were becoming the favorite of the early apostolic church, the selection of these books is a long story. Athanasius' list of books in 367 C. E. was the same as our New Testament. These books did not "officially" become canon until the Council of Trent in 1545.

[5] Tim Dowley, Editor, *Introduction to the History of Christianity*, (Minneapolis, Fortress Press, 2002), 115.

[6] James M Robinson, Editor, *The Nag Hammadi Library*, referred hereafter as *NHL*, (San Francisco: HarperSanFrancisco, 1978), the *Gospel of Philip*, 143.

[7] Robinson, *NHL*, *The Treatise on the Resurrection*, 54.

[8] Elaine Pagels, *Beyond Belief*, (New York: Random House, 2003), 129. This is a summarized statement by Dr. Pagels rather than a direct quote.

[9] Elaine Pagels, *The Gnostic Gospels*, (New York: Random House, 1979), 104.

[10] Pagels, *The Gnostic Gospels*, 53.

[11] Robinson, *NHL*, *Tripartite Tractate*, 92, (115:5).

[12] Robinson, *NHL*, *The Gospel of Truth*, 42, (20: 25-30).

[13] Ibid.

[14] Robinson, *NHL*, *Treatise on the Resurrection*, 54, (44:21-34).

[15] Ibid.

[16] For many examples, see, Bart D. Ehrman, *Misquoting Jesus*, (San Francisco: HarperSanFrancisco, 2005).

[17] Some have questioned if the *Gospel of John* might be gnostic because of its greater philosophical approach in telling the story of Jesus, but Elaine Pagels sets forth major differences in Chapter Two, "Gospels in Conflict: John and Thomas," in *Beyond Belief*.

[18] Robinson, *NHL*, the *Gospel of Thomas*, 126.

[19] Pagels, *Beyond Belief*, 164.

[20] Robinson, *NHL*, the *Gospel of Truth*, Pg. 41.

[21] Robinson, *NHL*, *Treatise on the Resurrection*, 56, (48:35). "It (resurrection) is the revelation of what is, and transformation of things, and a transition into newness."

[22] Robinson, *NHL*, the *Gospel of Philip*, 150, (67: 20).

[23] The Great Commandment is also found in Mark 12: 28-34 where it is noted that a Pharisee lawyer asks Jesus this question, "to test him."
[24] Robinson, *NHL*, the *Gospel of Thomas*, 126, (25). Knowing oneself is based on Jesus' words in the *Gospel of Thomas*, "When you come to know yourself, then you will become known."
[25] Pagels, *Beyond Belief*, 138.
[26] Pagels, *Beyond Belief*, 34. John 1:9
[27] Pagels, *Beyond Belief*, 34.
[28] Pagels, *Beyond Belief*, 41.
[29] Robinson, *NHL*, the *Gospel of Thomas*, 134
[30] Meyer, *The Gnostic Discoveries*, (San Francisco: HarperSanFrancisco, 2005), 8.
[31] Pharisees were teachers of the Jewish law. Luke 7:36. Sadducees were Jewish priest who accepted only the first books of Moses as their authority. Matthew 22:23.
[32] Matthew 19:16 The story of the rich man.
[33] Matthew 7:1 and Matthew 5:44
[34] Matthew 5:48
[35] Matthew 19: 16
[36] Matthew 9: 30 The story of Jesus healing two blind men — an example of "tell no one."
[37] A work which presents this concept of resurrection as happening in the present will be presented later and is named, the *Treatise on the Resurrection*.
[38] Elaine Pagels and Karen L. King , *Reading Judas*, 102.

Chapter Five

Who were the Gnostics: Heretics or Saints?

> The Christian heresiologists disagreed vehemently with Christian gnostics on matters of faith and life, and as a result they portrayed gnostic believers as vile heretics. Without a doubt the polemical intentions of the heresiologist influenced their understanding — or misunderstanding — of the gnostics. [1]
>
> - Marvin Meyer, *The Gnostic Discoveries*

The stereotype of the Gnostics being twisted and misinformed heretics is an unfortunate perception, but one that will be changed as the new story of the Gnostic Gospels is made known. These gospels bring to light specific information on why these Christians were treated as those who had no standing in the church, and why their voice was heretical. Because they have been portrayed as a group that opposed the apostolic church, their image has been that of a distinctive church, which was in vile disagreement with everything the established church believed.

In Chapter Two, the Gnostics' participation in the church was mentioned, and that it was not appreciated, at least, by Bishop Irenaeus. This new information of their participation is a helpful element in understanding that rather than being a separate religious cult that the Gnostics were not as "far out" as commonly assumed. An astonishing fact is that one of their principal leaders, Valentinus, was almost elected Pope, losing by just a few votes in 143 C.E. after the death of Pope Hyginus.[2] His election might have changed the nature and theology of Christianity, but that was not to be. As the literalist bishops grew in power, religiously and politically, Valentinus was to be condemned as a heretic.

Gnostic Churches later may have formed, becoming classified as schematics, or those outside the church. Although it could be argued some Gnostic Churches existed, such churches were few and not to endure. None ever became famous or a distinctive, well known church. Even if they existed, the greater issue for today is not the renewal of their churches, or what has been called Gnosticism. The Gnostics do not hold a set of new answers, and although their status as heretics needs to be reconsidered, their voice is a call that Christianity was a way of faith, led by hope and love, a process of endless spiritual maturing rather than insisting that one had to believe a certain way.

So who were the Gnostics, and how should they be understood? The Gnostics could be described as a movement or theological perspective within the rise of Christianity.[3] In essence, as the church was growing, they were those who challenged the dictate: "Just believe what you are told." By their protests and attempts to argue theology, and their disagreement with church policies, such as excluding women as priests, they could be known or understood as those who first questioned ecclesiastical authority or were the precursors for those who would be known as Protestants. Unfortunately, the axiom, "you are either with us or against us," was the position of most of the early bishops, and the Gnostics were deemed heretics. For some authorities, with their having some association to Christianity, they were sort of Christians, at best, were Christians who were "falsely so."[4]

Usually, described as being one heretical group, sect, or church, the codices of Nag Hammadi affirm the Gnostics, much like Protestants of today, had many theological beliefs and opinions. Classifying them as one voice was not fair to their many differences. The evidence, by studying their writings, indicates there were differing schools of thought, as was true in the Protestant Reformation, which had leaders such as Martin Luther and John Calvin. The Gnostics also had several influential leaders including Basilides, Heracleon, and Valentinus. Valentinus had a significant number of followers even though he didn't succeed as Pope. Not all that surprising, Valentinus, and his followers, the Valentinians, presented such a threat to the literalist bishops, beyond being identified as a heretic, he was excommunicated from the church![5]

Other theological positions deemed gnostic have been classified with titles such as Sethians, followers of Sophia, and those who because of their spiritual emphasis were called Montanists. These groups along with other theological perspectives will be explained more fully because today classifying those who were Gnostics, and those who were not, is a difficult task even for scholars.[6] The church fathers, on the other hand, were more than willing to explain exactly what the Gnostics believed and then to imply that Gnostics were one group who taught a basic set of beliefs. In so doing, the fathers established what most would consider the classical view of the Gnostics and their beliefs. However, the new resources dispute this view as being a fair and honest portrayal of them.

The classical view, used to explain the Gnostics, was that they were a different church whose beliefs weren't true and were totally mythical. As a group, their beliefs were straightforward, and these beliefs defined them as being Gnostics. Gnostics believed that all matter was evil. Creation was not good because a lower god or demigod, not the real God had mistakenly formed the earth. However, they believed that a few sparks of the true God fell from above into some of humanity. Jesus was the beholder of these sparks for a chosen few. They believed Jesus wasn't a real person and was only a spiritual being. Those few who were the real Christians would be awakened to the spark within them. Those so blessed possessed special, secret knowledge given to them by Jesus, and thus they would be saved, not by faith, but by their knowledge (gnosis). These beliefs represent the essence of their theology, according to their critics, and they describe their religion named Gnosticism.[7]

This classical explanation, still often used today, is a stark and skillful way to dismiss them as a bunch of theological lunatics! With the Gnostic Gospels before us, it is evident that the composite classical view is not accurate, as it takes parts and builds them to be a system of beliefs, giving the impression that all Gnostics believed the same. Some of these beliefs in the classical description were held by some Gnostics but not by all. Certain positions are highlighted and oversimplified, and these particular and usually strange beliefs become the explanation of whom the Gnostics were, and what they believed. However, the critical revelation is that these so-called descriptions of what they believed are derived primarily from their differing mythological stories. As discussed in the previous chapter, the critics then stress these myths over their strong belief in Christ.

In addition to setting forth the belief that the Christ of the Gnostics was simply mythological, the church fathers were able to establish an impression that the Gnostics were such bizarre outcasts and extreme spiritualist that they had nothing to offer for the good or truth of Christianity. By centering on their false myths as the essence of their faith, the Gnostics became a marginal and heretical group, easily vilified and denigrated as those who had unbelievable and ridiculous beliefs. With more information now available from the Gnostics themselves, a new understanding is emerging. As faith for many Christians is greater than believing certain myths or doctrines in the Bible, so it is now revealed by the Gnostic Gospels that Christian faith for the Gnostics was more than believing and insisting on their conflicting myths. Unfortunately, in spite of the new evidence, the image of their being delusional theological idealist is taking time to unravel due to the long historical prejudice against them.

An analogy would be if fifteen hundred years from now all Presbyterians were to be described as followers of John Calvin who believed in predestination – and not free will. Likewise, Lutherans would be those who were followers of Martin Luther and believed once one had been saved by grace that it wasn't necessary to do good works as heaven was guaranteed. It might be to say Roman Catholics were those who believed the only way to God was through the blessed Mother Mary and the Pope. Outrageous? Yes. Of course, such illustrations are only imaginary. It is obvious, in these examples, only part of the story is told. The partial emphases are selected as a means to establish derogatory, well placed, prejudicial arguments against a group whom one wanted to condemn. What is presented is highly exaggerated, misinforms, and would make it easy to categorize and explain away these groups.

Such a malignant scenario wasn't imaginative but was similar to the way the fathers portrayed the Gnostics as false Christians. As the Gnostic Gospels lain hidden more than fifteen hundred years, and were known only through second hand sources and hearsay, many gnostic scholars believe that such misinformation and exaggeration of their beliefs and positions is exactly what happened to those who were given by the church fathers, the name, "Gnostics."

In the writings of the church fathers, the word, Gnostics, is often capitalized.[8] By calling them Gnostics with a capital "G," the church could bring all these dissidents under one umbrella and make them one dissent group. Interestingly, although the fathers do not mention the word or term, Gnosticism, later critics would look as this group as those who believed in the religion, Gnosticism. As they did not hold the true beliefs in Jesus, they did not believe in the one true religion, which, of course, was Christianity. However, this attempt to categorize them as following a heretical religion has a substantial challenge!

As mentioned in Chapter Three, Karen King of Harvard University has written a book named *What is Gnosticism?* Her research helps us to better understand who the Gnostics were. Her first chapter is titled "Why is Gnosticism so Hard to Define?"[9] The message of Karen's book is quite different from those who want to explain Gnosticism as a belief system. She boldly states that "no religion called Gnosticism existed in antiquity."[10] With the Gnostic Gospels being firsthand resources, she argues that to codify the Gnostics as representing one collective religion was to impose a questionable stereotype.[11] The attempt was to create an essence for their beliefs, which is neither honest nor complete, and was used to simply them as a heretical group.[12]

She explains that the idea of Gnosticism was not a term used by the Gnostics in their own writings. Gnosticism was a *later* creation used for classification and a tainted explanation of their beliefs. To be more specific about the derivation of the term Gnosticism, Karen relates that the Yale scholar Bentley Layton's research indicates the term Gnosticism was first used, not by church fathers, nor by the Gnostics, but by Henry More in 1669 C.E. in the battle of Protestants against Roman Catholics.[13] Sir Henry More, a Protestant, characterized Catholicism as "a spice of the old abhorred Gnosticism, a kind of false prophecy that seduces true Christianity into idolatry."[14] Holy smoke! With a strange twist of prejudice, Catholics, their early antagonist, were themselves now identified with the Gnostics!

Talk about turning the table upside down! For a Protestant to condemn Catholics as Gnostics, such a charge shows how far so-called truth can be distorted and/or transposed in the battle for God. The obvious motive is to elevate one's own religion as superior over another. Without firsthand resources, Sir More took what he had heard about these Gnostics and jumped to the conclusion they believed in a foul and abhorred false prophecy called Gnosticism, and as he explains, further, a false religion which turned people away from true Christianity. Of course, Sir More would have been willing to tell you, as so many others have, what true

Christianity was. Indeed, with such confusing accusations and rumors similar to this against the Gnostics, these have persisted and worked well to define them as weird, non-Christians who believed in Gnosticism.

Before the Gnostic Gospels surfaced from near destruction, Gnosticism was deemed a bizarre religion, very simply, and negatively portrayed.[15] With the codices of Nag Hammadi now public, there is new information that radically challenges the classic summation of Gnosticism, whether one believes it was a later or earlier creation. If one is willing to go beyond what has been said about this abhorred false prophecy, the message of the Gnostics is more than persuading one to accept their beliefs and myths. Nor was it to believe in their non-Christian religion or their quasi-Christianity, Gnosticism. As Karen explains, the terminology was used to classify, simplify, and systemize their beliefs so they could be vilified and written off as heretics.[16]

Heretics? Interestingly, the root meaning of the word, "heretic," is "*choice*."[17] For the literalists, who were becoming established as the orthodox, there was no need for choice. To believe differently from their church was, in fact, a sin![18] The apostolic church possessed the correct, right, straightforward beliefs so why believe otherwise. Destruction of heretical writings was not unloving or un-Christian because those who accepted contrary beliefs to those of the apostolic church were choosing a path to hell, and hell was a literal fact and location! [19]

Gnostics were not alone in being called heretics. With the vision that the apostolic church had been given pure authority, a consequential reason that their theology would prevail was because of their aggressive, unrelenting, negative attack on all heretics who disagreed with them. Bentley Layton's assessment was that in the early church those called heretics numbered over half of the early Christians.[20] In the father's writings, these included such classifications as the Mariconites, Montanist, Ophites, Ebionites, Encratites, and the Tatians, to name a few.[21] In addition, the fathers mentioned wayward Christians who followed false leaders, such as Cerinthus, and Meander, indicating they were serious but minor players in the battle for Christ's truth.[22]

In essence, any who held beliefs different than the apostolic church were deemed as heretical by the bishops. Based on the volume granted in assailing them in the fathers' writings, it appears the Gnostics disturbed their church the most. Although the Marconites, who will be discussed, began in the church, and became immense in numbers in the Eastern part of the Empire, most of the heretical groups were outside or clearly detached from the Church of Rome. Originally believed to have been another of these separate groups, the new information reveals that the Gnostics were more like a cancer within, becoming the primary threat to the developing organized church and its strict theology. Most likely, because their threat was so direct within the church, the Gnostics were given the severest attacks and judgments by the church fathers.

Of course, the battle cry, heretics, against these early Christians was only the beginning of the term's malicious odyssey. Because the classification, heretics, proved to be so successful in condemning and identifying both wayward individuals and groups, the label would only gain in power and seriousness as the church grew. Used blatantly against early Christians, it was later to be used to condemn the priest, Martin Luther, the scientist Galileo Galilei, and hundreds of other individuals and groups documented in the *Encyclopedia of Heresies and Heretics* complied by Chas. S. Clifton.[23] Those considered heretical are numerous and astonishing!

Who were the Gnostics? The Gnostics were among the first of the heretics. They chose not to accept blindly that the truth of Jesus was possessed only by those in power in the apostolic church. They disagreed that the true beliefs and doctrines about Jesus were limited to the authority of this church. In a way, as heretics, the Gnostics were like David against Goliath, as they too had a stone to hurl. Their stone was in the form of a collection of gospels ascribed to different disciples including Philip, Mary, and Thomas – additional gospels to those in the Bible.

No, that couldn't be; there was no room in the "inn" of gospels because as Bishop Irenaeus explained there were only four true gospels; all other gospels were false. Therefore, had Muhammad-al-Samman not shattered the vase, the ancient messages that the Gnostics heard Jesus teach may have remained hidden, and the status of the Gnostics remained forever as being simply mythological Christians. Not pure in their beliefs, not saints without blemish or claiming to be so, the Gnostics were condemned as false believers, freethinkers, impious heathen, and infidels. Now, lo and behold, the table of truth may turn again! The Gnostics, by their so-called false gospels, may join other heretics who have aided in the advancement of Christianity and its greater truth. To understand Christians as being seekers of God may disturb those who believe that Christians alone know the facts about God. Without belittling the power of Christianity, for those who believe God is greater than the measure of any one religion, the message that we are all seekers of God will gain in importance as the Gnostics are better understood.

Notes: Chapter Five: Who were the Gnostics: Heretics or Saints?

[1] Marvin Meyer, *The Gnostic Discoveries*, (San Francisco: HarperSanFrancisco, 2005), 2.
[2] J. Michael Matkin, *The Gnostic Gospels*, (New York: Alpha Books, 2005), 41.
[3] For a discussion of the different understanding of the Gnostics after the Nag Hammadi discovery see Chas S. Clifton, *Encyclopedia of Heresies and Heretics*, (New York, Barnes and Noble Books, 1992), 49. As stated earlier, the Gnostics were not one group but were similar to the Protestants, and the reason for capitalizing them in this book.
[4] Matkin, *The Gnostic Gospels*, 41.
[5] Ibid.
[6] Karen L. King, *What Is Gnosticism?,* (Cambridge Massachusetts, Harvard University Press, 2003), 153.
[7] For a similar classical description see Bart D. Ehrman, *Lost Christianities: Christian Scriptures and the Battle over Authentication*, (Chantilly Virginia, The Teaching Company, Glossary, 2004), 55. For a refutation of the classical view see, King, *What is Gnosticism, 199.*
[8] Irenaeus, *Against Heresies*, hereafter noted as *AH*, 1: Preface.
[9] King, *What is Gnosticism?*, 4.
[10] King, *What is Gnosticism?,* 2.
[11] King, *What is Gnosticism?*, 14.
[12] King, *What is Gnosticism?*, 224.
[13] King, *What is Gnosticism?,* 7. For a longer description of Henry More's invention of the term, Gnosticism, see; David Brakke, *The Gnostics*, (Cambridge, Ma., Harvard University Press, 2010), 19.
[14] Ibid.
[15] King, *What is Gnosticism?*, 3.
[16] King, *What is Gnosticism?*, 20. Chapter 2 is titled, "Gnosticism as Heresy."
[17] Elaine Pagels, *Beyond Belief*, (New York: Random House, 2003), 184.
[18] Irenaeus, *AH*, 1: Preface.
[19] Irenaeus, *AH*, 5: XX, 1.
[20] Pagels, *Beyond Belief*, 174.
[21] Irenaeus, *AH*, 2: XXXII.

---

[22] Matkin, *The Gnostic Gospels*, 38.
[23] Chas. S. Clifton, *Encyclopedia of Heresies and Heretics*, (New York: Barnes and Noble Books, 1992)

Chapter Six

Protecting and Hiding the Gnostic Gospels

> Tertullian complains they [the Gnostics] refuse to accept and believe the rule of faith as others did: instead they challenge others to raise theological questions, when they themselves have no answers....[1]
>
> -*The Gnostic Gospels* by Elaine Pagels

Some scholars have suggested the blame for the early apostolic church, becoming so stringent and literal in its beliefs, was that the Gnostics forced its bishops to do so.[2] With the Gnostics putting their beliefs in writing, and accepting other gospels, they had to set the record straight as to which gospels were holy, and then in doing so, why Christian truth was limited to their four preferred gospels. In contrast to the bishops, the Gnostics never insisted that they had the exclusive truth and only their gospels were true. Never do they attack the gospels in the Bible as inauthentic, and as noted earlier, many of the same verses in the Biblical Gospels are included in the *Gospel of Thomas.*

Certainly, the Gnostics had their differences with the church, and in a few incidences, they attacked the bishops forthrightly, particularly, when they described them as being dry canals![3] Perhaps, because they had less power and organization, the Gnostics did not draw and swing the sword of religious truth as did the bishops of the developing church. In spite of this, the Gnostics were a perplexing threat to the authority of the church. Although they had "no answers," according to Tertullian, and did not accept the church's "rule of faith," the Gnostics' danger was that they dare challenged that the interpretation of Christianity was totally confined or limited to the church's truth.

In order to portray the Gnostics as a group who wanted to argue their truth, over and against that of the church, some have suggested that on the basis of the first verse of the *Gospel of Thomas* that the Gnostics were a religious sect who believed only they possessed the truth of Christianity. The verse says, "Jesus said, whoever finds the interpretation of these sayings will not experience death."[4] Thomas' Gospel, primarily, is a book that reports sayings of Jesus, and it can be assumed that many Gnostics believed they had found the correct interpretation. However, even with so much at stake as not experiencing death, never do the Gnostics say that their beliefs or their interpretation of his sayings is that which Jesus refers to in this verse. The *Gospel of Thomas*, as will be seen in Chapter Nine, proceeds to raise more questions than answers. Nor does the gospel provide any clear interpretation, or even a secret gnosis, which if accepted, would guarantee eternal life.

On the other hand, the apostolic church insisted, as some Christians do today, that only they had found the interpretation for eternal life. Their interpretations had come directly from Jesus, so there was no need for debate; their beliefs were orthodox. The Gnostics were not immune from the need for beliefs, but their understanding of their role in faith was greater than to establish the mantra, "we are right, you are wrong." As beliefs were open to change, so it was with their myths, which have taken center stage in defining them. Unfortunately, their myths are often understood as simply alternative answers to what some Christians would argue is *the* Christian answer as to how God created humankind and the world.

Today, several gnostic mythical stories, highlighted in the classical view, need to be dismissed with the modern knowledge of our earth and universe. For example, with new scientific information, the myth of many of the Gnostics that the creation of the universe was led by lesser gods, who designed the heavens, the earth, and its humans, doesn't make sense. Of course, the Gnostics might argue with the once popular belief that God's design of the universe was a three story plateau of heaven above, earth in the middle, and hell below. Again with the Gnostics, the belief of some who proposed that the earth or the material world was totally evil is as bizarre as saying that it is all good. Further, by declaring that everything the Gnostics believed was mythical was an effective way to propose all their beliefs were false. The implication was that the literalists possessed the correct knowledge of the world, the heavens, and God — and that the Gnostics did not. Clearly, the literalists won the argument over the Gnostics concerning myths, and even Christian beliefs, but the gift of the Gnostics is not a set of alternatives. Nor is it new gospels, which are without fault, as the literalists claimed for their four chosen gospels. Something much deeper was at stake with the Gnostics.

Rather insisting that only certain gospels told the true and complete story of Jesus, or that their beliefs were infallible, the Gnostics' focus was on the *spiritual* dimension of Christ and his teachings. Beliefs and myths were not ends in themselves and were more than final answers.[5] The Gnostics realized that beliefs were at their core, symbolic, pointing beyond themselves to a greater power and reality. Realizing this spiritual reality, strength for one's life came in bringing forth the spirit of God, and in doing so, opened the door to experience the presence of the living Christ.

An example of going beyond a belief in order to experience the presence of Christ would be the belief in the cross of Jesus. Surprisingly, the Gnostics believed in the Christian cross, not as doctrine, but as a dynamic force for living in the present. In one of their writings called, *The Apocryphon of James* it teaches, "But for those who have believed in my cross, theirs is the kingdom of God. Therefore become seekers...."[6] The message is, believe in the cross — and keep seeking! The goal in seeking was to experience the power of the cross, which spoke volumes about the understanding that Jesus had of the human condition. Many messages came from his cross including his identity with the reality of our suffering, forgiveness of our sins, and God's acceptance of us. Believing in the cross was to rest in a trust that God's spirit surrounds us in times of both suffering and blessing. The messages of the cross, more than just doctrines, were dynamic, and seeking these messages led one to experience the presence and power of Christ. Therefore, as James teaches, believe in the cross and seek its power for the living of one's life.

Christianity as a seeking faith, beyond a battle for correct beliefs, and even myths, was not the interpretation of Jesus which the world would embrace. The powerful and well organized church bishops and fathers would succeed in establishing that accepting their theology and beliefs would bring to the believer, salvation. Further, their view wasn't an interpretation; it was what God said! The beliefs of the apostolic church were unquestionable and the unmovable truths of God.[7] Therefore, believe in Jesus as their church and leaders did, and one would not experience death!

The Gnostics believed in the church but had a different vision for it. In variation to the literalists, the Gnostics believed the church's task was assisting in the development of faith; its purpose was not telling everyone what and how to believe. The church was a central place for fellowship and a home for worshiping the Master, but the church was not the Master. The Gnostics weren't isolationist or against the church's existence, but their image for it was a garden, not a vault for beliefs. The Gnostics viewed Christianity growing as a flower, not as a tundra of frozen doctrines. The church was one but had many branches and various flowering buds of color. Yes, as Tertullian charges in the introductory quote, it was fair to raise theological questions within the church! More than accepting and believing what he refers to as the rule of faith, which was believed to be an early statement of Christian facts, the attitude of not having all the answers was a more honest way to relate to God. Therefore, in Christianity, various interpretations aided its beauty and truth.

It is now learned that even in the earliest days of Christianity, not all heard Jesus saying to be his follower that everyone had to understand or experience God in the same way. These early Christians would not have identified themselves as Gnostics as they were less vocal in criticizing the church. However, with a disturbing letter sent to them from a hard line bishop, they also acted to preserve what they must have viewed as honest testimonies for the sake of Christ.

Some of the earliest monks are now known to have traveled to the Egyptian desert to experience God for themselves in a different way. Dedicated to Christ, scholarship, worship, and the hard work of printing by hand the gospels of believers, they are assumed to be the ones who hid the leather bound codices. Four miles from the cliffs of Jabal al-Tarif, there was once an ancient monastery of Pachomius.[8] As a matter of record, in 367 C.E., the monks at this monastery received a Festal Letter, sent annually from the Bishop of Alexandria, to announce the date of Easter. This Festal Letter of 367 C.E. had further instructions. It contained the ecclesiastical "Order" that books and writings with heretical tendencies be purged! [9]

Thankfully, not all agreed with this Order to purge, which most believe meant that heretical books should be burnt. Although no one can be certain what happened exactly, or prove how the thirteen, leather bound books were hidden, their discovery brings forth firsthand information on Christian materials that had been only rumored to exist. Therefore, the basic assumption is that some of the monks were upset with the decree from the bishop to destroy writings, which quite likely they had translated from Greek into Coptic, and then personally had copied onto delicate papyrus. Defying this Order, possibly more than one monk, because of the large size of the vase, decided to hide and bury the books near the monastery, either at the base of the cliffs or in one its high caves.[10] Wherever the original burial site, the effort was extraordinary in order to save these dangerous, heretical books. Heretical and dangerous books? Of course, they were! Bishop Athanasius, who wrote this Festal Letter, declared that books with gnostic leanings were "defiled, polluted, full of myths and empty."[11] Reason enough these books should be purged. Bishop of Alexandria, who will be seen to become more powerful in the church than Constantine, believed to eradicate heresy was a service to uphold the will and truth of Christ!

In spite of this astonishing Order from an authoritarian, literalist Bishop, who reportedly physically struck other bishops who disagreed with him, and once cut off the arm of an opponent, the assumption is that the monks of this monastery defied his written dictate.[12] Perhaps, they hid the codices in the jar because they believed the wider message of Jesus was being suppressed. Although we cannot know what these monks believed exactly, it is obvious that they did respect views other than those of Bishop Athanasius. With their greater attention to the spiritual dimension of Christianity, they could have appreciated the gnostic perspective as such a seeking way to be Christian would be discovered in the books they hid.

For example, the monks would have read in the *Gospel of Thomas*, found within four miles of their Monastery, sayings of Jesus that would have included its first verse about seeking, and such teachings as: "From me did the all come forth, and unto me did the all extend. Split a piece of wood, and I am there. Lift up the stone, and you will find me there."[13] "The kingdom is inside of you and it is outside of you."[14] Further, the prophetic words, "recognize what is in your sight, and that which is hidden from you will become plain to you. For there is nothing hidden which will not become manifest."[15]

Interestingly, all of these hidden sayings of Jesus do not reveal new beliefs, but ways to find and develop faith. Implications from these particular sayings are that seeking is the way to find the presence of God and his Spirit. God is both within and beyond us. Revelations from God are not complete and finished because new knowledge, and even things that are now hidden, will become apparent as time unfolds. In these verses, the concept of theology changes from being the establishment of a set of revelations from God. Rather, knowledge of God is an ongoing process open to discovery. Like most other verses in the Gnostic Gospels, they do not lend themselves to authoritarian doctrines, but they engage the person so that one must seek for oneself both meaning and truth in the quest for spiritual maturity.

Within the collection or library of books, from Nag Hammadi, are five new gospels. Also, as in the Bible, there are other books that are classified as epistles, acts (of the apostles), theological discourses, liturgical hymns/poems, and several books of apocalypse — stories depicting a future victory over evil and the end times of the world — much like the Book of Revelation in the Bible. There are different stories of creation, and as reported, direct challenges to the virgin birth, to a physical bodily resurrection, and to belittling women as religious leaders. These books are neither a Bible unto themselves nor do they replace or negate the Bible. What seems more than likely, early gnostic Christians would have read these books alongside those in the Bible for understanding and inspiration from Jesus.[16]

Contrary to some impressions, the writings that were found do not encourage persons to compromise or reject their Christian faith, give up or leave their preferred churches, accept a set of gnostic beliefs, or even join a modern Gnostic Church. These gospels affirm that the necessity of believing certain doctrines in order to obtain salvation, as many still assert today, was questioned even by early Christians. By affirming that Christianity was not as unified in beliefs as assumed, they challenge Christians to move beyond insisting that what they believe is the only meaning of faith. Rather than being defined by beliefs, faith takes on a greater spiritual focus. Faith doesn't exclude beliefs, but when beliefs define faith, the dynamic spiritual trust in Jesus and God becomes secondary and lost.

In this modern age or milieu, when it is much more acceptable to question elements of faith and belief, rather than just accepting what you are told, the discovery and availability of these hidden Christian resources could not have been brought to light in a better era in history. For many Christians, it is time for Christianity to move beyond fighting over who has the correct interpretation of Jesus, or the Bible, which church is the only true church, and what doctrines must be believed to avoid hell! These books open a window to encourage persons to search for the deeper spiritual message of Jesus. They offer the new opportunity for modern Christians to be inspired in one's own faith by the gnostic or seeking way of Christianity.

In summary, the Gnostics believed that Christianity was more than a set of final beliefs and a finished story. As the beautiful and engaging Christ story continues, there will be various interpretations. All interpretations are challengeable, and the Gnostics would affirm that no one interpretation can make claim to absolute truth as that would be idolatry — claiming equality with God. Not hearing Jesus say that all his followers had to believe the same, they accepted the words of the Apostle Paul, who taught that Christianity was a body with many parts.[17] Agreeing with St. Paul, whom interestingly both the literalists and the Gnostics would claim as their own, the Gnostics seem to understand that diversity was a natural and desirable fact of life.[18]

More importantly than the fact of diversity, they also agreed with Paul who wrote in 1 Corinthians 13, known as the love chapter in the Bible, love "does not insist on its own way."[19] Surely, the monks must have had some feeling why St. Paul may have written these words, especially, when they received the official Order from on high. Of course, perhaps, the Bishop could argue this wasn't insistence but was based on authority and was done for the protection of the truth. Often, as seems the case in many religions, including Christianity, the need for being right and fundamental has surpassed basic teachings of their founders. Then, political and ecclesiastical authority takes hold to lock in certain beliefs and positions as the true way to God. Ironically, it was the Gnostics who were successfully portrayed as the ones who insisted on their secret gnosis and were the narrowed minded ones who claimed they knew the only path to God. Now, with the discovery of the Gnostic Gospels, an altogether different understanding of the Gnostics is being rediscovered. Never do they say in any of their writings you must believe as we do; they did not call themselves the only true Christians, but they embraced a style of faith that proclaimed honestly seeking God was more truthful than insisting, "we have the truth."

The Gnostics were believers in Jesus, but more importantly, because of Jesus, they were "Seekers of God."

Notes: Chapter Six: Protecting and Hiding the Gnostic Gospels

[1] Elaine Pagels, *The Gnostic Gospels*, (New York: Random House, 1979), Pg. 131.
[2] Williston Walker, *A History of the Christian Church*, (New York: Charles Scribner's Sons, 1959) 58.
[3] James M. Robinson, *The Nag Hammadi Library*, hereafter referred to as *NHL*, San Francisco, HarperSanFrancisco, 1978), *Apocalypse of Peter*, 376.
[4] Robinson, *The Nag Hammadi Library, Gospel of Thomas*, 126
[5] The myths of the Gnostics, which will be examined in Chapters 16, 17, and 18, may appear to be the gnostic answers to the makeup of the divine world, but as will be presented, these myths were attempts to explain unsolved mysteries of how and why our world was created.
[6] Robinson, *NHL*, *Apocryphon of James*, 32.
[7] Walker, *A History of the Christian Church*, 26. For the story of Pachomius and the establishment of the earliest monasteries in Egypt.
[8] Irenaeus, *Against Heresies*, 1: X, 5.
[9] Elaine Pagels, *Beyond Belief*, (New York: Random House, 2003), 97.
[10] Robinson, *HHL*, "Introduction," 22. As noted in Chapter One, endnote # 2, there is minor debate over the original hiding place of the jar. Some believe in could have been in a cemetery at the base of the cliffs or perhaps was originally placed in one of the caves. As there was only one jar as opposed to the many scrolls found in caves near the Dead Sea, exactly where it was hidden is open to conjecture. The major fact is that it was found!
[11] Pagels, *Beyond Belief*, 177. Of interest, Athanasius list twenty seven books he calls the books of the New Testament. His list constitutes the books in today's New Testament!
[12] Tim Dowley, ed, *Introduction to The History of Christianity*, (Minneapolis: Fortress Press, 2002), 171.
[13] Robinson, *NHL,Gospel of Thomas*, 137, 77.
[14] Robinson, *NHL,Gospel of Thomas*, 126, 25.
[15] Robinson, *NHL,Gospel of Thomas*, 126, 5.
[16] Pagels, *The Gnostic Gospels*, XV.
[17] I Corinthians 12: 12.
[18] Elaine Pagels, *The Gnostic Paul*, (Minneapolis: Fortress Press, 1975).
[19] I Corinthians 13: 5.

Chapter Seven

The Gnostic Meaning of Gnosis — Relationships!

> The truth proclaimed by the Church is immoveable, and the theories of these men are but tissues of falsehoods. [1]
>
> -Bishop Irenaeus, *Against Heresies*

By the late second century, the apostolic church was well on its way in unifying their system of bishops and also establishing the criteria for membership in their church. As Elaine Pagels explains that by the second century, "Whoever confessed the creed, accepted the ritual of baptism, participated in worship, and obeyed the clergy was accepted as a fellow Christian."[2] The power of this church was growing in defining what it meant to be a Christian and at the center was being a devoted church member. This devotion wasn't just too any church, but to the church led by bishops. In their writings, when the fathers referred to the church, they were beginning, not always, but as in the quotation above, to capitalize "Church." They could do this because there was the only one true church. There was no need for any others, because, as stated, their church's truth was *immoveable.*

With the claim of having exclusive truth, all other beliefs that did not agree with *the* Church were simply theories and not the facts of faith. In the case of the Gnostics, an obvious reason they did not possess Christian truth was because of their various and differing beliefs among themselves. Truth was one, according to the bishops; therefore, the Gnostic's knowledge of God was unreliable because they were not one voice. Not being united in beliefs, early critics then claimed this meant they taught that it was acceptable to believe "whatever one wanted to believe." Bishop Irenaeus was one such critic. In regard to their theology, Irenaeus writes that "everyone of them generates something new every day."[3] The Gnostics knew that this claim of believing whatever without discretion meant going beyond the theological boundaries set by the church. Bishop Irenaeus makes this exceeding clear when he adds that they were false believers because the Gnostics "seek revelations of God on their own, in defiance of the church's truths."[4]

Oh, my! The Gnostics might have answered, "Yes, we do." Do you not know that *knowledge* is the safeguard against believing just anything, and it is precisely the reason not to believe blindly, as you propose? Knowledge and self examination are essential for building honest faith. We believe the truth of Christ is greater than the measure of the bishops' minds!

For the Gnostics, Jesus was the truth, and as their *Gospel of Truth* declares, Jesus was a great joy for believers.[5] His truth was found foremost in the daily experience of seeking newness of life with the living Christ and having an openness to the Spirit of God. This seeking opened the door for knowledge being a part of one's relationship and an understanding of God. Because the Gnostics understood knowledge as a tool in the process of faith, and not faith's facts, their respect and use of the term, "gnosis," would add to their trouble with the church.

The bishops charged, "You free thinking Gnostics believe in gnosis for your salvation and not faith. You believe your own self knowledge is greater than the wisdom of the church. In order to save you from the pits of hell, be it known your beliefs are wrong. You are heretics." [6]

Such charges were critical in giving them the name Gnostics, and at the center of the name was the term, "gnosis." Understanding the difference of its meaning between that of the fathers and that of the Gnostics is key in freeing one's appreciation for the Gnostics. Gnosis is a Greek word which translates into English as knowledge and can refer to different kinds of knowing.[7] As explained previously, for the church fathers, their understanding of the word had a narrow meaning. Gnosis meant one's theological beliefs that was equivalent to one's knowledge of God, and in regards to the Gnostics, gnosis meant their secret and erroneous knowledge of the divine.[8] Therefore, to expose their invalid beliefs, the fathers expanded the term gnosis, giving them the name Gnostics. They could not be called Atheist; they believed there was a God.

They were not Agnostics; they didn't doubt or question the existence of God. So, the fathers highlighted the word gnosis to describe them as being Gnostics.[9]

The fathers applied this label for three basic reasons. First and foremost, as has been stated, the fathers were disturbed that the Gnostics held beliefs, or gnosis, contrary to those of their church. Next, the fathers could use this label because these Christians assumed they possessed special knowledge or a secret gnosis, which when known by initiation, would lead the way to salvation. Finally, these Christians were Gnostics because by their secret knowledge they believed they were those in the 'know' about Christianity and God, but were not![10]

"Gnostic" was not a complimentary name! Gnostics was an imposed name in order to identify these people as having a false understanding of God. *Imposed?* Yes! A surprising and telling revelation from the materials is that these Christians did *not* call themselves Gnostics. Richard Smith writes in the "Afterward" of The *Nag Hammadi Library in English* that "none of the Nag Hammadi texts use 'gnostic' as a term of self-determination."[11] Within their writings, they do not refer to themselves as Gnostics. Nor is the word gnosis used by the Gnostics to refer to some secret teachings, which had often been assumed to be the primary reason for their name. Indeed, this exaggeration of secrecy in the term, gnosis, implied they were a sect or cult – exactly how the fathers wanted them to be known. What becomes clear is that the fathers wanted all to know that gnostic theological views were unacceptable and had nothing to do at all with true Christianity!

By limiting the meaning of gnosis to being the beliefs one held, this description of these uninformed Christians fit the needs of the fathers quite well. This allowed them to expand the word heretic from its general meaning, referred to earlier, from "those who believed in choice of beliefs." Now, with the growing power and authority of the church, even more precisely beyond choice, heretic meant, particularly for those groups and persons, like the Gnostics, those who did not believe *correctly*! In the words of Bishop Irenaeus, "It is a matter of necessity that every church agree with this Church, on account of its pre-eminent authority."[12] His church possessed not only the truth, but the authority to condemn all who did not accept the true beliefs of God.

Far more relevant, than whether the church made harsh judgments that were fair or not, comes a lesson from the Gnostic Gospels that brings a positive message about the meanings of gnosis and faith. For the Gnostics, the word gnosis was used to describe a part of the process of faith and not the end result of faith. Gnosis was a dynamic term that allowed beliefs to change and faith to grow and mature. Importantly, gnosis had two basic dimensions or aspects for the Gnostics which went beyond the church fathers' definition. Understanding these two dimensions further helps clarify the fathers' choice to call them Gnostics, and why the Gnostics believed that gnosis to be a critical and essential part of faith.

The first dimension of gnosis included beliefs, and this complicates the gnostic meaning of the term somewhat, but not when understood in context. The Gnostics had beliefs, and they would have gladly admitted their beliefs didn't always agree with those who held positions of power in the church. Agreeing with the fathers, they recognized beliefs were convictions necessary for understanding the world and God. Disagreeing, a difference was that part of gnosis, meaning beliefs, could be subject to change with new knowledge and insight. Sounds reasonable?

Not so, said Bishop Irenaeus. Clearly, he would have repeated his statement that the truth of the Church is "immoveable."[13] Specifically referring to the Gnostics' beliefs he writes, "the theories of these men [and he would have included women] are but a tissue of falsehood!"[14] According to Irenaeus, unlike that of the church, the gnosis of the Gnostics was unreliable and nonsense. His reasoning behind this charge was that he thought the Gnostics upheld beliefs, mystical truths, and visions not sanctioned by his church. The problem was that Jesus had not given these misguided teachings, at least to any bishop's knowledge, to his church. Because these unorthodox teaching went beyond blessed knowledge, they were, therefore, mere theories, not Christian truth.[15] Simply stated, because their gnosis was false, the Gnostics did not understand Jesus or Christianity.

"No," said the Gnostics! They were convinced that their own beliefs were true, but also that truth was not limited or confined by what one believed. Nor was the meaning of gnosis limited to one's beliefs. Their beliefs were a part of their understanding of the term gnosis, but only a part. To say the definition of Christianity was dictated by one's beliefs was to overlook a greater message of Jesus, as there was another overriding side to the coin of gnosis. This side of the coin, or second dimension of gnosis, was its most valuable aspect as it exposed the heart and soul of Jesus' message and the true power of Christianity.

Gnosis had a dynamic side that was the key to unlocking faith. In their writings, when the Gnostics used the word gnosis, it referred to a way of believing and not simply beliefs alone. Essential to understanding the gnostic seeking way of faith is for these Christians that gnosis was not knowledge as knowing the facts or giving consent to a rational system of beliefs. Gnosis in this dynamic dimension was experiential knowledge, intuitive, emotional, and was more spiritual than religious. Information wasn't excluded, but gnosis primarily meant knowing defined as to know or to relate to another. As mentioned in Chapter Two, gnosis was foremost a knowing in the sense of *he or she knows me*![16]

Overshadowed by the teachings of the bishops and the purging of the gnostic writings, this dynamic meaning for gnosis was unknown until the Gnostic Gospels could be read in recent times. What is discovered is that gnosis for the Gnostics predominately meant "*acquaintance*." Therefore, Bentley Layton explains term gnosis in the introduction to his book *The Gnostic Scriptures.* He writes regarding gnosis, "In English one can call this kind of knowledge 'acquaintance.' The corresponding word is gnosis. If one is introduced to god, one has gnosis of god." To emphasize the point he adds, "the English word 'acquaintance' always translates gnosis or its equivalent."[17] Throughout the gnostic works, gnosis signifies much more than their beliefs, and surprisingly, more than mystical visions and secrets. Gnosis is a beautiful term about an acquaintance and is about relationship to others, particularly, to Jesus and God.

Also, in our acquaintance with God, there is a very important passage related to the dynamic meaning of gnosis within the *Gospel of Philip.* This verse teaches, "Faith is our earth, that in which we take root. And Hope is the water through which we are nourished. Love is the wind through which we grow. Knowledge (*gnosis)* then is the light through which we ripen."[18] In this beautiful and thoughtful teaching, gnosis did not stand alone as the meaning and equivalent of faith, nor was it limited to what one believed. Knowledge (gnosis) was one of the dynamic dimensions for enriching life along with faith, hope, and love! Using our knowledge could grow our faith and life, or in their words, to "ripen" both.[19] Gnosis was only one of the critical building blocks in developing our relationship to God. What one believed needed to be tempered with knowledge!

Far ahead of their time, the Gnostics were thinking Christians who went beyond following those who insisted on their truth because of their authority and power. To claim what one believed was the exact and exclusive knowledge of God, was not only vain, but suspect. Gnosis was more than a certain wisdom; it was a word or tool to help our faith be honest and grow, and most importantly, to assist in our relating to Jesus and God.

A more personal example of this dynamic dimension of gnosis is in the *Gospel of Thomas.* It also stresses gnosis as knowing or understanding oneself in relationship to God. In verse 3, Jesus says, "When you come to know (gnosis) yourself, then you will become known, and you will realize that it is you who are the sons of the living Father."[20] Knowing oneself was an essential part of gnosis, and as the verse teaches, doing so can lead to a positive relationship with God.

This teaching of Jesus of knowing oneself implies the need for understanding in more than a cursory way; obviously, to gain deeper understanding involves many kinds of knowledge. Marvin Meyer in the Introduction to *The Gnostic Bible* writes, "Gnosis is a common word in Greek, and it can designate different types of knowledge."[21] Different kinds of knowledge included rational facts, logical reality, and one's beliefs, but importantly, it also involves dimensions of knowledge such as emotion, imagination, intuition, and for the Gnostics, mythical thinking.[22] Mythical thinking would get them further in trouble because that implied they accepted only Greek philosophy and myths and not Christian truths.

Of some significance, the gnostic concept of knowing oneself, based on Jesus' words, wasn't just Greek philosophy dependent upon on Socrates' wisdom, in his famous statement, "know thyself." In addition to the philosophical knowledge, especially, for the Gnostics, knowing oneself included spiritual understanding, and this was a part of gnosis. For Thomas, "know thyself" wasn't just a wise saying, and although its wisdom should not be denied, Jesus expands upon its wisdom with his call for faith. Thomas heard Jesus teaching that faith in God helps us understand ourselves more deeply, and as stated earlier, allows us to realize and know we are children of God. Earlier, the concept of self knowledge was discussed, but now it can be seen as related to the term gnosis. Gnosis, if there be any secret, is about our own personal understanding of ourselves and direct relationship to God.

Knowing (gnosis) ourselves as a child of God may seem trite, as it is a fairly popular concept today, but for the Gnostics truly believing this for ourselves presents a radical departure from a belief called the doctrine of original sin. Understanding ourselves as a child of God would suggest we relate to God as a parent. As a child is related to its parents at birth, so it would be that at birth one is not separated from God. Certainly, one can separate oneself from God by one's own choice or way of life. To say that when a child is born that there is no good or spiritual dimension in them, until they are baptized, would be nonsense to the Gnostics. Therefore, their Christian understanding of knowing oneself would be different from the belief that all persons were born in total depravity, also known as the doctrine of original sin. This understanding of the totally sinful self was established by St. Augustine and became official church doctrine some 300 years after the Gnostics' time.[23] Therefore, the Gnostics would not have not known of such a doctrine, but the argument here is that if their view of our being children of God had been allowed, such a totally negative view of humanity could at least be debated within Christianity.

Today, this belief of original sin is often taken, particularly by fundamentalist Christians, as an unmovable dogma. However, Robin R. Meyers explains in his book *Saving Jesus From the Church*, such a doctrine creates what he calls a salvation monopoly or franchise. He adroitly remarks, "We are pronounced bad by birth and given only one possible cure by the same entity that provided the diagnosis!"[24] In its extreme form, this doctrine of total depravity, according to Augustine, was a condition that all babies inherit at birth.[25] Unfortunately, being born in total depravity has encouraged many to believe that they are bad, and there is no good in them, unless they accept Jesus as their Savior from sin. The Gnostics would have been appalled at such a totally negative way to understand oneself and such a circular way to understand the message of Jesus. Jesus' message wasn't a threat, nor that we were all good or all bad, but rather, there was good news from a loving God.

Not denying the existence of evil or sin, according to Thomas' account, knowing oneself can lead one to realize that you are a son (also as a daughter) of the living Father.[26] As Thomas' gospel records in Verse 70, "Jesus said, that which you have will save you if you bring it forth from yourselves."[27] Thus, in this sense of knowing oneself, gnosis means coming alive to God's spirit within. Without denying the existence of sin, there is also something good in us. This awakening or realization that comes is not salvation from degradation or one's original sin, so herein the Gnostics have a subtle but crucial difference with the orthodox on the conception of sin. More than being the focus of one's damnation, or the fact of sin, the emphasis is on the beginning and building of a relationship or gnosis with Christ. Gnosis was a positive and dynamic blessing for life, yet, even far more significant than differences with the doctrine of original sin, and other beliefs, comes its overall and foundational dynamic dimension.

Elaine Pagels explains gnosis well when she suggests the concept for the Gnostics means "insight."[28] Insight is not finding enlightenment as the complete answer, but is to be enlightened as to what is true either about oneself or the world. Insight is like gaining a collection of knowledge from various realities, which allow one to understand or see or even feel meaning. The Gnostics might express it as finding deep peace, or spiritual rest, particularly, when one affirms and desires to *ripen* their God given spirit within. It might be a moment, a revelation, or experience of ah-ha! This illumination is not final knowledge; it opens the mind to new knowledge and understanding that allows us to change our visions, wisdom, and faith.

Because the fathers believed new religious knowledge or insight wasn't necessary, this dynamic and active understanding of gnosis was not even considered and most likely not understood by them. Insight for the fathers meant coming to the realization that what they taught was truth and should be believed and accepted on faith. However, for the Gnostics, faith was a verb, not a noun, and likewise was the word, gnosis — meaning to ripen one's faith.[29]

Understanding what the Gnostics themselves meant by gnosis is critical in reversing the quite common perspective that the Gnostics believed they were saved by their gnosis — their beliefs. The Gnostics do not say this! The Gnostics never say believe our beliefs or prepare yourself for damnation and hell. The fathers do! The primary bishop who led the charge against the Gnostics, and vehemently declared that accepting the beliefs of his "Church" was necessary for the gift of salvation, was the Bishop of Gaul.[30] In other words, as implied in the statement above by the Bishop, the gnosis of the Gnostics meant "tissues of falsehood" and only the apostolic church understood gnosis.

Bishop Irenaeus in his writings, and particularly in his book *Against Heresies*, would make certain that gnosis would be understood as meaning beliefs and that these heretical believers should be called Gnostics.[31] Because he is recognized as the prime source in explaining and demonizing the gnostic positions, Irenaeus possibly could have been the creator of the label, Gnostics — with a capital "G." His book, *Against Heresies*, is actually a massive five volume attack, particularly against the Gnostics, who are his primary target. However, there are many others whom he accuses as not accepting the doctrines and positions of his Church as truth.[32]

Against Heresies is the common, shorter, abbreviated name for quick reference to Irenaeus' voluminous work, but his official title for them is quite illuminating in how the Gnostics were given their name. In Greek, the full title of his collective five volumes is translated *The Refutation and Overthrow of Falsely So-Called Knowledge.*[33] No wonder modern scholars refer to it as simply *Against Heresies*! The last word "Knowledge" in the title is the Greek word "Gnosis." The critical words are the combination, "So-Called Knowledge." Then to make his point more emphatic, it expands to "Falsely So-Called Knowledge." Also within this descriptive title is the declaration, because their Gnosis is false, this knowledge not only should be refuted but overthrown! Throughout the five volumes, he charges that gnostic beliefs are off the mark of truth. Clearly, as Irenaeus believed, destroying/overthrowing their writings and gospels, which almost happened, would eliminate their teachings and heresy. By making reference within *Against Heresies* to other gospels such as the *Gospel of Truth* and the *Gospel of Judas*, ironically, he gave evidence for existence of other gospels in early Christianity, which otherwise might never have been known historically to exist.[34] In one general comment pertaining to *all the other* gospels than those his church approved, his judgment is straightforward when he says, "how inconsistent with the truth are their statements."[35] Truth, for this theologian, was either/or, and as he begins his book, the charges of heresy become quite bold!

In the Preface to *Against Heresies*, in Volume 1, the Bishop's first words are directed to those who did not accept the church's teachings as truth. He writes, "Inasmuch as certain men have set the truth aside, they err."[36] He then decries, "These men falsify the oracle of God, and prove themselves evil interpreters of the good word of revelation."[37] He says that his purpose in writing is "to make the doctrines known to thee, but also to furnish the means of showing their falsity."[38] Then speaking specifically of the Gnostics in his opening remarks, he says, "They also overthrow the faith of many by drawing them away, under a pressure of superior knowledge from him who founded and adorned the universe."[39] If that wasn't enough, Irenaeus adds,

"Their sentiments are very different. They have not sufficiently purged their brains to avoid such an abyss of madness."[40] Their knowledge was not only superior, but an "abyss of madness." Purge their brains? The Gnostics might have argued this purging of the brain, which would eliminate any need to question beliefs, was exactly what the literalists wanted for all their own believers. Avoid madness, cleanse your souls, by believing what you are told!

Obviously, Irenaeus was a skilled writer for his time, an imposing Bishop, and a virulent leader against all heresies. However, for those who disagree with his charges and authority, there are within his work some rather humorous statements. In his introduction he explains, "I shall also endeavor, according to my moderate ability, to furnish the means of overthrowing them, by showing how absurd and inconsistent with the truth are their statements."[41] "Moderate ability?" Although not shy in his vicious attacks, was he trying to suggest for himself the virtue of *humility*? In another remark he writes, "I intend with brevity and clearness to set forth the opinions of those who are now promulgating heresy."[42] Five volumes is *brevity*? For those who are promulgating heresy, there is one fact he does state rather boldly, "they are evil interpreters of the good word of revelation."[43] *Evil*?

With more information, particularly with the sources in *The Nag Hammadi Library*, today some might want to reconsider just how evil these heretics were. Beyond the judgment of being evil, could it be possible they might have some positive gnosis to offer? Certainly, gnosis meaning one's openness to new knowledge, insight, and one's living relationship with God provides an entirely new appreciation of the word. With the power of his pen, Irenaeus was able to argue and convince many who would read his works that not only the gnosis of the Gnostics meant false theology, but that anything gnostic was anathema. In addition, they were also simpletons, according to Irenaeus. As he states, referring to both the Gnostics and their gnosis, "these *simple ones* are unable to distinguish falsehood from truth."[44]

Unfortunately for Christian faith, the narrow interpretation of truth by leaders of the apostolic church, represented well by Irenaeus, would become known in its essence, as the orthodox beliefs of Christianity. In contrast, the meaning of "gnostic," would come to mean false and mythological beliefs, and this assumption lasted long into history — until now. More momentous than the demise of the Gnostics, the revelation of their works makes clear that one form of interpreting Christ was won, not by openness to what Christ taught, but by attitudes of power and selfishness. Such attitudes seem contrary to the teachings of Christ, and particularly again, to those of Paul, about love not insisting on its own way, highlighted in his first letter to the Corinthians.[45]

All this authoritarian and strict theological haranguing against those who did not believe properly may seem unreal with its boldness and arrogance, particularly, in its relationship to the early church. However, using negative arguments against all heretics wasn't the only way the apostolic church would defend their right to know and preach the gospel truth. With an unusually positive argument and message, they also presented a bold reason for their privilege to claim the exclusive right to speak for Jesus and God in a doctrine named Apostolic Authority. The content of this doctrine would be another powerful, central means to condemn all gnostic beliefs, keep their voice silent, and more importantly, to raise high the literalists' banner of their Christian truths over all others.

Notes: Chapter Seven: The Gnostic Meaning of Gnosis — Relationship

[1] Irenaeus, *Against Heresies*, hereafter noted as *AH*, 1:X.
[2] Elaine Pagels, *The Gnostic Gospels*, (New York: Random House, 1979), 126.
[3] Irenaeus, *AH*, 1: XVIII, 1.
[4] Ibid.
[5] James M. Robinson, Editor, *The Nag Hammadi Library*, hereafter noted as *NHL*, the *Gospel of Truth*, (New York:HarperCollins, 1978), 40.
[6] Pagels, *The Gnostic Gospels*, XXII.
[7] J. Michael Matkin, *The Gnostic Gospels*, (New York: Alpha Books, 2005), 13. Matkin shares an excellent definition of gnosis that is more reflective of the Gnostics' deeper understanding of the term.
[8] Pagels, *The Gnostic Gospels*, Pg. 127.
[9] Irenaeus, *AH*, 1: XVIII,1. The exact origin of the label, Gnostics, is not known, but Irenaeus clearly refers to those who believe in gnosis as Gnostics.
[10] Pagels, *Beyond Belief*, (New York: Random House, 2003), 33
[11] Robinson, *NHL*, 549.
[12] Irenaeus, *AH*, 3: III, 2.
[13] Irenaeus, *AH*, 1: X, 5.
[14] Ibid.
[15] Ibid.
[16] Bentley Layton, *The Gnostic Scriptures*, (New York: Doubleday, 1987), 9.

[17] Ibid.

[18] Robinson, *NHL*, the *Gospel of Philip*, 156.

[19] Ibid.

[20] Robinson, *NHL*, the *Gospel of Thomas*, 126.

[21] Willis Barnstone & Marvin Meyer, *The Gnostic Bible*, (Boston: New Seed Books, 2006), 8.

[22] The primary myths of the gnostics will be presented in Chapters 17 & 18.

[23] Robin Meyers, *Saving Jesus From The Church*, (New York: HarperOne, 2009), 97.

[24] Ibid.

[25] Ibid.

[26] Robinson, *NHL*, the *Gospel of Thomas*, 126.

[27] Robinson, *NHL*, the *Gospel of Thomas*, 134.

[28] Pagels, *The Gnostic Gospels*, XVIII. Here, also, is a good explanation of "gnosis."

[29] Robinson, the *Gospel of Philip*, 156.

[30] For a thumbnail sketch of the Bishop of Gaul, see, Tom Dowley, ed., *Introduction to the History of Christianity.*

[31] For a discussion of the word, gnosis, being expanded upon by Irenaeus, see, Marvin Meyer, *The Gnostic Discoveries*, (San Francisco, HarperSanFancisco, 2005), 40.

[32] Pagels, *Beyond Belief*, 128. Bishop Irenaeus' *Against Heresies* also can be attained by www. earlychristianwriters.com/Irenaeus or www.thegnosticlibrary.com.

[33] Pagels, Beyond Belief, 141. For the history of Irenaeus' text from Greek to Latin, see Layton, *The Gnostic Scriptures*, XXV.

[34] Layton, *The Gnostic Scriptures*, 181. Also, Irenaeus, *AH* 1:XXXI,1

[35] Irenaeus, *AH*, I: Preface

[36] Ibid.

[37] Ibid.

[38] Ibid.

[39] Ibid.

[40] Ibid.

[41] Ibid.

[42] Ibid.

[43] Ibid.

[44] Ibid.

[45] I Corinthians 13

Chapter Eight

Apostolic Authority Revisited

> The Truth is to be found nowhere but in the Catholic Church, the sole depository of Apostolic Doctrine. [1]
>
> -St. Irenaeus, *Against Heresies*

As the bishops of the apostolic church were denouncing the Gnostics for their false gnosis, the underlying implication was that their own "gnosis" was the true knowledge of God. Irenaeus, for example, writes in *Against Heresies*, "True gnosis is that which consists in the doctrines of the apostles...."[2] The apostolic doctrines to which he refers are first found in certain beliefs expressed in the baptismal questions. Baptismal questions might not seem to be that critical to the beliefs of the church or its theology, because today, they often are asked rather routinely and ceremonially. As the early church became more organized, confessing beliefs before baptism became essential in the process of becoming a Christian. The questions were central because they framed a number of doctrines that the apostolic church taught were the beliefs that true Christians should accept, believe, and confess.

Interestingly, it was unlikely any questions were asked in the first baptisms of Christians. The earliest records in the New Testament indicate that baptisms by both Peter and Paul did not include questions but were simply administered with the baptismal words "in the name of Jesus Christ" (Acts 2:38 and 19:5). In these Biblical verses, only forgiveness of sins and the gift of the Holy Spirit for believers are mentioned following the baptisms, and they are presented as *results* of baptism and are not required questions for the believer.

By the time of Hippolytus, a Bishop of Rome who lived from c.a. 170 C.E. to 235 C.E., in his writing titled *Apostolic Tradition*, he states that there were at least three questions that were necessary when one was baptized. The questions included confession of faith but also involved affirming beliefs about Jesus' life, his death, and resurrection. The rational was that these beliefs had been taught to his earliest disciples directly by Jesus. Then, particularly, through the apostle Peter, his truths and wisdom had been passed on to the church. To include them in the ritual of baptism was only expressing what Jesus wanted people to believe about him. Thus, the baptism ritual evolved, from an affirmation of belief, to consent to beliefs.

Hippolytus reports the person being baptized would be asked, "Do you believe in God, the Father Almighty?"[3] Then, the believer would go under water. The second question, quite more complicated and lengthy, was, "Do you believe in Christ Jesus, the Son of God, who was born by the Holy Spirit of the Virgin Mary, and was crucified under Pontius Pilate, and was dead and buried, and rose again the third day alive from the dead, and ascended into heaven, and sat at the right hand of the Father, and will come to judge the living and the dead?"[4] The new Christian says, "I believe," and is baptized in the water again. Then the question, "Do you believe in the Holy Spirit, in the holy church, and the resurrection of the body?"[5] After responding, "I believe," the believer is baptized a third time.[6] Well, one would think being dunked three times and affirming all these doctrines would be sufficient to prove one's faith! However, further evidence indicates that later, as the apostolic church grew in power, even up to three years of pre-baptismal instruction were required before the ritual was administered.[7] Why?

Baptism was coming to be interpreted as dealing with a person's past, their repentance, and less with one's future; therefore, the person had to prove oneself worthy for baptism. As Tertullian taught, "purity was required before baptism."[8] No, he does not explain what constituted purity! However, the appearance seems to be that purity meant a willingness to confess the core beliefs of baptism. These beliefs, altogether, constituted the doctrine of the church that explained the life, meaning, and messages of Jesus; they expressed in detail, the truths of Christianity. As Elaine Pagels says, "The orthodox, by contrast (to the Gnostics), were beginning to identify their own doctrine as itself the truth — the sole legitimate form of

Christian faith."[9] Interestingly, the questions at baptism were beginning to be summarized in a new form, as well.

Although not found as a sole ancient document, all these baptismal beliefs were to be expressed in what several church fathers called the **Rule of Faith**, or in what Bishop Irenaeus refers sometimes in his writings to as the **Rule of Truth**. Irenaeus details these beliefs of this Rule in *Against Heresies*; they are quite in line with the baptismal questions. As the contents of these questions will be discovered as the same doctrines found in the Apostles' Creed, these baptismal questions are quite revealing. Why? These questions demonstrate how faith in Christ came to mean accepting beliefs, and how Christianity as a religion became defined primarily by these doctrines. Although the Gnostics tried to protest that one's relationship to Christ was far more central to faith than agreeing to doctrines, the church would win the argument that believing these beliefs was <u>the</u> way to know Jesus and God. Their argument that all the details in the baptismal questions were the true teachings of Jesus, interestingly, would not end there. Growing out of the baptismal questions, there were additional beliefs and doctrines which told the true or orthodox story of Christ and Christianity.

For example, the apostolic church began to argue for their belief that the story and meaning of Jesus could be found only in gospels *approved* by the church. Perhaps, there was a reason. In contrast to other gospels, the four favored gospels gave the clearest support to the beliefs and doctrines of the bishops stated in the baptismal questions. Tim Dowley in the book *Introduction to The History of Christianity* reports that in regard to the canonical selection for a gospel, "Above all, it had to be written by an apostle, and also be recognizably orthodox in its content."[10] Certainly, the four gospels of Matthew, Mark, Luke and John met that criteria, and by making them holy and the true word of God, the stories and other beliefs within them could be added as the facts of Christianity. Therefore, from these four gospels and the baptismal questions, the literalists' theology could take its form and build its extended system of beliefs in order to make the Christ story clear and fundamental. To this story, however, there would be additional beliefs that the apostolic church also established as being the truths of Christ and Christianity.

Including beliefs of the baptismal questions, but going beyond with the help of the four holy gospels, the bishops declared not only the virgin birth but the miracles of Jesus were actual events in his lifetime. He was crucified, but then after his death, an additional belief, not in the early baptismal questions, was that he made a visit to hell before his resurrection to life again on earth. Upon his return to earth, he met and spoke with certain disciples establishing his truths with them before his assent into heaven. Now, Jesus would be sitting at the right hand of God, casting judgment on both the living and the dead, as to those who would join him in heaven. Of course, these beliefs are commonly known in conventional Christianity, but early in their development as doctrines, the bishops stressed all these were literal events and were to be accepted as nothing but the truth. Within these doctrines are facts that happened both before Easter and afterwards, and all should be accepted by faith. All reports of what happened post-Easter were as actual as those events which were pre-Easter, a distinction expanded by Marcus Borg, particularly, in his book *Meeting Jesus Again for the First Time.*[11] Something had changed subtly. More than developing faith or belief in Jesus, the message of the church was to believe in their form of Christianity!

In addition to these pre and post Easter realities about Christ, the orthodox theology would be expanded to include some beliefs that were not necessarily required, but expected, because they conveyed the literal teaching about God and the creation. Interestingly, these additional beliefs still hold power in regard to some of today's theological debates, and often not recognized is that these creations stories helped to build a foundation for other orthodox beliefs and doctrines. In the creation story, which would be central to the description of God, as it was for the Gnostics, the literalists were to teach that the creation story told in the Bible's Book of Genesis was exactly how all was created.[12] Although there are differences in the details and order of creation in Genesis 1 and Genesis 2, both of these were the literal truth.[13] More importantly, all other religious and pagan creation stories were myths, but not theirs. The story told in *Genesis* was not mythical, and rather, as noted earlier, was historical.[14] Today, it would be like saying the details in the story of Genesis were the scientific truth and were the exact order of how creation of all things happened on earth.

Accepting that the creation stories were correct in their details, the next step would be to affirm theological truths derived from them. This step would be critical for the literalists' development of theology, because from creation's details, the truth of God's plan for humankind could be discovered and made clear. From the events described in Genesis, the theological lesson was that all was good in the creation of this world. Then, humankind tempted by the serpent, ate of the tree of knowledge, sinned, and this became their fall.[15] The message from the fall was that there was now evil in the world brought forth by the first humans separating themselves from God and disobeying the benevolent Creator.[16] This story, of sin and shame by these actual human persons, Adam and Eve, was the total truth of why there was evil in the world, and no other interpretation of this remarkable event and saga should be considered.

From this historical rebellion against God, the theological message was that since all have fallen short of the glory of God, sin reigns; we need to be saved, or we have no afterlife.[17] Here, the story particularly moves to the advantage for Christians over other religions. One can be saved, not just by believing in God as did the Jews, doing good works, or following religious laws, but salvation was awarded only to those who accepted Jesus as the messiah — the Christ.[18] With the coming of the Messiah, the way to be forgiven of all sin and be considered righteous before God, to be his blessed, chosen ones on earth and ready for heaven, was to believe in Jesus as the only way to God.[19]

This summary of the early church's primary beliefs was regarded as the teachings of Jesus, and the doctrines that Jesus would have approved. There was no need to vary from these primary beliefs because according to the apostolic church's wisdom and authority, these beliefs came directly to their church through Jesus. To move beyond anything but a literal interpretation of these beliefs would not be fair to Jesus, to his first disciples, and particularly, to his apostles.[20] The task according to the church wasn't to question these truths but to accept them all — by faith. Faith was gained when one was baptized and confessed these beliefs; doing so allowed one to become a true Christian.

Obviously, most of these beliefs are commonly known today by many as the basic and fundamental truths of Christianity. They may sound quite familiar, because for some Christians, faith still means what one believes, and for many churches, accepting and confessing these beliefs, developed by the apostolic church, mark the true Christian.

Now, enter the Gnostics, to question whether accepting this system of theology was the only way to be a believer and follower of Jesus. Not that they didn't accept many of its assertions, but their question was whether it was necessary, to be deemed a true Christian, that one had to believe all these theological statements and positions as indisputable truths.

For the Gnostics, this literal theology could not only be questioned but challenged in many of its details. Their effort wasn't to dismantle Jesus, but to understand his message in a broader context than that his mission was to establish doctrines which God required for belief, and if not accepted, one's path to hell was paved. Against such a powerful system of theology and ecclesiastical authority, the Gnostic Gospels affirm that the Gnostics were far more than those who just presented alternative beliefs to the literalists. They were those who had the courage and audacity to question, not just authority, but doctrines which were declared as absolute and certain truth.

Some of their questions to the literalists might be summarized: As believers in Jesus, why can't we hold different interpretations about such beliefs, as his virgin birth, his visit to hell, his status as now sitting and judging at the right hand of God? Since these beliefs weren't asked in early baptisms, why are these questions and others now asked at baptism? Although not required at baptism, why cannot we differ from you in the interpretation of the creation story told in Genesis?" Why is it that we and pagans, and those of the Jewish faith, and all who disagree with you, have no chance for salvation or eternal life?

In essence, these questions were why was it not fair to have differing interpretations of the meaning of Jesus and his messages? There was an answer! The reason was because the bishops' beliefs had been passed from Jesus directly to his apostles. From the apostles, their beliefs had been conveyed to the church that they had established. This process was given a name by the church fathers and was declared early in the proto-orthodox writings as a doctrine of the church. This truth was called, officially, the "Doctrine of Apostolic Succession," and sometimes, "Apostolic Authority."[21]

Although there is no evidence for this in the Bible, it became the dogma or truth proclaimed by the church. The bishops of this church represented an uninterrupted line of inherited wisdom from Jesus and the apostles, and this blessed privileged gave them the exclusive right and authority to explain and detail Christian truth.

Now, because of the Gnostic Gospels, there is what might be called a fork in the road or a different possible path that might have been taken in regard to apostolic authority. Apostolic authority might have meant more than only one orthodox way to believe in Christ. New evidence suggests the road to authority wasn't as straight as have been assumed. Before the discovery of the gospels of Thomas, Philip, and Mary Magdalene, it was believed that this right to authority had been granted to the church by all the apostles of Jesus, excluding the betrayer, Judas, who was replaced by Matthias. The apostles have been assumed to be one voice. All of the twelve disciples have been considered as apostles because of their closeness to Jesus and their commitment to witness and be his follower. With their importance, of some interest, there is limited information on several of the original disciples including Thaddaeus, Bartholomew, and Simon the Zealot — not to be confused with Simon who would become Peter.[22] From these disciples, no works or writings are known. Perhaps, gospels or writings by some of these could be found someday, but because they are not mentioned by the early fathers, most do not believe these apostles had any written sources or works. So, it cannot be known whether or not these disciples or apostles also passed on apostolic authority and wisdom to the bishops. Without their written witness, the assumption has been that all these apostles agreed with each other or gave their blessing, as spokesmen, primarily, to St. Peter and St. Paul.

However, the Gnostic Gospels raise a serious question. Who was an apostle? The question is critical because this early church based its sole authority for its theological truth on the apostles.[23] What could be a greater authority than those who knew Jesus, heard him speak, and teach, and then met with him after his resurrection? Beyond the twelve disciples, a complex question is what made one an apostle? Although some would argue that knowing Jesus during his lifetime was critical in order to be called an apostle that would exclude Paul, who often claimed he was an apostle — particularly to the Gentiles. So who were apostles?

Ann Graham Brock, in her book *Mary Magdalene, The First Apostle* relates, "…in the New Testament we have no unified concept of the apostle but rather a number of definitions which seem to stand in contradiction to one another."[24] And then she explains with Paul being regarded as an apostle, two aspects emerge as essential. First, one of the credentials was witnessing an appearance of the risen Christ; second, it was receiving a divine call or commission to proclaim Christ's message.[25] Now, for a shocking fact: *Mary Magdalene*, other than being a woman, met the criteria for being an apostle, plus the additional factor of knowing Jesus during his lifetime!

In the New Testament, Mary Magdalene meets the two theological conditions for apostleship. Matthew, Mark, and John record Jesus' appearance to her and then her commission to spread the good news.[26] Even in an early writing of the Bishop of Rome, Hippolytus referred to Mary Magdalene as the "apostle to the apostles."[27] However, as the tradition grew that men only could be priest, so grew the assumption that being a man was required to be an apostle. Mary's status as an apostle was soon forgotten, and particularly so, as Peter's status as the most trusted of the original twelve disciples, rose. Peter, as the leader of the apostles, was the one on whom Jesus would build his church. Surely, Mary, as a secondary and female disciple, although very close to Jesus, would have given her complete devotion and approval to Peter.

Mary Magdalene, with her gospel now extant, named the *Gospel of Mary* in the Nag Hammadi collection, clearly shows that she did not support Peter as the disciple who knew and understood more about Jesus than any other disciple. In her gospel, Mary argues directly with Peter, and then other disciples boldly attack Peter's mistrust of her.[28] In the text of this gospel, after Mary shares a vision from Jesus, Peter expresses his disdain and disbelief by asking,

> Did he really speak with a woman without our knowledge and not openly? Are we to turn about and all listen to her? Did he prefer her to us?"[29] [It gets worse!] Levi says to Peter, "You have always been hot-tempered. Now I see you contending against the woman like the adversaries. But if the Savior made her worthy, who are you to reject her? Surely the Savior knows her very well. That is why he loved her more than us.[30]

With every right for apostleship, except not being a male, the possibility of Mary Magdalene being consulted for apostolic authority and wisdom seems unlikely! Mary was not given anything near apostolic status by the church, and historically, got little respect. Because the story of the adulterous woman came right before the first mention of Mary Magdalene in the Gospel of Luke, she was long portrayed in history as the prostitute in the preceding story.[31]

Pope Gregory the Great (540 C.E.–604 C.E.) is credited with making such a pronouncement in a sermon that he delivered in 591 C.E. teaching that Mary Magdalene must have been the sinner at the well.[32] Beyond this effective means to belittle the importance of Mary, and to overlook her early recognition as being an apostle, her feminine voice now rises to affirm and uplift the status of women in Jesus' ministry. On a positive note, even the Roman Catholic Church officially now refutes the status for Mary as the prostitute whom Jesus converted at the well, and although denying a marriage to Jesus, recognizes her closeness, even as a Saint.[33]

In addition to the Apostle Mary's gospel, two other of Jesus' original twelve disciples are now known, by the Gnostic Gospels, to be responsible for witnesses that don't lend themselves to the doctrine of apostolic authority. Well, at least, their wisdom from Jesus wasn't deemed as needed or necessary. Before the *Gospel of Philip* was found, what was known of Philip was primarily from verses in the Gospel of John. In John 6, in a text not highly recognized, it reports Jesus tests Philip's faith by asking, how are they going to feed the multitude that had gathered on the other side of the Sea of Galilee? Philip answers, "Six months' wages would not buy enough bread for each of them to get a little."[34] Jesus doesn't reprimand Philip, but Andrew, Peter's brother, shows his faith by sharing that there is a boy who has five loaves of bread and two fish.[35] Of course, that's enough. Philip, in contrast, didn't show much faith it seems!

Later, in his gospel, John indicates that Philip is also slow to comprehend the truth. In John 14, Philip asks Jesus, "Lord, show us the Father, and we will be satisfied. Jesus said to him, have I been with you all this time, Philip, and you still do not know me."[36] Philip isn't presented as the wisest or most trusting of the twelve, yet, in the Book of Acts it reports that Philip was one of the disciples who met with Jesus after his resurrection in the Upper Room.[37]

Philip is presented as a weaker disciple in these stories, but because Jesus doesn't boldly scold him after his remarks, he has been accepted in a fairly positive light as one of the original twelve disciples. However, his gospel would not be too welcomed by the literalists. Why? Within his gospel, Philip presents a different interpretation about Adam and Eve; he does not accept their story as a literal event, and he speaks of five sacraments that were different from those taught by the church. Probably, most disturbing of all, he refutes the literalist's doctrine of the virgin birth![38] Whoops! His gospel does not support the message that all the apostles were of one voice! Then, there is another fairly well known disciple whose story is interesting.

Thomas, also an original disciple, was known primarily because of the description of him given in the Gospel of John. The portrayal of Thomas is clearly more critical and severe than that given to Philip by St. John. In his gospel, John reports that Thomas doesn't even show for the first gathering with Jesus after his resurrection — what true apostle would want to miss that?[39] Then, John, quite successfully, intentionally or not, applies the label, "doubting Thomas," to this apostle.[40] Although St. Augustine explained Thomas' doubting was in order that others might not doubt, by his confession to Jesus as the Lord, Thomas has been immortalized as a weak and wavering disciple.

In contrast, Peter was the strongest disciple, according to the church, and to him would be given the title, the first Bishop of Rome, and eventually honored as the first Pope.[41] Therefore, the historical assumption was that Thomas also humbly consented to the leadership of Peter as the primary apostle. Peter had been given the keys to the kingdom, recorded only in the Gospel of Matthew; therefore, the impression became that he was the most trusted apostle and had been given superior status above all the other disciples.[42]

Even more than the gift of the keys to the kingdom, the primary ecclesiastical and historical argument for Peter's status as the first Pope has been that Peter was first to encounter Jesus after his resurrection, an event recorded only in Luke's gospel.[43] Being the first disciple to whom Jesus would choose to make his resurrection known somehow conveyed that he was the leader and most special of the disciples. Herein lies a substantial conflict.

In the Gospels of Matthew, Mark, and John, *Mary Magdalene* is the first to witness and to stand in awe of the resurrected Jesus![44] In spite of this fact, it was Luke's account of the first resurrection appearance, in contrast to all the others, that became the truth and tradition. By the church's accepting the Luke account, Peter was honored as the Pope. His wisdom was holy, true, and orthodox.

Especially, because Peter, as the first Bishop of Rome, had passed on the true interpretations of Jesus to the church's priests, this became the reasoning why they were closer to Jesus and God; therefore, they knew more than common believers.[45] To search for or question religious beliefs beyond the holy church, which was established and blessed by Peter, was not only futile but sinful. How sinful was it for others like the Gnostics to question religious beliefs and the church's positions? Irenaeus writes, "Let...all the falsely so called 'Gnostics' be recognized as agents of Satan."[46]

The Gnostic Gospels make it clear that Gnostics disagreed that Jesus had embedded his authority and his wisdom foremost or primarily to Peter. Further, they disagree that the other disciples had given their consent to his special status and authority.[47] Rather surprisingly, as will be seen in latter chapters, the Gnostics highly revered Peter and his authority, as was Paul's, as both of their names are used as titles in several of the writings found in the Gnostic Gospels. For the Church of Bishops to claim that Jesus had chosen Peter as superior to all the other disciples became a compelling argument. It was an insightful, positive way to say that those chosen as bishops, who followed Peter, were privy to pure truth and privy to the correct articles of faith and doctrines. But with new information from the Gnostics about other disciples, to claim that Peter somehow gathered all the apostles and received their consensus, seems unlikely. And yet, who can argue with Apostolic Authority?

With the prestige and power that bishops were granted, perhaps the Gnostics would have been wise to create their own system of bishops. That apparently wasn't even a consideration. The Gnostics believed there were different levels of Christian maturity, but believed all had direct access to God. Therefore, they had little respect for those who claimed superlative knowledge and relationship to God because of their ecclesiastical positions.[48] Bishops were never called evil by the Gnostics, or even evil interpreters of the Word, as was done to them, yet, they felt free to criticize the bishops' assumed, holy wisdom and power. For example, as referred to earlier in one of the gnostic writings *The Apocalypse of Peter*, the resurrected Christ explains to Peter that those "who name themselves bishop, and also deacon, as if they had received their authority from God, are in truth, waterless canals."[49] Although accepting of the church, the Gnostics believed a person could experience God directly without a need for mediation by rabbis, priest, bishops or other holy officials.

In the Protestant Reformation this democratic concept was a major issue and was called the "priesthood of all believers." Early on, the church fathers had cried such a belief was foul and dangerous. The bishops knew the true way to God, and to challenge or disagree with their wisdom was to disagree with the plan of God! How crucial was it to agree with the bishops? Elaine Pagels explains the necessity of obedience to them in her chapter called "One God, One Bishop." In *The Gnostic Gospels,* she shares that "Bishop Ignatius warns the laity to revere, honor, and obey the bishop 'as if he were God.' For the bishop, standing at the pinnacle of the church hierarchy, presides in the place of God."[50] Whether all Ignatius' flock agreed with his near deity is not known, but obviously, although respected, today, most bishops don't appear to hold themselves so highly.

Significantly, contrary to what might be assumed by their differences, the Gnostics accepted some of the basic tenants that the bishops believed. From the information above, it might appear that the Gnostics had no respect for the bishops and their teachings. As indicated earlier, Gnostics weren't entirely against literalism, for within their own gospels there is evidence that they too held such positions, as Jesus being a historical person, that he was crucified, that he was resurrected, and once again, that Jesus was "Lord and Savior."[51] Because the Gnostics have been assumed to be a group who were totally mythological in their beliefs, these familiar beliefs sound out of place for them. The surprise, and disbelief for some, is that all these beliefs are found in their writings!

The fact that the Gnostics held some of the literalists' tenets is not what one usually hears. Their writings overwhelming lift up the same Jesus as do the four gospels of the Bible. The Gnostics never disowned the apostolic church; remember, one of their most famous teachers, Valentinus, almost became Pope. The Gnostics wanted to be a part of Christ's church.[52] That they wanted a different way of believing and the freedom to disagree with the bishops' teachings was clear, but as has been so often repeated in history, the Gnostics were silenced by those who were able to claim political and ecclesiastical power. In the Gnostics' case, the establishment of the doctrine of Apostolic Authority, which set Peter over the other disciples, effectively closed the door on other disciples such as Thomas, Philip, and Mary Magdalene. With the voices of other apostles now known, however, the portal of authority is widened as well as what it means to be a believer and disciple of Jesus.

The argument isn't to negate the place and power of Matthew, Mark, Luke, John, Peter, and Paul. Their witness and writings are still invaluable in building Christian faith. However, the argument is that because the apostles, Thomas, Philip, and Mary Magdalene in their gospels supported such views as a spiritual resurrection, questioned the virgin birth, upheld the right of women to be priests, the result was that these apostles were given secondary status and their views were silenced. Their gospels were purged as there was no room for gospels that did not support what was becoming the Christian orthodox position. In essence, what was Christian truth was established politically and ecclesiastically, meaning one group in power, insisting on its own way, won what would be known as the true beliefs of Christianity. Now, it is known that there were other interpretations that had merit, or at least, could be judged so by others. It is clear one group that would claim Christian orthodoxy as theirs alone would grow and take the name "Catholic," and more precisely "Roman Catholic" implying its beliefs were not only correct but universal.

What became the Roman Catholic Church would then accept the literalist's theology of this early church as their own, but in their defense, so have many others! Their apostolic beliefs would be adopted as normative Christianity not only by the Catholic Church but by most churches in the Western hemisphere. Many churches have defected from the polity or ecclesiastical structure of the Roman Catholic Church, but the theology based on the baptismal questions and the early Rule of Faith, now expressed in the Apostles' Creed, is also the standard for many non-Catholic Churches.

Therefore, the message isn't to condemn the Roman Catholic Church, and although they would disagree with this criticism of the doctrine of Apostolic Succession, it must be conceded that this doctrine has given them much strength and respect. Indeed, many changes have happened in the development of the Roman Church and to equate them with the narrowness of several early church fathers, who declared all other churches heretical and other theologies false, is an unfair assumption. Today, the ecumenical movement isn't without its defectors, but the message is that Christian orthodoxy goes beyond the Roman Catholic Church; empathically, many other churches owe their heritage to these early Christians.

Today's Fundamentalist Christians, who believe only they possess the true beliefs and insist that those who disagree with their interpretation of the Bible are doomed to hell, come closer to the passion and style of faith of the early church. Mainline Protestant Churches also are not without substantial influence, particularly, for their normative beliefs, from the early orthodox Christians. The Protestant Reformation was a major break from many of the policies of the Roman Church, and although it may appear that as with the Gnostics that the division was complete and separate, roots of orthodoxy, both in their beliefs and style, did not vanish within Protestantism.

Even at the beginning of their protest, the peace of Christ did not bode well. Protestants became as adamant about possessing the truth as those before them. Protestants killed Catholics, and Catholics killed Protestants, and the wars continued for some time.[53] Even with serious differences over the interpretation of the Bible, again, the beliefs of the Apostles' Creed, and in time, the latter Nicene Creed came through many religious trials unscathed for both Catholics and Protestants. Although these Creeds may be at times today a part of the Catholic liturgy, these Creeds are often exalted far more in their prominence and expression in mainline Protestant churches. These articles of faith, or statements of beliefs, are the doctrines which would become for many churches as the unquestionable truths of Christianity and reflect the literal, orthodox theological system established by the early apostolic church.

The lesson from the Gnostic Gospels, therefore, isn't that they are another protest against Roman Catholicism, those known today as Fundamentalist, nor about a theology of Gnosticism, but the criticism is much wider. Rather, they are a call to all Christians and church denominations to reexamine what they believe, and how they believe. Reformation and repentance doesn't stop at any one church's door. The Gnostics offer no simple or alternative answers but bring a voice that Christ's messages rise above many different churches that march forth with bold banners declaring absolute truth. Jesus' message to his followers wasn't to assume truth, but always because of him, to seek truth, not with arrogance, but with love using one's heart, soul, and mind.[54]

The Gnostic Gospels are not about rejecting Christianity as a true religion, nor building other churches upon them. The Gnostics also were not about setting their beliefs and myths in stone. What is so surprising, informative, and meaningful is how Christian and thought provoking are many of these other long hidden gospels and writings. Gospels of Thomas, Philip, and Mary provide bold new apostolic perspectives on a way to be Christian that emphasizes a dynamic faith over accepting a system of beliefs. The argument being presented is not to declare their gospels should become a part of the Bible, but to dismiss them as not being acceptable for Christian inspiration and instruction is unmerited. Unbelievable to some, but inspiring to others, will be how faithful and dedicated the Gnostics are in trying to be honest to Christ. The best example of their understanding of faith, as a process of seeking both truth and God, without having to declare doctrines as unquestionable truths, stands foremost in the gem of the Gnostic Gospels, the subject of the next chapter, the *Gospel of Thomas.*

Notes: Chapter Eight: Apostolic Authority Revisited

[1] Irenaeus, *Against Heresies*, hereafter noted as *AH*, 3: IV.

[2] Irenaeus, *AH*, 4: XIVIII: 8.

[3] Tim Dowley, ed., *Introduction to The History of Christianity*, (Minneapolis, Fortress Press, 2002), 116.

[4] Ibid.

[5] Ibid.

[6] Ibid.

[7] Dowley, *Introduction to The History of Christianity*, 117.

[8] Dowley, *Introduction to The History of Christianity*, 118.

[9] Elaine Pagels, *The Gnostic Gospels*, (New York, Random House, 1979), 137.

[10] Dowley, *Introduction to The History of Christianity*, 109. Also, Pagels, *The Gnostic Gospels*, 127.

[11] Marcus Borg, *Meeting Jesus Again For The First Time*, (New York, HarperOne, 1994), 15.

[12] Genesis 1:1--2:3 and Genesis 2:4--4:6.

[13] For the classic attempt to make the two stories one see *Halley's Bible Handbook*, (Grand Rapids, Michigan, Zonderman, ***), 83-95. However, making a list of the order of the elements of creation affirm major differences.

[14] Andrew Welburn, *The Beginning of Christianity*, (Edinburg, Floris Books, 1991), 39. Leonard Shlain, *The Alphabet Versus The Goddess*, (New York, Penguin Putman, 1998). 71, and 119. Shlain's theory is that the Hebrews were the first to develop the alphabet and used that to enforce the notion that their myths were recorded historical events.

[15] *Genesis* 3:1-24.

[16] Ibid.

[17] *Romans* 5:18-21.

[18] Gospel of John 3:18.
[19] Gospel of John 3:16.
[20] Irenaeus, *AH,* 3: XVI.
[21] Irenaeus, *AH,* 3: IV.
[22] Halley, *Halley's Bible Handbook*, 554.
[23] Irenaeus, AH, 3: IV.
[24] Ann Graham Brock, *Mary Magdalene, The First Apostle: The Struggle For Authority*, (Harvard, Ma., Harvard Theological Studies, 2003), 9.
[25] Brock, *Mary Magdalene, The First Apostle: The Struggle for Authority*, 6.
[26] Brock, *Mary Magdalene, The First Apostle: The Struggle for Authority*, 65. Matthew 28:10, Mark 16:1, John 21:23
[27] Brock, *Mary Magdalene, The First Apostle: The Struggle for Authority*, Quoted from Hippolytus, *De Cantico*: XXIV—XXVI.
[28] John M. Robinson, The Nag Hammadi Library, hereafter quoted as *NHL*, San Francisco, Harper SanFrancisco, 1978) *Gospel of Mary*, 526.
[29] Ibid.
[30] Ibid.
[31] Luke: 7:36-50.
[32] Brock, *Mary Magdalene, The First Apostle, The Struggle for Authority*, 168.
[33] Bart D. Ehrman, *Truth and Fiction in The Da Vinci Code*, (Oxford, University Press, 2004), 161.
[34] John 6:1-13.
[35] Ibid.
[36] John 14:8-14.
[37] Acts, 1:13.
[38] Robinson, *NHL*, the *Gospel of Philip*, 143.
[39] John 20:19-35.
[40] John 20: 24-29.
[41] For a discussion of the Gospel of Luke heightening Peter's prominence over other disciples far more than the other Gospels, see Brock, *Mary Magdalene, The First Apostle: The Struggle for Authority*, 39.
[42] Matthew 16: 13-20. For a different view of the power and status of Peter traditionally given to Peter see, *Halley's Bible Handbook*, 602.
[43] Luke 24: 33-35.
[44] Matthew 28:9-10, Mark 16:9-11, John 20:1-2.
[45] Irenaeus, *AH,* 3: III.
[46] Irenaeus, *AH,* 5: XXVI: 26.1
[47] The *Gospel of Philip* and the *Gospel of Mary*, particularly, challenge the higher calling of Peter, but as will be seen in Chapter Twelve, "St. Peter – a Gnostic?," Peter was highly honored and revered by the Gnostics, but not as a Pope.

[48] For a discussion of early gnostic leaders, who did not call themselves Bishops, J. Michael Matkin, *The Gnostic Gospels*, Alpha Books, New York, Chapter 4, "The Gnostic Lineup," Pg. 35.
[49] Robinson, *NHL*, *Apocalypse of Peter*, 376.
[50] Pagels, *The Gnostic Gospels*, 42
[51] See Robinson, *NHL*, the *Gospel of Mary*," 523, for an example.
[52] Pagels, *The Gnostic Gospels*, 39.
[53] Williston Walker, *A History of the Christian Church*, (Charles Scribner's and Sons, New York, 1959), See the discussion of what is called the Thirty Years War, 392.
[54] Matthew 22: 37.

Chapter Nine

The Gospel of Thomas — New Sayings of Jesus

> The Gospel of Thomas is without question the most significant book discovered in the Nag Hammadi Library.[1]
>
> -Bart Ehrman, *The New Testament*

The *Gospel of Thomas* is powerful, evocative, and is the only gospel of *The Nag Hammadi Library* that some have suggested should have been considered for inclusion in the canon of the Bible. Why? The Gospel contains one hundred fourteen sayings of Jesus. Surprisingly, seventy nine sayings are similar and often the same verses found in the New Testament. Significantly, in the *Gospel of Thomas* are thirty five new and different sayings of Jesus.

These new sayings and teachings are not extreme or radical. However, like most of the teachings in the New Testament, Jesus' words are not simple or understood easily. His sayings in this gospel are similar to his parables in that not just one meaning but several conclusions can be drawn. The beauty is that these verses make one think — and think for oneself. They do not lend themselves to authorities who can tell others exactly what they mean. You are the hearer and the interpreter; implicit is what do these teachings mean to you?

What follows are selected examples of the new sayings of Jesus found in the *Gospel of Thomas.* After a verse from the gospel is quoted, there follows a possible interpretation, and the remarks should be read as commentary. The comments are subjective insights and illustrate possible meanings. These verses encourage one's affirmation of the spirit of God within oneself and one's development of a spirituality using one's heart and mind. The selections are verses that have been chosen because they represent some of the texts that Elaine Pagels suggests have the potential to transform Christianity.[2] Interestingly, the focus of these verses is not on what one believes, but how one believes.

> Thomas: Verse #2: "Jesus said, Let him who seeks continue seeking until he finds. When he finds, he will become troubled. When he becomes troubled, he will be astonished, and he will rule over the all."

This is the complete verse referred to earlier regarding how the Gnostics would interpret faith as a process of seeking rather than just accepting beliefs. Seeking God is a central theme found in many of the Nag Hammadi texts and is a core value for the Gnostics' way of faith.[3] The complexity of the verse is apparent. Finding and knowing God is certainly possible and happens, yet seeking is the true dynamic of faith. In the gnostic interpretation, finding God is a continual process and is never complete. "When he finds, he will be troubled" implies finding God is more than feeling comfortable or overconfident. However, finding insights and truths of God can be astonishing when being one with God is experienced. The term "the all" in the verse is a gnostic concept that sometimes means Jesus himself, as will be seen in Verse 77, or at times, it refers to the total spiritual world, or to the supreme God. Of course, ruling over the all could be interpreted as the right to dominate others, but that is contrary to gnostic seeking and other teachings of Jesus. What Jesus meant by ruling over the all is quite unclear; perhaps, it is a spiritual relationship.

> Thomas: Verse # 3: "Jesus said, If those who lead you say to you, see the kingdom is in the sky, then the birds of the sky will precede you. If they say to you, it is in the sea, then the fish will precede you. Rather, the kingdom is inside of you, and it outside of you. When you come to know yourselves, then you will become known and will realize that it is you who are the sons of the living father. But if you will not know yourselves, you dwell in poverty and it is you who are that poverty."

In Chapter Seven, on the meaning of gnosis, part of this verse was discussed, and in its context here, the suggested meaning of gnosis as meaning relationship is amplified. This verse is an imposing text in that it contains several significant themes found in the Nag Hammadi writings. A central message of the gnostic material is that the primary place to find God is within oneself, not in externals as in beliefs, dogma, creeds, or dictates of the church. It teaches, "The kingdom is inside you." You don't need a bishop, priest, or preacher to tell you what to believe to experience God. The divine is found by an inward direct experience. Also, the "kingdom is outside of you." You are not God, and your experience is not absolute nor the norm for all. God's Spirit can be awakened within us, but God is greater and beyond ourselves.

In trusting the spirit of God within us, it is also important to "know yourself." We have a serious responsibility to try to understand, honestly, who we are and why we exist? As discussed earlier, this knowing oneself can lead, not only to the discovery of God's spirit within, but also the realization "you are the sons of the living father."

Whoops! Even the Gnostics weren't perfect. What about the daughters of the living Father? As will be seen in an upcoming passage in Thomas, Jesus declares, in the sight of God, sons are daughters, and daughters are sons — implying we are all children of God![4] If we ignore that we are children of God, Jesus says "you will *not* know yourselves," the consequences are "you will dwell in poverty and it is you who are that poverty." Like so many of the theological related words that Jesus used such as love, sin, grace, peace, etc., he does not give an exact definition for the word poverty. Clearly, poverty can mean different things to different people. To some it might be translated as sin, to others a state of misery, or a lack of well being. So whatever poverty means to you, if you don't understand yourself, Jesus says you "dwell in poverty." The beauty is that poverty is not precisely defined, but one doesn't have to be a priest or scholar to get its basic message. Doesn't Jesus seem to be saying move beyond that which enslaves you; awaken to the gift of life and live in the strength of God's spirit, which is within you?

> Thomas: Verse # 5: "Jesus said, Recognize what is in your sight, and that which is hidden from you will become plain

> to you. For there is nothing hidden which will not become manifest."

In this verse, Jesus seems to be opening the door to the future without being specific about it. Perhaps, he was talking about himself and what he would mean to the world. That could well be, as his small voice has become immense and manifest to the world. As a prophetic voice, some might even say that the Gnostic Gospels themselves, which were hidden, have become manifest and are now plainly before the world to see and hear, but there are other implications from this provocative verse.[5]

As the world comes of age, it is also true that we are learning almost unbelievable, mind-boggling, new realities about God's created and vast universe. In studying God's cosmos, although mysteries still abound, much that has been hidden is "becoming manifest." Theological views, which were based on the earth being the center of the world, are being challenged. New truths are being found such as the humble location of earth and the totally unimaginable size of our universe, informing both science and religion. This verse supports the belief that these facts are not threats to the reality of God but are a revelation about what is true and real about God's incredible universe. Our understanding of the universe has been too small and not recognizing or accepting its vastness, we have allowed our vision of God to be too small!

> Thomas: Verse 22: "Jesus saw infants being suckled. He said to his disciples, These infants being suckled are like those who enter the kingdom. Jesus said to them, When you make the two one, and when you make the inside the outside, and the outside the inside, and the one and the same, so that the male not be male nor, the female, female; and when you fashion eyes in place of an eye, and a hand in place of a hand, and a foot in place of a foot, and a likeness in place of a likeness; then will you enter the kingdom."

Within this teaching Jesus said, "When you make the two one, so that the male not be male nor, the female, female...then you will enter the kingdom." Dr. Carl G. Jung would have loved this verse with its emphasis on the oneness of male and female, because one of Jung's teachings was that all of us have both male and the female characteristics intermingled within us. So too would those who now celebrate the importance and equality of women, as this verse stresses the oneness of our being. The gnostic perspective supports not just equality but the leadership and central place of women in the church and Christianity.[6] Thankfully, churches of almost every denomination amazingly have broken tradition and allowed women to be ordained. Unfortunately, division and differences have been emphasized over oneness.

Traditional Christianity, often, has assumed men are superior to women. In the Bible, but not in Jesus' teaching, women are told to keep quiet in church, and at home to obey their husbands.[7] They do not have the wisdom, nor the spiritual understanding and closeness to God as men. Therefore, men only must lead the church, and so it was even for the early apostolic church. Although support for such male dominance is found in the Bible, if the gnostic style of Christianity had been accepted, the world and the church would be different. In the Gnostic Gospels women are powerful, intelligent, and highly respected by Jesus. They too are his disciples and even apostles. Male and female are not different before God. The important message, which by now may seem redundant, is a basic belief in gnostic thinking: we are all children of God!

> Thomas: Verse 70: "Jesus said, "That which you have will save you if you bring it forth from yourselves. That which you do not have within you will kill you if you do not have it within you."

Traditional Christianity has said our salvation depends totally on God and is often expressed as "only by his grace." All we need to do is believe in Jesus, as that is all that matters, and then we will be saved. The deathbed repentant, the Roman Emperor Constantine, a person who did not live an exemplary life, but was critical in establishing the power of the church and its orthodox theology, would have loved such a concept of grace that all that was required for salvation was belief.[8]

However, the *Gospel of Thomas* suggests being saved is not all up to God. We have a responsibility! Since we all have the capacity to know and love God and others, we have a personal responsibility ourselves to realize God's Spirit within and as the verse says, "to bring it forth." It does not say it is all up to us to save ourselves, as opponents like to charge. Rather, salvation happens by a relationship that involves the interaction both of persons and God together. As will be seen in other quotations from other gnostic writings, the Gnostics believe in the concept of grace. The Gnostics do not deny grace as meaning forgiveness, but it is not automatic just because you have accepted Jesus, believe the correct dogma, or belong to a particular church. As Christians, we have a continuing responsibility to seek forgiveness for a new and more loving life."That which you have will save you if you bring it forth from yourselves."

> Thomas: Verse 77: "Jesus said, It is I who am the light which is above them all. It is I who am the all. From me did the all come forth, and unto me did the all extend. Split a piece of wood, and I am there. Lift up a stone, and you will find me there."

Jesus is the highest light ("above them all"), and his light can be found in this world. Finding God is not limited to ourselves but is also revealed in the wonder of nature. Lifting a stone or splitting wood may reveal a light or something more than just what is physical creation. Jesus teaches that reality is both physical and spiritual. Although some gnostic myths teach that the material world is totally evil, this saying of Jesus from Thomas does not support that concept. Here, Jesus suggests even his spirit can be found in the midst of the world.[9]

Jesus identifies himself as the light and himself as the "all," ("It is I who am the all"), a new description of Jesus. Herein brings the specific distinction of the theological differences between Thomas and John in the understanding of God's light. Jesus as the light of the world is not a new concept. However, this metaphor to light illustrates how different persons can understand Jesus differently but still be Christian.

As mentioned previously in Chapter Four, the theological understanding of the light of God has a serious divergence between the two disciples, John and Thomas. In addition to Elaine Pagels' comments stated in that chapter, she further explains in her book *Beyond Belief*, for the writer of the *Gospel of John*, the teaching is that Jesus is the only true light of the world.[10] In other words, the light of God is in Jesus alone, and the only way to experience the light is to believe in Jesus. Therefore, because God's light is only in Jesus, John's gospel makes the exclusive claim for Christianity in verse, 14:6, "no one comes to the Father except through me."

In contrast to John's interpretation, Elaine argues the *Gospel of Thomas* has a different understanding of the light of God. In her words, "John says that we can experience God only in Jesus. But certain passages in Thomas' gospel draw a quite different conclusion: that the divine light Jesus embodied is shared by humanity since we are all made in the image of God."[11]

John's gospel makes the way to God exclusive–only for those who believe in Jesus. Thomas' gospel is inclusive in that the divine light is shared beyond Jesus. Jesus is unique, and believing in him is a true way to God, but as will be seen in the gnostic mythological stories, there were other ways to relate to God and receive his light.[12] The distinction between John and Thomas is profound and thought provoking, particularly, for those who believe other religions can be valid and that the light of God can extend beyond Jesus.

The metaphor of light ("It is I who am the light") suggests God is more than an anthropomorphic form, but more profoundly, a spiritual light. Because light is neither male nor female, God, transcends male or female classification. Of course, traditional Christianity has strongly promoted God as a male or only as a Father. For the Gnostics, God is not simply a male or a female but is androgynous, having both characteristics. Often, in the gnostic books, God is referred to as "God the Father, God the Mother."[13] Beyond these descriptions, the nature of God is a Spirit, and Jesus reflects God's light and Spirit.

These passages, examples of the new sayings of Jesus, and many others, in the *Gospel of Thomas*, project a style of Christianity that is about seeking without finding finished or final answers for what is true about oneself, the world, and God. Because Thomas shares only sayings of Jesus, doesn't involve himself in so-called classic gnostic themes, such as creation is all bad, and because there are no creation myths in his gospel, some have argued that this gospel should not be classified as gnostic.[14] However, by avoiding the trap that the Gnostics were all about mythology, many scholars believe this gospel reflects the very heart and soul of gnostic theology.

To summarize, the *Gospel of Thomas,* particularly, from the new teachings of Jesus, teaches God's light shines in Jesus, and because we were created in his image, we have the innate capacity to know God and let his light shine in us. God's spirit, his light, can be found within us, and our belief or trust in Jesus brings forth that light. The responsibility is ours to turn on that light and let that light and the living Jesus lead us in our Christian life. Our ethical responsibility is to seek and develop a loving life as did Christ. Because the Gospel's emphasis is on seeking, in contrast to John's emphasis on believing, it may have been part of the inspiration for the Gnostic who argued that the true call of Jesus was to go beyond primary beliefs, to seek, find, and grow in spirituality.[15] Christian maturity was more than becoming Biblical scholars or theological experts but building one's positive relationship to one's self, others, and God through Jesus. In essence, doesn't Thomas' gospel extend and expand what the phrase, "to believe in Jesus" means?

The *Gospel of Thomas* is the starting place for those who want to read the Gnostic Gospels. Selections from other gospels and writings will be shared in Chapter Eleven, but because Thomas' gospel doesn't directly enter the battle over beliefs, has many verses similar to those in the Biblical Gospels, and concentrates on Jesus' words and teachings, it is considered the Nag Hammadi's gem. The *Gospel of Thomas* was never given consideration by the church that chose the canon for the Bible, quite likely, because of the early tradition that there were only four authentic Gospels. If there was room for only four gospels, or "no more and no less," as Irenaeus teaches, John's gospel may have been chosen because it more clearly reflects the literalist position that Jesus was the only way to God.[16] Wouldn't it have been interesting, however, if Thomas' gospel, which presents a more inclusive meaning to Jesus being the light of the world, was included in the canon of the Bible?[17] Such possible conflict was perhaps why Thomas's gospel was excluded, as according to the apostolic church, such debate was not needed; the issue was settled.

According to the Gnostics, this debate would have been healthy and truer to Jesus' way of trusting all his disciples to interpret his messages and their meanings. However, even though this gospel was dismissed for whatever reason, by its inclusion in the Nag Hammadi Library and the discovery of its Greek fragments, it is known to be an ancient gospel. The *Gospel of Tho*mas is inspirational, particularly, for those who will engage themselves beyond believing Jesus' teachings are straightforward and direct. Both by the inclusion of many verses found in the Bible, and the addition of thought provoking new sayings of Jesus, much in the tradition of his parables, the *Gospel of Thomas* is powerful and evocative. This gospel's inclusion in the Bible is not the issue, but its messages should be heard and placed in the quest for religious and Christian truth.

What is surprising is that this gospel, and the discovery and revelation of other Gnostic Gospels have not had the same impact that the Dead Sea Scrolls had on the Christian community. Part of the reason may be that the relationship between the two has been muddled. Indeed, the direct relationship of the Dead Sea Scrolls to the Old Testament and the separate relationship of the Gnostic Gospels to the New Testament has not been that well understood. The Scrolls' value for the study of the Old Testament cannot be undermined as they bring new information and historical support for it, but the rising importance of the Gnostic Gospels to New Testament Christianity will someday be realized as also as being equally exciting and significant.

Notes: Chapter Nine: The Gospel of Thomas — New Sayings of Jesus

[1] Bart Ehrman, *The New Testament*, (Oxford, Oxford University Press, 200), 208.
[2] Elaine Pagels, *Beyond Belief*, (New York, Random House, 2003), 29.
[3] Pagels, *Beyond Belief*, 240.
[4] James M. Robinson, *The Nag Hammadi Library*, hereafter noted as *NHL*, the *Gospel of Thomas*, (San Francisco: HarperSanFrancisco, 1978),129:2
[5] See Chapter Six, "Protecting and Hiding the Gnostic Gospels"
[6] Ann Graham Brock, *Mary Magdalene, The First Apostle*, (Boston, Mass.: Harvard University Press, 2003), 171.
[7] I Timothy 2: 1-15
[8] James Carroll, *Constantine's Sword*, (New York: Houghton Mifflin Company, 2001), 188.
[9] Karen King, *What is Gnosticism?*, (Harvard, Mass.: Harvard University Press, 2003), 200
[10] Pagels, *Beyond Belief*, See Chapter Two, "Gospels in Conflict," 30.
[11] Pagels, *Beyond Belief*, 40.
[12] The primary myths of the Gnostics will be examined in Chapter Sixteen which show they believed there were other paths to know God than by Christ.
[13] Pagels, *Beyond Belief*, 233.
[14] Meera Lester, *The Everything Gnostic Gospels Book*, (Avon Massachusetts: Adams Media, 2007), 158 and 164.
[15] Pagels, *Beyond Belief*, 139.

---

[16] Irenaeus, *Against Heresies*, 3: XVI.
[17] Pagels, *Beyond Belief*, 38.

Chapter Ten

The Gnostic Gospels and The Dead Sea Scrolls

> I think the Dead Sea Scrolls belong to what I would call the old days; the Sons of Light against the Sons of Darkness. That's tied to the historical concept, and the symbols are read historically: 'we are the Sons of Light,' and 'they are the Sons of Darkness,' and we're going to be the glorious ones. Whereas in the Nag Hammadi finds, those Coptic papers talk about the brotherhood of all — which is a Gnostic tradition. [1]
>
> -Joseph Campbell, *An Open Life*

Ancient manuscripts on thin sheets of papyrus, with beautifully inscribed letters, would naturally excite most historians and cryptologists. However, the thirteen, leather bound books found near the small hamlet of Nag Hammadi go far beyond professional archeological excitement because they contain words and teachings ascribed to Jesus. Although it seems that all teachings of Jesus would have been recorded, there is reason to believe that some were omitted or overlooked, purposely, because of religious bias. Now, with the discovery of the nearly destroyed Gnostic Gospels, new information emerges on the Gnostics. More importantly, they contain new teachings and insights into the meaning and messages of Jesus.

Most scholars believe Jesus spoke in Aramaic, the prominent language of his time in Palestine.[2] When his teachings were put into written form, rather than Aramaic, they were translated into the more common and popular language of the Roman Empire, Greek. The generally accepted belief is that his words and teachings were carried on by his disciples in what is called the oral tradition. The oral tradition meant his sayings, stories, and teachings were first passed on verbally by one person or a group to others. Then, what he said was transferred and translated for a wider audience in books. The long-held assumption was that the teaching and words from Jesus recorded from the oral tradition could be found only in the four Gospels of Matthew, Mark, Luke, and John. However, the cache of books discovered at Nag Hammadi significantly challenges the long-held position that the wisdom and words of Jesus were limited to the gospels that are in the Bible.

The usual attack against these newly revealed gospels is that they were false, because they were later creations, composed by persons who wanted to add or edit the story of Jesus. Such a charge is fair for a number of gospels that have surfaced throughout history because of their being clearly exaggerated, romantic, or enhanced tales of Jesus.

For example, a book believed to be written fairly early in the development of Christianity is called *The Infancy Gospel of Thomas*, which was not found in the books of Nag Hammadi.[3] One of the stories that the book relates is of Jesus as a youngster being divine, but a brat. Jesus throws a young friend named Zeno off a roof, and Zeno dies from the fall. Miraculously, Jesus brings him back to life again![4]

Another example of a gospel believed to be created after the New Testament period would be a book named the *Proto-Gospel of James.*[5] Called "Proto" because it describes events prior to Jesus' birth and infancy, this gospel implies that the mother of the blessed Mary, who would be Jesus' grandmother, Anna, was, as her daughter, also a virgin! Mary, herself, in this account is kept pure by living in the Temple in Jerusalem; she is fed by an angel, and before puberty, God chooses the widower Joseph to be her earthly husband. Joseph takes an extended trip, and while away, Mary conceives a child by the Holy Spirit — to the shock of Joseph![6] Indeed, there are a fair number of gospels that are later fabrications used to support some religious doctrine, or to idolize Jesus, and in this case, Mary.

Because of such contrived writings, other gospels than the four in the Bible are often written off as fabrications. However, after extensive study, there are about twenty gospels that have been discovered or that are believed to be very early and legitimate gospels.[7] An example would be what is called the *Signs Gospel*, a document not extant; however, it is one that many believe was a source for the miracle stories or "signs" of Jesus that are found in the Gospel of John.[8] Others would be the *Gospel of Peter* which is surprisingly anti-Semitic.[9] In contrast to Peter's gospel, there are the *Gospel of the Hebrews*, and the *Gospel of the Ebionites*, both of which support a Jewish/Christian way of following Jesus.[10] The dating of these gospels is quite complex, but the point is that it is now believed early in the development of Christianity, there were more gospels than the four canonical gospels.

Interestingly, the question had hardly been raised before Nag Hammadi, why more of the first disciples had not written accounts of Jesus' life and ministry? With the Gnostic Gospels, it appears that the oral tradition of telling the story of Jesus and his teachings was wider than had been believed. Now, there is evidence that some of the other original twelve disciples also had remembrances, which were put in writings by them or their disciples. One can find translations and commentary on these gospels, which are believed to be early and authentic in *The Complete Gospels*, edited by Robert J. Miller.[11] Included in the book are all the gospels found at Nag Hammadi, and as Robert Funk says in the "Forward" to *The Complete Gospels*, these gospels are important in understanding the "full story of how Christianity took its rise."[12]

The Gnostic Gospels are pre-eminent in the midst of all these gospels because being found together as a collection, bound in separate leather codices, indicated they were considered worthy enough to be hand copied and preserved. Even the fact of their being hidden makes their value evident. Beyond the additional fact that other gospels weren't included, such as the *Gospel of Judas*, and the *Gospel of Peter*, doesn't mean these other gospels and writings, which are considered early authentic reports and responses to Jesus, weren't valuable. Perhaps, they were not available for the monks to copy, or it might have been that the monks were selective in their choice of books. However, with Athanasius, the Bishop of Alexandria, having the power within his Egyptian territory in 367 C.E. to order books with gnostic leanings destroyed, these monks probably had little choice but to protect these gospels by hiding them.[13] The find of these hidden gospels make it not just hearsay, but brings the remarkable proof that there were more than four early gospels in circulation, in early Christianity.

Certainly, the church fathers wanted these gospels with gnostic leanings to be known as false writings about Jesus. It might be easier to accept that claim if it were not for the strong words of belief about his life, and resurrection, and the deep meaning Jesus had to these followers. If all these books were totally imaginary and mythical tales, and were just bizarre stories of Jesus, as was expected, they would have need of little respect. Indeed, there is no question, within some of the books there are myths and some strange tales, like Jesus laughing on the cross. For the most part, these gospels reveal a deep belief in Jesus, and they yield different understandings of the one whom they also called Savior.[14]

Even if the canonical books were deemed the best accounts of Jesus, it is unfortunate that other gospels were not allowed to exist. Little imagination is required to understand why the four gospels in the Bible would be the preference of those who wanted their literalistic viewpoint and interpretation of Jesus to be the only accepted Christian truth. In fact, the bishops were so successful in silencing the works of other Christians, there was little else to rely on until the discovery of these gospels. Now discovered and evaluated as being gospels which the fathers attacked and tried to destroy, the truth of Jesus is not confined, but widened. All indications are that these teachings, which also would have come from the oral tradition, are legitimate. They would be words that other close disciples of Jesus heard and passed on to those who believed in him, and these disciples, or their followers, believed strongly enough to put them in writing!

Amazingly, the world and most Christians don't seem to know, don't care, or don't realize that there are newly discovered teachings of Jesus. New words! New verses from Jesus! One would think the Christian world would be turned upside down, or at least quite excited, that additional sayings of Jesus had been discovered. Precisely, because they tell us more about Jesus, one would think these gospels would be books of greater interest and attention than the Dead Sea Scrolls.

A shocking fact or realization for many people is that the Gnostic Gospels were found in December 1945 — nearly two years before the discovery of the Dead Sea Scrolls![15] A natural question then is why was there more excitement over the Scrolls than these new gospels?

The answer lies in one word — tradition! The Scrolls were seen to support the traditional understanding of Christianity; on the other hand, these new gospels threaten the tradition of there being only four authentic gospels. As has occurred, a number of times in history, rightly or wrongly, as with the case of Galileo's affirmation of the earths' rotation around the sun, religious tradition triumphed over other wisdom. In this case, the strong tradition of only four true gospels trumped the reality that other gospels existed shortly after the time of Jesus. Now, in spite of what was ingrained, as with Galileo' insight, new evidence changes or expands what has been assumed. Despite the shock to tradition, the discovery of these gospels can be monumental in opening a new way to strengthen one's Christian faith. Once the understanding that the Gnostic Gospels are not a threat to the four Biblical Gospels, the transforming power of these gospels will be more fully understood and realized. When this is recognized, they may at least rise to the level or exceed the grandeur and enticing popularity of the Scrolls. For such recognition to happen, however, requires a deeper understanding of both the Gnostic Gospels and the Dead Sea Scrolls.

In regard to the Gnostic Gospels, skepticism was a natural response. The very idea that there were other and different gospels brought alarm and disbelief. Christians had been taught for centuries that there were only four true gospels. Surely, if there were other gospels, they had to be fake or forgeries, and if Gnostic Gospels, mythological. Other authentic gospels? No, that couldn't be! If God had wanted other gospels, they would have been included as books in the Bible.

Further, the new sayings of Jesus were fairly complex and different which made them difficult to relate to or recite. Because these gospels didn't tell the story of his life, emphasize his passion, and retell the story of his death and resurrection, these omissions made them suspect. More disturbing was that they challenged traditional doctrines and did not emphasize the miracles. Also, these gospels were a correction to the assumption that early Christians, for the most part, believed in Jesus in the same way. Then, there was the tradition of heresy which taught that there were many strange, heretical groups who just didn't get the true message of Jesus. Long rumored, even by those who thought these gospels actually might exist, was the belief that when and if they were found, they would not be worthy of respect.[16] Therefore, these questions and concerns suppressed early excitement about the possibility of new, authentic gospels.

On the other hand, early releases of material found in the Dead Sea Scrolls seemed to support and give credence to the well-established story of Jesus. There was reason for great interest and fanfare as there appeared to be an obvious connection to the development of Christianity before the coming of Jesus. Many wondered if Jesus could have been a part of the religious community which produced the Scrolls. If not a member, perhaps there was some direct influence upon Jesus.[17] As these Scrolls contained astonishing similarities to Christianity, the Scrolls were more appealing and attractive than the new and different earlier discovered Gnostic Gospels.

The Scrolls revealed, for instance, stories about a Teacher of Righteousness, which many thought could be Jesus, or at least, a reference to him.[18] There was a clear anticipation of a coming Messiah within many of the Scrolls. Messiah?[19] This Greek word translates into English, as "Christ." Could this not point to Jesus?

Of interest to Biblical scholars, the Scrolls contained what would become the oldest complete manuscript, by a thousand years, of the Old Testament.[20] The Book of Isaiah was given central importance amongst its books. Christian tradition taught that the Book of Isaiah had foretold the coming of a suffering servant, a virgin birth, and even death on a cross. It was hoped that there might be additional prophecies in the writings of the Scrolls that would conform to the ministry and life of Jesus.

Indeed, writings in the Scrolls told of ceremonies of baptism and a special meal of communion, using bread and wine [21] Wow, reason for excitement, particularly in the Christian community, as it appeared the Scrolls could lift up the truth of Jesus and Christianity.

After having translating and reading more than nine hundred documents, found in eight caves, northwest of the Dead Sea, most scholars believe their direct relationship to Christianity is minimal.[22] Their primary value is historical information before and after the time of Jesus.[23] The Scrolls reveal evidence for a growing conflict between the Roman authority and some who held strongly to the Jewish religion. They expose many details about a group of Jewish ascetics, who lived in a monastic setting named Qumran, located on a high terrace above the Dead Sea. They are believed to be people whom the Jewish writers, Josephus, Philo, and Pliny the Elder referred to as Essenes.[24] Essene is a word, which in Greek, means holy or saintly. Interestingly, in their writings they do not call themselves, Essenes, and some recent scholarship questions those of Qumran as being those named Essenes.[25] However, whoever they were, the Scrolls reveal the people at Qumran were extremely ritualistic, religious, and Jewish.[26] Although the Scrolls have many similarities to Christianity, there are major differences.

In the Scrolls, those who lived in the community of Qumran identify themselves as being the children of light.[27] Being such, they believed other Jewish groups were not truly righteous or pure in their worship of God. As children of light, particularly, for those who would be initiated after at least a year's participation in their community, they would be blessed, not by one messiah, but two![28] One messiah would be priestly and spiritual, ruling in the heavens; the other messiah would be secular or royal and would rule on earth.[29] Their baptisms were not administered just once but were repeated often for purification. A daily common, communal meal, often with bread and wine, was taken in a large structure somewhat like a church or a holy meeting place that was not used for housing.[30] The goal of the community was to develop purity of life and true worship of the Hebrew God, Yahweh.[31]

Much more upsetting and threatening than the sins of Jewish impurity and apostasy were those they identified as the children of darkness! Most likely, this designation referred to their prime enemy, the Roman government.[32] The children of darkness were portrayed as evil, totally godless, and an adversary, but there was no reason to fear the enemy! For those, who committed themselves to this sect, they could expect a final holy battle in which the children of darkness, or the Roman army, would be annihilated.[33] They, as the children of light, would triumph over evil, and their messiahs would reign.[34] One can hear echoes of Armageddon, the final battle or war, which brings triumph to Christians and God, highlighted in the Book of Revelation, in the New Testament.[35]

Obviously, there are some close resemblances to Christianity, but the Essenes are not mentioned in the Bible, or by Jesus![36] There is no evidence in the Scrolls of a foretelling of Jesus other than an expectation of some kind of messiah.[37] Perhaps, Jesus was influenced by the Essenes, but such a claim is circumstantial. It is clear that if Jesus knew of the Essenes, it was his desire, by his teachings, to move beyond their isolation from the world and their arrogance as the pure ones of God. Jesus may have appreciated their rite of baptism and their practice of a meal that signified communion with God, as he did institute these with his followers. Still, Jesus did not identify himself as an Essene.[38]

Further, in spite of believing God would be on their side in the final battle on earth, the conflict did not go well for them. Archeologists know that Qumran was totally destroyed by the Roman Army in what is called the Jewish Revolt, or Jewish War, from 66-70 C.E.[39] Thirty years after the life of Jesus, the tensions with Rome had only increased. The Emperor Nero blamed the famous fire of 64 C.E., in Rome, on the sect of Christians, but his wrath was no less on the Jews — a fact often overlooked. Nero sent sixty thousand Roman soldiers to Judea in 66 C.E. to destroy the Jewish temple and Judaism, which most Emperors also believed to be a false and rebellious religion.[40] At the beginning of this war, Jewish forces, led by those who were known as Zealots, fared better than what one might have expected.[41] As Neil Silberman writes that in the early stages of the war, "Just as in the detailed vision of the War Scroll, the Sons of light seemed to have been aided by heaven-sent forces."[42] However, with the arrival of General Vespasian, who would succeed as the Emperor after Nero, his even larger army would begin to achieve one victory after another. In the spring of 68 C.E., the settlement at Qumran was destroyed and burned.[43] It was rumored that Emperor Vespasian issued a decree to end the Jewish religion for all time, if true, so much for a decree![44] However, Judea as a Jewish Province was conquered, and Judea as a State then became known as Palestine, from the old regional name, Philistia.[45]

One of the closing and deciding battles of the Jewish War was led by Titus, Vespasian's son, in 70 C.E. The result was the destruction of Jerusalem. Its horrid details were recorded by the contemporary Jewish historian Josephus.[46] Of note, Titus followed Vespasian as Emperor, building a triumphal arch in Rome, which still stands, to celebrate his suppression of the Jewish Revolt.[47]

Before this monument could be erected, after the destruction of Jerusalem, which essentially ended the war, the last obstacle in the defeat of the Jews took place at the high mountain fortress of Masada. In this final skirmish, the Zealots, and some believe also a few surviving Essenes, because a few of their scrolls were found in the ruins of Masada, were defeated.[48] Those who had fled to Masada held out for a few years, but when the Romans broke through its unusually high, sheer escarpments, Josephus reports many committed suicide rather than give in to the Romans.[49] The archeological ruins at Qumran and Masada tell the destructive story. Without question, the children of light were not saved, at least, on earth!

There is a popular belief, without much evidence, that John the Baptist, who baptized Jesus, may have been an Essene.[50] If John was an Essene, Jesus does not confirm that relationship, and neither does John.

However, if John came from the Essene or unnamed community, Jesus certainly goes beyond their claim to religious superiority. More to the point than John's possible relationship is that this is another case study of a Jesus who rebels not only against the very religious and self righteous Pharisees, and the Sadducees who were the priests of the Temple. Here, again, Jesus rebukes the self righteousness of those who were extremely holy and ritualistic, upholding their own purity above others. As Joseph Campbell teaches, the identity of the Sons of Light against the Sons of Darkness illustrates the historical symbol of what he calls the old days or the perennial concept, we are the righteous; they are the evil ones.[51]

Certainly, the similar cry, 'God is on our side,' has been used to justify religious wars and create national arrogance; unfortunately, this justification still happens in Christianity and other religions. Jesus, obviously, by his teaching to love one's enemies had a wider conception than God's blessing was for those who claimed it only for themselves. Jesus' vision of moving beyond religious self-righteousness too often has taken a back seat to the mentality of a closed minded group, or tribal need, to possess religious power and privilege in order to make ones' group seemingly better than others. Being the chosen ones, as certainly the children of light dreamed, has plagued too many religions and forms of Christianity.

Thankfully, there are new Christian resources that can move us back to the more humble and visionary message of Jesus. Instead of claiming to have all the answers, or being the only ones whom God loves, the Gnostic Gospels support the perspective we are in this struggle together. Even they are not pure in avoiding self righteousness all together, and where so, underline that the message of Jesus is greater than reproducing Gnostic beliefs, myths, or Gnosticism. However, overall, as Joseph Campbell attests, the Gnostic Gospels, or what he calls the Nag Hammadi finds, go beyond this attitude of being "the glorious ones" but rather uplift the brotherhood and sisterhood of all.[52]

The historical value of the Scrolls cannot be dismissed. They give added evidence surrounding the time of Christ that describes the tension and conflict between the Roman government and religious groups. Clearly, those religions that did not support the Roman government, enthusiastically, were regarded as a threat to both their pagan religion and the Empire. The Dead Sea Scrolls are particularly valuable in the studies of the Old Testament, the sect at Qumran, and later Judaism. Other than Old

Testament prophecies, which relate to Jesus, there is limited relationship to Christianity. This fact is well illustrated in Bart Ehrman's book *Truth and Fiction in The Da Vinci Code*. Referring to Dan Brown's book, Ehrman corrects remarks made by a main character, Leigh Teabing, who is a wealthy aristocrat and expert on the Holy Grail. Teabing in his teaching about the Grail relates the Dead Sea Scrolls to Christianity and suggests they contained lost gospels. Bart writes:

> But it is not as Teabing explains, because the scrolls [do not] contain anything explicitly Christian. They are thoroughly and completely Jewish. And it is not because they contain Gospels that are more accurate than those of the New Testament. There are in fact no Gospels among the hundreds of documents found at Qumran.[53]

Bart Ehrman's message is that in building his story, Dan Brown's research was not correct when he related the Scrolls to Christianity, as is commonly done. The Gnostic Gospels were not part of the Dead Sea Scrolls. Certainly, Dan's reference and use of use of some material from the Gnostic Gospels has heightened interest in them. Beyond that factor, the bottom line, which many Christians have yet to realize, is as Bart teaches, "The first thing to stress, again, it that there are no Christian documents of any kind here; they are all Jewish texts."[54] Of course, that these Jewish texts help with the understanding of the Bible's Old Testament is vital, and hopefully someday, the Gnostic Gospels also can be understood as vital to the further understanding of the Christian New Testament, as well.

Particularly for Christians, the Gnostic Gospels may be eventually realized as significant and powerful as the Dead Sea Scrolls, and as the understanding takes hold that these gospels are a joy and not a threat, they too will be highly honored and appreciated. Of course, such a positive recognition will take time. However, as it is recognized and understood that the Gnostic Gospels bring positive new insights for Christianity, they will be lauded as revolutionary for Christian faith. These gospels are revolutionary in that they provide a fresh break from the forms of Christianity that are much like the Essenes; for clearly, the Essenes are not alone as those who have believed they were the children of light and all others lived in darkness. This break allows Christians to continue in their faith and to expand its emphasis on being foremost a dynamic spiritual trust rather than consent to beliefs. In the next chapter, one will see this dynamic attitude which is supported by verses from various, gnostic writings that were silenced because they did not support Christianity as being a religion of unquestionable beliefs.

Notes: Chapter Ten: The Gnostic Gospels and the Dead Sea Scrolls

[1] Joseph Campbell, *An Open Life*, (New York: HarperPerennial, 1990), 33.
[2] Bruce Manning Metzger, *The New Testament*, (New York: Abingdon Press, 1965), 98.
[3] Bart D. Ehrman, *The New Testament*, (Oxford: Oxford University Press, 2008), 214.
[4] Ibid.
[5] Ehrman, *The New Testament*, 225.
[6] Ibid.
[7] Robert J. Miller, Editor, *The Complete Gospels*, (San Francisco: HarperSanFrancisco, 1994), 5.
[8] Miller, *The Complete Gospels*, 174.
[9] Ehrman, *The New Testament*, 215.
[10] Ehrman, *The New Testament*, 206
[11] Miller, *The Complete Gospels*, V.
[12] Miller, *The Complete Gospels*, VIII.
[13] Elaine Pagels, *Beyond Belief*, (New York: Random House, 2003), 176.
[14] James M. Robinson, Editor, *The Nag Hammadi Library*, hereafter noted as *NHL*, *The Dialogue of the Savior*, (San Francisco: HarperSanFrancisco, 1978), 244.
[15] Pagels, *The Gnostic Gospels*, (New York: Random House, 1979), Pg. XI.
[16] Pagels, *Beyond Belief*, 31.
[17] Edmund Wilson, *The Dead Sea Scrolls*, (Oxford: Oxford University Press, 1969), 77. Also, Michael Wise, Martin Abegg, Jr., and Edward Cook, *The Dead Sea Scrolls; A New Translation*, (San Francisco: HarperSanFrancisco, 1996), 291.
[18] Wilson, *The Dead Sea Scrolls*, 77.
[19] Hershel Shanks, *The Mystery and Meaning of the Dead Sea Scrolls*, (New York: Random House, 1998), 65.
[20] Wise, Abegg, and Cook, *The Dead Sea Scrolls: A New Translation*, 11.
[21] Robert H. Eisenman and Michael Wise, *The Dead Sea Scrolls Uncovered*, (New York: Barnes and Noble Books, 1994), 230. Concerning baptism see Shanks, *The Mystery and Meaning of the Dead Sea Scrolls*, 75.
[22] Bart D. Ehrman, *Truth and Fiction in the Da Vinci Code*, Chapter Two, "The Discoveries of the Dead Sea Scrolls and the Nag Hammadi Library,"(Oxford: Oxford University Press, 2004) 25.

[23] James H. Charlesworth, "The Dead Sea Scrolls: Fifty Years of Discovery and Controversy," The Princeton Seminary Bulletin, 1998, Vol. XIX # 2.
[24] Neil Asher Silberman, *The Hidden Scrolls*, (New York: Riverhead Books, 1994) 89
[25] Andrew Lawler, "Who Wrote The Dead Sea Scrolls?," Smithsonian Magazine, January 2010, Pg. 40. This article raises questions whether the Essenes or other self-reliant groups may have occupied Qumran. The evidence is not conclusive. Also Weston W. Fields, *The Dead Sea Scrolls; A Short History*, (Brill: Boston, 2006), 95.
[26] Ehrman, *The New Testament*, 48.
[27] Silberman, *The Hidden Scrolls*, 177.
[28] Millar Burrows, *The Dead Sea Scrolls*, (New York: Gramercy Publishing Company, 1986), 265.
[29] Shanks, *The Meaning and Mystery of the Dead Sea Scrolls*, 75.
[30] Wise, Abegg, and Cook, *The Dead Sea Scrolls, A New Translation*, 19
[31] Wise, Abegg, and Cook, *The Dead Sea Scrolls, A New Translation*, 205.
[32] Wilson, *The Dead Sea Scrolls*, 65.
[33] Wise, Abegg, and Cook, *The Dead Sea Scrolls, A New Translation*, 291.
[34] Ibid.
[35] Revelations: 19: 11-16.
[36] Ehrman, *The New Testament*, 48.
[37] Ehrman, *Truth and Fiction in the Da Vinci Code*, Ibid., Pg. 31.
[38] Ehrman, *The New Testament*, 48.
[39] Shanks, *The Meaning and the Mystery of the Dead Sea Scrolls*, 106.
[40] Max Margolis and Alexander Marx, *History of the Jewish People*, (New York, Meridian Books, 1958), 196.
[41] Ehrman, *The New Testament*, 250.
[42] Silberman, *The Hidden Scrolls*, 258.
[43] Ibid.
[44] Margolis and Marx, *History of the Jewish People*, 204.
[45] L. Michael White, *From Jesus to Christianity*, (San Francisco: HarperSanFrancisco, 2004), 223.
[46] William Whiston, *Josephus: Complete Works*, (Grand Rapids, Michigan: Kregel Publications, 1960), 502.
[47] White, *From Jesus to Christianity*, 222.
[48] Silberman, *The Hidden Scrolls*, 259.
[49] White, *From Jesus to Christianity*, 226.
[50] Wilson, *The Dead Sea Scrolls*, 132. Also see, Fields, *The Dead Sea Scrolls*, 88, for a discussion about John the Baptist being an Essene or not.
[51] Campbell, *An Open Life*, 62.
[52] Ibid.
[53] Ehrman, *Truth and Fiction in The Da Vinci Code*, 35.
[54] Ehrman, *Truth and Fiction in The Da Vinci Code*, 28.

Chapter Eleven

The Gnostics Speak for Themselves

> For centuries, our understanding of Gnosticism was limited to inferences drawn from what the Gnostic's enemies (the proto-orthodox) said about them; in 1945, however, a cache of original Gnostic documents was discovered near Nag Hammadi, Egypt. With these texts, we are able to reconstruct more reliably what Gnostics actually believed. [1]
>
> -Bart D. Ehrman, *The New Testament*

In *The Gnostic Gospels*, Elaine Pagels writes that she first learned of the gnostic discoveries in 1965 as a graduate student at Harvard.[2] In many of her public lectures, Dr. Pagels tells how she and other scholars assumed the first transcriptions of the manuscripts simply would contain strange and weird writings from Christian antiquity. Furthermore, because these papers were written in Coptic, they did not get much attention. Who could translate them?

Dr. Pagels decided to learn Coptic because her Professors George MacRae and Helmut Koester were convinced that the extraordinary find of these codices could possibly "revolutionize the traditional understanding of Christianity."[3] To her surprise, she found the intuitions of her professors to be correct. She discovered different interpretations and perspectives of Christianity, and beyond the highly rumored myths of the Gnostics, she found a cache of inspiring Christian texts, which were to deepen and change her understanding of Christianity. After years of study of the gnostic scriptures, in her 2005 book *Beyond Belief*, her testimony is "we find that these remarkable texts, only now becoming widely known, are transforming what we know as Christianity." [4]

More important than the text's academic value, she relates how these Gnostic Gospels have had an effect on her own personal faith and life. She writes:

> These discoveries challenged us not only intellectually, but — in my case–spiritually. I had come to respect the work of the 'church fathers' such as Irenaeus of Lyons (c.180,), who had denounced such secret writings as an abyss of madness and blasphemy against Christ. Therefore, I expected these recently discovered texts to be garbled, pretentious, and trivial. Instead, I was surprised to find in some of them unexpected spiritual power.... [5]

This spiritual power is being discovered by others, as well. These books contain many verses that challenge us to think more deeply about our faith, and they also call us to review how we exercise our Christianity. The focus, as explained earlier, is about our knowing and relating to Christ, emphasizing our spiritual relationship without detailing how that has to be. The beauty and commitment to Christ, as witnessed in these verses, give insight into why the Gnostics heard the message; faith is activated by the spiritual experience of seeking love and God.

Earlier selected verses from the *Gospel of Thomas* illustrated this seeking style of Christianity. What follows are a few verses from some of the other gospels and writings found at Nag Hammadi. In these verses, one will be able to extract that the Gnostics were not just about different beliefs and myths. These verses, which have much more power and relevance than the intrigue of the gnostic creation myths, are often overlooked. Being so distinctively Christ centered, it is amazing that these verses would be deemed heretical and false. To say they are evil and un-Christian, as was charged, is truly beyond belief![6] All quotations are from the gnostic books found in *The Nag Hammadi Library in English*, edited by James M. Robinson.

The Gospel of Truth

Verse 1: "The gospel of truth is joy for those who have received from the Father of truth the grace of knowing him." [7]

The author of this gospel is unknown, but some believe him to be Valentinus. The title is taken from this first verse.[8] Gnosis, or knowing him, is clearly about ones relationship as to a friend. The emotion of joy comes in the experience of grace and knowing the Father.

Verse 16: "...the one who is addressed as the Savior, (that) being the name of the work he is to perform for the redemption of those who are ignorant of the Father, while in the name [of] the gospel is the proclamation of hope, being discovery for those who search for him."[9]

Jesus is the Savior, but more powerful than the name is the work of redemption, which brings hope to seekers or "for those who search for him".

Verse 20: "Jesus...he was nailed to a tree; he published the edict of the Father on the cross. Oh such great teaching! He draws himself down to death though life eternal clothes him. Having stripped himself of the perishable rags, he put on imperishability which no one can take away from him.[10]

Being "nailed to a tree" is a rather direct way to express the crucifixion. Also, "he published the edict" is a fascinating way to express what otherwise might be known as the revelation of the cross. The theme of putting on imperishability is similarly described in Paul's First letter to the Corinthians, Chapter 15, in the Bible.[11]

Verse 33: "Make firm the foot of those who have stumbled and stretch out your hands to those who are ill. Feed those who are hungry and give repose to those who are weary, and raise up those who wish to rise and awaken those who are asleep."[12]

One of the many charges against the Gnostics found often in the writings of the church fathers was that the Gnostics had no morals or morality.[13] Since they believed the world was totally evil, and their whole desire was to escape it, they had no need to care for it. It is hard to argue that this verse doesn't affirm a strong, moral ethic and responsibility to others!

The Gospel of Philip

Verse 25: Some said, "Mary conceived by the 'holy spirit.' They are in error. They do not know what they are saying. When did a woman ever conceive by a woman?"[14]

In Aramaic, "spirit" is a feminine word.[15] Therefore, the question of conception by two women is raised. The Gnostics did not believe in the virgin birth in the literal, physical sense, but conceived of it as a symbolic belief. Of course, with the virgin birth being a literal fact for those who would decide which books should be included in the Bible, the *Gospel of Philip* didn't have a chance to make it into the canon, especially with this verse!

Verse 56: "Jesus is a hidden name, Christ is a revealed name. For this reason Jesus is not particular to any language; rather he is always called by the name Jesus. While as for Christ, in Syriac,* it is Messiah, in Greek it is Christ. Certainly all the others have it according to their own language. The Nazarene is he who reveals what is hidden. Christ has everything in himself, whether man or angel or mystery and the father."[16]

Although this is a fairly complicated passage, it is clear that Jesus was extraordinary beyond his name. Often asked is whether the Gnostics believed Jesus was the Messiah. The answer is revealing and bold; Jesus was the Messiah–in whatever language — the Christ! *Syriac is also a name for Aramaic, the language spoken in Palestine by the common people of Jesus' day and believed to be spoken by him, as well.[17]

Verse 63: "And the companion of the (Savior) Mary Magdalene...(he)...loved her more than (all) the disciples (and used to) kiss her (often) on her (   )–{the word is missing!} The rest (of the disciples) they said to him, 'Why do you love her more than all of us?" The savior answered and said to them, 'Why do I not love you like her?"[18]

Some say not much imagination is needed to fill in the missing word as being that Jesus kissed her on the lips, but here is a good example of omissions that happen often in the gnostic texts.[19] *The Da Vinci Code* uses this verse to support its theory of Jesus being married to Mary Magdalene.[20] That is also imagination as there is no solid evidence to prove Dan Brown's contention one way or the other.[21] Whatever the case, more important to the issue of faith, this verse gives evidence that the Gnostics believed in Jesus as Savior and that Mary Magdalene was a truly special, close, and beloved disciple of Jesus.

Verse 67: "Truth did not come into the world naked, but it came in types and images. But one receives the unction of the (   ) power of the cross. This power the apostles call the 'right and the left.' For the person is not longer a Christian but a Christ."[22]

Truth, for the Gnostics, came in types and images, not just in the literal or "naked truth." So it was for the power of the cross. To become a Christ, taken in its literal sense, might seem impossible, but as a goal to lift ones' way of life as Christ-like seems an admirable calling. Martin Luther said it was our goal to become "little Christ," and clearly to seek such a way of life was part of faith for Philip.

The Gospel of Mary (Magdalene)

Verse 8: [The blessed one says] "Peace be with you. Receive my peace to yourselves. Beware that no one lead you astray, saying, 'Lo here!' or 'Lo there!' For the Son of Man is within you. Follow after him! Those who seek will find him." [23]

Mary uses the term, "the son of Man," a phrase that commonly means the one who understands being human.[24] Mary's witness is that Christ brings peace to those who follow and seek. Mary Magdalene, who was maligned thorough the years, might have liked the thought, "trust the process of life, trust Christ, and you will be at peace." Clearly, she witnesses to the peace that can be found in Christ.

Verse 10: "I said to him, Lord, how does he who sees the vision see it (through) the soul (or) through the spirit? The Savior answered and said, 'He does not see through the soul nor through the spirit, but the mind which (is) between the two..." [25]

What a beautiful teaching! Faith utilizes the mind — even our God given brains — in our seeking!

Verse 17: (Peter is complaining) "Did he really speak with a woman without our knowledge (and) not openly? Are we to turn about and all listen to her? Did he prefer her to us." [26]

Peter is speaking to the other disciples but is also asking us, "What do you think?" The *Gospel of Mary* should be read carefully because it reveals deep wisdom and faith from this feminine Apostle. Not to be overlooked, this gospel includes many theological teachings, which are more thoughtful than even the knowledge of her close companionship with Jesus.

The Apocryphon of James

(Apocryphon is a word that translates as secret) James was a brother of Jesus.

Verse 4: "Hence become full of the Spirit, but be in want of reason, for reason belongs to the soul; in turn it is the nature of the soul."[27]

Sometimes religion or faith is defined by blind trust in doctrines or beliefs. Not so for the gnostics, faith should include reason! If using one's reason was one of their "secret" teachings, then secret surely has a deeper meaning than the implication of being bad, exclusive, or evil. Using reason or one's mind over blind trust, even when filled with the Spirit, could well have been one of the primary issues that bothered the literalists!

Verse 8: Become earnest in the word! For as to the word, its first part is faith; the second, love; the third, works; for from these come life."[28]

For Christians who believe in the "word," this verse suggests it is not about believing alone, but also calls for love and works. Faith, love, works; not bad admonitions from suspect and false Christians!

Treatise on the Resurrection

Verse 48: "It is the revelation of what is, and the transformation of things, and a transition into newness. What then is the resurrection? It is no illusion, but it is the truth! Indeed, it is more fitting to say that the world is an illusion, rather than the resurrection which has come into being through our Lord, the Savior, Jesus Christ."[29]

Because the Gnostics interpreted the resurrection event differently from what they were told, the apostolic church got the message out successfully that they didn't believe in the resurrection. Right? No, wrong! They appear even to outdo them in this passage! A not so common but beautiful interpretation of resurrection is presented as being a transformation and transition into newness. Resurrection in this treatise is presented as something we can experience now as well as after death

The Prayer of the Apostle Paul

This short prayer actually begins the writings of the collection of Nag Hammadi as it is the first book found in the First Codex, more commonly known as the Jungian Codex. This book is a prayer attributed to St. Paul which begins after the introduction:

Verse 2: "Redeemer, redeem me, for I am yours…." [30]

Verse 35: The prayer ends: "yours is the power and glory and the praise and the greatness forever and ever. Amen. Prayer of Paul, the Apostle. In Peace. Christ is holy."[31]

Paul was vital to the Gnostics – not the Paul of harsh judgments – but the Paul of dedication and often imagination, also a quality which can be found in his writings in the Bible. St. Paul is usually assumed to be the spokesman and the hero of the literalists alone, but as will be seen in

Chapter Thirteen, Paul was also the mentor of the Gnostics and revered highly by them.

In review, from these selected verses, several themes of the Gnostics can be derived or discovered. One theme of these Gnostic Gospels is the importance of being seekers of God, which is the message of this book. Another theme of these gospels is using reason and our minds in seeking both truth and God. Gnosis, as presented earlier, is about relating ourselves to others and God, not believing a set of beliefs. Faith is a dynamic process that matures and grows and does not stop in unquestionable beliefs such as the virgin birth. Everyone doesn't have to interpret beliefs in the same way, even for the meaning of the resurrection of Jesus. It is clear that there is a moral and ethical responsibility to care for others. Male chauvinism has no place in the church or its ministry. One is to become full of the Spirit, as James the Lord's brother exhorts, and one can become earnest in the word of God, which is made up of faith, love, and works.

As can be deducted from these verses from the Nag Hammadi manuscripts, these Christians did believe in Jesus. Rather shocking, is how inspiring, thought provoking, and as stated, Christ centered these passages are! These teachings are just a small sampling of the multitude of teachings in which Jesus is lifted up and praised by most of the fifty two books found at Nag Hammadi. Not all the books were Christian, as exemplified by one book being a two page section from Plato's *Republic*![32] However, most are directly related to Christ and Christianity, although each varies in style and content. Reading *The Nag Hammadi Library in English* can be a daunting task, and as with the Bible, commentaries and books about the different writings are helpful and in some cases essential in understanding the framework of their contents. As one goes beyond the *Gospel of Thomas* to other books found at Nag Hammadi, many other verses and themes, like these highlighted above, will be found that encourage faith and a living relationship with Christ.

Not to be denied, particularly in certain of the gnostic books, is that the influence from their myths often seeps in and makes them less appealing. Some books are dedicated to explaining different mythologies, and, unfortunately, these are the books most commonly used to define the Gnostics. For example, *The Apocryphon of John* is a book which totally sets forth the Sethian myth of the creation of the fall and salvation of the world;

with many unusual names and figures, it is quite difficult to understand without some background and knowledge of the Sethians.[33] The same can be said for a book named *The Tripartite Tractate*, a long, complex treatise in three parts, and thus its name.[34] In its case, an understanding of the Valentinian myth is needed to grasp its contents. Both of these myths will be more fully explained in their separate chapters dealing with gnostic mythologies.

Not all the gnostic books are equal in their quality, prose, or content, and to define the Gnostics on the basis of only a few books misses the message of faith expressed in most of gnostic gospels, as illustrated in the verses above. To dismiss all their writings as myths is to look beyond the reality that most of the books center on the praise and truth of Christ. However, as freethinking Christians, they believed that truth was not bound by acclaimed authority and that conventional beliefs and myths could be challenged by the very freedom that Christ preached and instilled in believers.

This freedom to believe openly, honestly, and differently brings forth another shocking revelation which was totally unexpected. The Gnostics deeply revered St. Peter and St. Paul! So ingrained in Christian tradition that Peter and Paul were the sole property of the orthodox, being their founders and leaders, it is unimaginable that others might have held these blessed apostles as exposing their views. Peter and Paul had more to do than any other apostles in the development of the church and to consider even the possibility of them upholding the faith of the Gnostics seems absurd. However, as will be illustrated in the next two chapters, several writings within the Gnostic Gospels make it abundantly clear that the Gnostics held Peter and Paul in the highest esteem; Peter and Paul, for the Gnostics, also were their mentors and brothers in Christ.

Notes: Chapter Eleven: The Gnostics Speak for Themselves

[1] Bart D. Ehrman, *The New Testament*, (Oxford: Oxford University Press, 2008), 202.
[2] Elaine Pagels, *The Gnostic Gospels*, (New York: Random House, 1979), XXIX.
[3] Ibid.
[4] Elaine Pagels, *Beyond Belief*, (New York: Random House, 2003), 29.
[5] Pagels, *Beyond Belief*, 32.
[6] Irenaeus, *Against Heresies*, 1: Preface.

[7] James Robinson, Editor, *The Nag Hammadi Library in English*, hereafter noted as *NHL*, (San Francisco: HarperSanFrancisco, 1978), the *Gospel of Truth*, 40.
[8] Robinson, *NHL*, the *Gospel of Truth*, 38.
[9] Robinson, *NHL*, the *Gospel of Truth*, 40.
[10] Robinson, *NHL*, the *Gospel of Truth*, 42.
[11] I Corinthians 15:42.
[12] Robinson, *NHL*, the *Gospel of Truth*, 47.
[13] Pagels, *Beyond Belief*, 121.
[14] Robinson, *NHL*, the *Gospel of Philip*, 143.
[15] J. Michael Matkin, *The Gnostic Gospels*, (New York: Alpha Books, 2005), 134
[16] Robinson, *NHL*, the *Gospel of Philip*, 144
[17] Matkin, *The Gnostic Gospels*, 132.
[18] Robinson, *NHL*, the *Gospel of Philip*, 148.
[19] In manuscript studies, the term "lacunae" is used for omissions, as in the text here.
[20] Dan Brown, *The Da Vinci Code*, (New York: Anchor Books, 2003), 323.
[21] Bart D. Ehrman, *Truth and Fiction in The Da Vinci Code*, (Oxford: Oxford University Press, 2006), 98.
[22] Robinson, *NHL*, the *Gospel of Philip*, 150.
[23] Robinson, *NHL*, the *Gospel of Mary*, 525.
[24] Pagels, *The Gnostic Gospels*, 123.
[25] Robinson, *NHL*, the *Gospel of Mary*, 525.
[26] Robinson, *NHL*, the *Gospel of Mary*, 526.
[27] Robinson, *NHL*, *The Apocryphon of James*, 31.
[28] Robinson, *NHL*, *The Apocryphon of James*, 33.
[29] Robinson, *NHL*, *The Treatise on the Resurrection*, 56.
[30] Robinson, *NHL*, *The Prayer of the Apostle Paul*, 28.
[31] Robinson, *NHL*, *The Prayer of the Apostle Paul*, 29.
[32] Robinson, *NHL*, Plato, *Republic*, 588A-589B (VI.5), 318.
[33] Robinson, *NHL*, *The Apocryphon of John*, 104.
[34] Robinson, *NHL*, *The Tripartite Tractate*, 58.

Chapter Twelve

The Apostle Peter — A Founder of the Church — a Gnostic?

> It is interesting that the Gnostic writer of the *Apocalypse of Peter* chose Peter to star in his account, since Peter was seen as Jesus' chief disciple and was venerated by the traditional Christian community. In fact, the emerging orthodox hierarchy saw Peter as its human spiritual anchor, referring to him as its first bishop or pope. [1]
>
> -Meera Lester, *The Everything Gnostic Book*

The Gnostic Gospels bring not only new words and teachings of Jesus but also fresh insights into the beginnings of the church. Christianity, of course, as a religion, traces its roots to the life of Jesus. By his death and resurrection as Christ the Messiah, Jesus became its founder. Motivated by Jesus, now the Christ, to spread his gospel, the primary founders of his church were the disciples Peter and Paul. Christianity and the church were to develop and expand significantly because of their missionary zeal. Other disciples were involved, but these two men have been given the most credit and respect for establishing the early churches of Christianity. Because of their prominence, Peter and Paul have been considered the champions of orthodoxy in the Christian tradition; therefore, surely, they had no connections to the Gnostics.

Although the first churches were founded in the Mediterranean region, and particularly, in locations where there were Jewish synagogues, Rome, eventually, was to exceed Jerusalem as the primary center for the expansion of Christianity. Being the political and social hub of the Roman Empire,

Rome was essential in the dissemination of the gospel. In addition, the church at Rome had the special privilege of claiming as its founders both Peter and Paul. From Paul's Letter to the Romans, now in the Bible, this church had received its theological wisdom and the primary doctrines for faith. From Peter, as its first bishop, it had received its ecclesiastical wisdom and authority. Because both were recognized as the leading disciples on how Jesus wanted his message to be explained and shared, they were to become the primary pillars for the literalist interpretation of Christian theology and the polity of the church.

Now, because of the Nag Hammadi books, the baptismal bowl of Christian orthodoxy has developed a crack! Could Peter and Paul be associated with other interpretations of Christianity than those blessed by the apostolic church? Shockingly, the Nag Hammadi discovery affirms that the Gnostics believed both Peter and Paul represented and supported their theological positions. By using the names of Peter and Paul in the titles of several of their writings, the Gnostic Gospels bring the surprising information that these two saints were also considered as theological authorities for the Gnostics.

The gnostic books bearing the names of Peter and Paul were unknown, expect perhaps for some privileged scholars, before Nag Hammadi. Now, it is revealed that in early Christianity that these saints were not the sole theological possession of the literalists. It is known that not only was there a cover up of gospels, which did not support the church's theology, but, now in addition, books were silenced that would indicate that Peter and Paul were sympathetic to anything gnostic. The reason this is rather shocking is because throughout most of history, these two ecclesiastical giants were not considered anything other than exclusive saints for orthodox Christianity. Therefore, not only is there the shock of the Gnostic Gospels; also, there comes the news that there was what can be called a gnostic Peter and a gnostic Paul.

In contrast to the little known knowledge that Peter and Paul could be gnostic, what is widely known is that the Apostle Peter was to be regarded by the church at Rome as their primary priest and saint. As the most trusted of Jesus' twelve disciples, their primary leader, and the one whom Jesus confided in to build his church, Peter was to gain special status. Peter was recognized as the first Bishop of the Church at Rome. Being privy to the direct teachings of Jesus, both before and after his resurrection, how could

St. Peter not be blessed with the correct and orthodox desires of Jesus for his church?

Peter, as presented in the New Testament is a highly honored and loveable character. He was energetic, impulsive, very human, capable of mistakes, and a natural born leader. Originally, known as Simon, Jesus changes his name to Peter, or Petra, which means the rock.[2] Particularly, the gospels of Luke and Matthew, more than the gospels of Mark and John, elevate the importance of Peter above the other disciples. In the Book of Acts, which is attributed to the gospel writer Luke, it is recorded that Peter preaches a sermon in which three thousand people were converted to Christianity.[3] This sermon was at an annual Jewish Festival called the Feast of Harvest.[4] As it was held this particular year on the fiftieth day, or pente-day, after the resurrection of Jesus, Christians renamed this event, Pentecost, celebrating Peter's harvest of souls.[5] Pentecost became known officially as the beginning or the birthday of the church.[6] The Holy Spirit promised by Jesus was reported to have descended upon the people at Pentecost with a roaring, powerful wind.[7] At its birth, the church was not an institution or singular body but a gathering of many people from various countries to whom Peter preached. The people spoke different languages, yet they could understand each other, and Peter.[8] Those present at Pentecost were overwhelmed and emboldened by the spirit of Jesus and by the power of God. Representing diverse tongues and people, they were to be the seedlings for spreading the gospel and establishing the church throughout the world, even as far as Rome.[9]

After this event, Peter in his ministry performed miracles, and seeing the positive response to Jesus by persons others than the Jews, Peter partially begins to accept that Gentiles, or those, not of the Hebrew faith or lineage, could become Christians.[10] Synagogues were the first meeting place for Christians, and Paul's Letter to the Galatians in the Bible indicates that Peter's vision for Christianity and its church was to be an extension of Judaism.[11] Thus, Peter was reluctant at first to accept Jesus as the Messiah for Gentiles, but Paul was able to convince him otherwise. According to the Book of Acts, Chapter 15, Peter was to give his official support to Paul's strong stance of accepting Gentiles as Christians at the Council of Jerusalem.[12] This Council was clearly the first of many such deliberative meetings to decide the structure of the church and how Christianity would be defined. With Peter's direct blessing, the critical decision was made to welcome Gentiles, importantly, without the necessity for circumcision and Jewish restrictions or customs.[13]

Surprisingly, in the Book of Acts, which is considered the primary source for the story of the development of the early church, Peter is not mentioned after this first Council in Jerusalem. Tradition has it that Peter ultimately settled and established his ministry in Rome, where he would be martyred for his Christian faith during the reign of Nero.[14] Legend says he was crucified on a cross upside down at his request because he did not want to claim equality with Jesus.[15] According to another tradition of the church, his crucifixion took place at the location where the Vatican's Basilica of St. Peter now stands.[16]

Upon St. Peter, the rock, bishops and the church fathers were to build their church. Although Paul has been given credit for the primary establishment of the church in Rome, Peter's martyrdom gave him lasting prestige. Reportedly given the keys of the kingdom by Jesus, and revered particularly by the two mentioned gospel writers, Luke and Matthew, Peter was given prominence, not only with the title, Bishop of Rome, but in time, was to be recognized as the first Pope of the Holy Roman Catholic Church.[17]

With Peter being the powerful Bishop of Rome and the Pope, why would one even suspect that those who weren't accepted as legitimate members of the church, or were heretics, would have any respect or venerate St. Peter? The Gnostic Gospels contain a major surprise. The Nag Hammadi books clearly show that the Gnostics also honored and appreciated Peter, not quite as a Pope, but certainly as saintly. Not only is their respect for Peter, but surprisingly four of these gnostic books relate directly to Peter. Peter's name is used in their titles. Although there is a variance in his authority within these books, his voice as a bold, central disciple of Jesus is now known to have extended beyond the apostolic church.

What follows are synopses of these four books, which were a part of the Gnostic Gospels, found at Nag Hammadi and have Peter's name as part of their titles:

The Acts of Peter and The Twelve Apostles tells the story of Peter and the other disciples taking a journey to a city where they meet a pearl merchant.[18] This merchant also appears as a doctor who gives Peter a bag of medicine. The pearl merchant/doctor identifies himself as being Jesus Christ. He tells Peter and the disciples to go heal the bodies and the hearts of people. Jesus also teaches that his name is more valuable than gold and silver — and precious pearls![19] Certainly, this is an imaginative story, but within it, both Peter and Jesus are central characters, and Jesus' teachings are given directly to Peter.

The Apocalypse of Peter, sometimes translated as *The Revelation of Peter* (apocalypse means revelation), is a book that elevates several gnostic themes. Peter is given strong spiritual authority and power.[20] Jesus even chooses Peter as the foundation for those who would become his disciples. Peter has visions, and they are interpreted by none other than Jesus Christ. Just as the bishops claimed direct revelation from Jesus, here the Gnostics assert such privilege for themselves. In this account, Jesus is depicted as laughing at the foolishness of those who think they are crucifying him. Jesus speaks directly to Peter and says, "He whom you saw on the tree, glad and laughing, this is the living Jesus."[21] The text teaches that those who crucified Jesus were killing someone, but they did not kill the immortal Christ! The crucifers are described as blind ones who have no guide. However, the crucifers are not the only blind ones, as Jesus then tells Peter, those who call themselves bishops and deacons overlook the little ones and are dry canals![22] Hum? Peter, the Bishop of Rome, might not take too well to Jesus' comment.

The Act of Peter is about an unusual healing by St. Peter.[23] The recipient is Peter's own daughter. The daughter had been paralyzed to protect her from a sexual advance by a man named Ptolemy. In a strange twist, Ptolemy repents from his advance and gives a parcel of land to Peter and his daughter, and she is healed. Then the text says because it was "beneficial for you and me," apparently to protect his daughter, Peter reverses the miracle, and the daughter becomes an invalid again! [24] Peter sells the parcel and then gives the proceeds to the poor.

The lessons appear to be that of protecting the purity of his daughter, and Peter's charity in giving to the poor. This healing and then un-healing is a rather strange tale, but as unusual as it is, does affirm the power of Peter to heal and lead.[25]

The Letter of Peter to Philip is a gnostic text but has elements that the literalists might support.[26] Interestingly, this letter was found also as one of the books included with the newly discovered *Gospel of Judas.* Whereas Peter is given a central place in the other books, significantly, in this letter he is given status as being a primary leader of the apostolic group. This letter speaks of the reality of Jesus suffering, a literalist teaching, and then, strongly presents the gnostic theme of the attainment of fullness through the light of Jesus. As it has both theological positions, scholars believe it is written by a Gnostic who was trying to convince or placate the literalists.[27]

In all these books, support for Peter's role as a leader of the church, definitely, was recognized. The surprise was that these books give witness that the Gnostics believed Peter was also critical to their theology. However, in spite of their respect, they fall short of elevating him above all the other disciples as did the early bishops.

Interestingly, in the Bible, other disciples are given special prominence as well as Peter. The Apostle John is described as the most loved disciple.[28] For many, Paul was the most insightful and was recognized as an apostle because of his unique relationship with Jesus.[29] Utterly shocking is that Judas is described as Jesus' "favorite" in the *Gospel of Judas.*[30] Yet, for the early bishops, there was no question as to whom was the closest and most trusted by Jesus — St. Peter. Elevated to be the leader of leaders, especially blessed by Jesus, the church declared him, as is well known, the first Pope. However, if the Gnostics had been given a chance, the first Pope might not have been Peter, but Pope Mary Magdalene! What? Why?

Both in the *Gospel of Philip* and the *Gospel of Mary*, Mary Magdalene is the closest to Jesus, and he endows her with special visions and leadership.[31] Mary is given higher regard than Peter. Philip, in his gospel, makes the case that Jesus loved her more than all the disciples.[32] Particularly, in the *Gospel of Mary*, differences and conflict with Peter come to life.[33] Unfortunately, ten pages are missing from this Gospel, but the exchanges between Peter and Mary are quite intense. Although the conflict was mentioned in part in the last chapter, the details are revealing why the Gnostics held her as valuable as Peter. What follows is the specific account that gives at least nearly equal support to Mary:

> First, Mary receives a vision and teachings from the Lord and Savior. Andrew, a disciple, says her teachings are strange.[34] Peter then questions her integrity and says:
>
> "Did he really speak with a woman without our knowledge and not openly? Are we to turn about and listen to her? Did he prefer her to us?" Then Mary wept and said to Peter, "My brother Peter, what do you think? Do you think I made this up myself in my heart or that I am lying about the Savior?" Levi answered to Peter, "Peter, you have always been hot-tempered. Now I see you contending against the woman like the adversaries. But if the Savior made her worthy, who are you indeed to reject her? Surely, the Savior knows her very well. That is why he loved her more than us."[35]

Mary Magdalene was never considered as a candidate for Pope of the Church, of course, and that is not the issue. Interestingly, however, both the Gnostic Gospels of Philip and Mary present her as an apostle as strong as Peter.[36] If women had been allowed to be priests, and the Gnostics respect for Mary had been recognized, she might have been the holy angel instead of Peter 'up there,' or at least with him, guarding the pearly gates to heaven! For sure, the church would have been different, and because of Mary's high respect and closeness to Jesus, women would have been given their rightful place in the early church as priest and ministers — not having to wait all these years.

Another noteworthy gnostic book that should be recognized is the *Gospel of Peter*.[37] This Gospel was not included in the Nag Hammadi collection, yet it was believed to have been extraordinarily popular in the developing church. The reason for its exclusion is not known, but it is quite severe on the Jews for the crucifixion of Jesus. In addition, it has quite a strong docetic Christology.[38] Docetic means that Jesus appeared to be human, but wasn't.

A common charge against the Gnostics was that all held a docetic view of Jesus. This docetic charge will be elaborated more fully with the discussion of the early church heretic, Marcion, who most scholars believe should not be categorized as a Gnostic.[39] However, the argument or belief that all Gnostics were docetic, as Marcion clearly was, doesn't hold with the new knowledge from the Gnostic Gospels. Docetic elements are found in some books, as in the *Apocalypse of Peter*, but are not as dominant as expected.[40] The docetic view of Jesus is not present in the majority of gnostic books found at Nag Hammadi. In other words, for most Gnostics, Jesus was a real person. Perhaps, the excluded *Gospel of Peter*, with its anti-Jewish tact and its strong docetic interpretation of Jesus, was too much for the monks of Nag Hammadi?

Beyond the question of why the *Gospel of Peter* was not found at Nag Hammadi, the new story of Peter expands what was known of him, and yet, does not negate the Roman Catholic interpretation of him. Clearly, they won the primary interpretation of Peter, and to their credit, it has served their church well, and also for the strength and vitality of all Christianity. These books, however, mean that there were other interpretations, making the understanding of Peter more complex.

To summarize, because Peter was the chief disciple for the apostolic church, and in their ecclesiastical formation crowned him as the first Pope, the assumption that the Gnostics resented Peter would seem reasonable. Although the Gnostics did not grant his status as superior to other disciples, the Gnostics highly respected him. However, to say that Peter was the sole property of the literalists can now be questioned based on the books in *The Nag Hammadi Library*, because the Gnostics also believed he supported their perspective and theology.

So was Peter a Gnostic? From the information, it would be fairer to say there was a gnostic Peter rather than Peter was a Gnostic. Just as those who claim Peter as a literalist, it might be fairer to say that they also took the person of Peter and aligned their own interpretations with him. Obviously, a powerful disciple, to use his authority to affirm one's viewpoint and theology makes perfectly good sense. There is no question that the literalists established quite solidly that he was theirs alone, but such purity of ownership is challenged by a gnostic Peter.

A gnostic Peter would mean the Gnostics interpreted Peter as one who supported and inspired them. By the titles of some of their books, their gnostic stories of his talking directly with Jesus, his recognition as a healer and miracle worker, and by their use of his authority to affirm their theological positions, the Gnostics, at least, wanted to claim Peter. Clearly, such an allegiance did not prevail, and as Peter cannot speak for himself now, who knows what he would say? It cannot be denied that Peter was an influential figure in the gnostic understanding of Christianity, and although his high regard by the Gnostics is interesting, even more astonishing is the stronger relationship of the Gnostics to St. Paul.

Notes: Chapter Twelve: Saint Peter — A Founder of the Church — a Gnostic?

[1] Meera Lester, *The Everything Gnostic Gospels Book*, (Avon, Massachusetts: Adams Media, 2007), 230.
[2] Henry Hampton Halley, *Halley's Bible Handbook*, (Grand Rapids, Michigan, Zondervan Press, Revised, 2000), 554.
[3] Acts 2: 1-13.
[4] Halley, *Halley's Bible Handbook*, 725.
[5] Ibid.
[6] Ibid.
[7] Acts 2:2.
[8] Acts 2:4.
[9] Halley, *Halley's Bible Handbook*, 763.
[10] Acts 3: 1-10.
[11] Halley, *Halley's Bible Handbook*, 800.
[12] Acts 15: 1-35.
[13] Halley, *Halley's Bible Handbook*, 743.
[14] Halley, *Halley's Bible Handbook*, 872.
[15] Ibid.
[16] Tim Dowley, Ed., *Introduction to The History of Christianity*, (Minneapolis: Fortress Press, 2002), 60.
[17] Helen Keeler and Susan Grimbly, The *Everything Catholicism Book*, (Avon, Ma., Adams Media, 2003), 32.
[18] James M. Robinson, Ed., *The Nag Hammadi Library in English*, hereafter noted as *NHL*, (San Francisco: HarperSanFranciso, 1978), *The Acts of Peter and the Twelve Apostles*, 287.
[19] Robinson, *NHL*, *The Acts of Peter and the Twelve Apostles*, 287–294.
[20] Robinson, *NHL*, *The Apocalypse of Peter*, 372.
[21] Robinson, *NHL*, *The Apocalypse of Peter*, 377: 81.
[22] Robinson, *NHL*, *The Apocalypse of Peter*, 372-378.
[23] Robinson, *NHL*, *The Act of Peter*, 528.
[24] Robinson, *NHL*, *The Act of Peter*, 530.
[25] Robinson, *NHL*, *The Act of Peter*, 528--531.
[26] Robinson, *NHL*, *The Letter of Peter to Philip*, 431.
[27] Robinson, *NHL*, *The Letter of Peter to Philip*, 431–437.
[28] John 13:23.

[29] Bart D. Ehrman, *The New Testament*, (Oxford: Oxford University Press, 2008), 291.
[30] Elaine Pagels and Karen L. King, *Reading Judas*, (New York: Viking Press, 2007), 3.
[31] Robinson, *NHL*, the *Gospel of Philip*, 139 and the *Gospel of Mary*, 523.
[32] Robinson, *NHL*, the *Gospel of Philip*, 148.
[33] Robinson, *NHL*, the *Gospel of Mary*, 524.
[34] Robinson, *NHL*, the *Gospel of Mary*, 526.
[35] Robinson, *NHL*, the *Gospel, of Mary*, 526.
[36] Ann Graham Brock, *Mary Magdalene, The First Apostle*, (Harvard, Ma.: Harvard University Press, 2003), 161.
[37] Robert J. Miller, Ed., *The Complete Gospels*, (San Francisco; HarperSanFrancisco, 1992), the *Gospel of Peter*, 399.
[38] Ehrman, *The New Testament*, 216.
[39] J. Michael Matkin, *The Gnostic Gospels*, (New York: Alpha Press, 2005), 43.
[40] Robinson, *NHL*, *The Apocalypse of Peter*, 372.

Chapter Thirteen

The Apostle Paul — a Founder of the Church — a Gnostic?

> From such elements of earlier tradition which the Valentinians ignored, Irenaeus and his followers construct the antignostic Paul, reinterpreting his letters in an orthodox direction: by the late second century he becomes the church's champion, the challenger of the gnostic Paul.[1]
>
> -Elaine Pagels, *The Gnostic Paul*

Undoubtedly, Peter was a powerful figure in establishing the church, but some consider the Apostle Paul to have been as influential if not more so than Peter in the development of Christianity. Paul was an aggressive missionary and the founder of churches in many cities and regions of the Roman Empire. His letters are full of exhortations for the churches as well as theological teachings. His influence has been so lasting that some have made the unconventional proposal that Paul, not Jesus, was the true founder of Christianity.

A. N. Wilson's book *Paul, The Mind of the Apostle* argues that Paul was Christianity's true creator.[2] He explains, "The fact that the Gentile world adopted Christianity is owing almost solely to one man: Paul of Tarsus. Without Paul, it is highly unlikely that Christianity would have ever broken away from Judaism."[3] Of course, this overlooks Jesus as the primary source for the religion, but Wilson concludes his book by saying, "Paul, and not Jesus, was — if anyone was — the Founder of Christianity." [4]

Paul, the Founder of Christianity? Maybe the Gnostics aren't as far out as critics would like to portray them, because they would stand with the literalists that Jesus, not Paul, was their Founder. Wilson makes only one comment about the Gnostics in his book. He refers to them as possibly being the false teachers that Paul mentions in some of his letters, and joining this tradition, he writes them off as such a group.[5] Although it is now known, bishops attacked many others who were considered false teachers, the Gnostics would agree with one of Wilson's indictments. He states that the religion, Christianity, was an "institutional distortion of Paul's thought."[6] The Gnostics would applause the charge of "institutional distortion." Clearly, the apostolic church, which became the institution, convinced the world that Paul had preached their literalist theology, their strict morality, and their stance of male dominance. The Gnostics had a much different reading of Paul.

Whereas, many today accept Paul's teachings as the literal laws and truths of Christianity, others disagree and believe his teachings are extreme – particularly, those verses that can be found which denigrate women, express hostility to Jews, support slavery, and declare that only those who believe in Jesus are saved. Often, Paul is loved or hated. Therefore, another, significant, unexpected gift from the Gnostic Gospels is that they may help to bring forth a new, more honest, and refreshing view of Paul.

Two questions come to the forefront in revising the understanding of Paul. Could Paul have been a Gnostic? Secondly, could there be more than one Biblical Paul, meaning different authors named Paul? At first, such thoughts may sound ridiculous, but both Biblical research and the Gnostic's appreciation of Paul bring new light on what has been taken for granted. Serious questions are raised about all his letters being authentic, and what truly was his theological stance.

Scholarly studies of the writings of St. Paul in the Bible now argue by critical analysis that all the letters of Paul were not written by the same person.[7] This may sound like a modern day heresy, but it can be helpful for those who have trouble with Paul's teachings, such as women should keep quiet in church and need to obey their husbands! What is instructive is that such harsh teachings of Paul are found primarily in the three books of the Bible, I Timothy, 2 Timothy, and Titus. These books are commonly known as the Pastoral Epistles.[8] Studies reveal that their writing style, Greek phrases, vocabulary, and theology contrast significantly with those which are referred to as the Pauline Corpus.[9] The Corpus letters are believed to be the undisputed authentic letters of St. Paul. They are the books of Romans,

I Corinthians, 2 Corinthians, Galatians, Philippians, 1 Thessalonians, and Philemon.[10] The direct denigration of women in these letters is within two verses of 1 Corinthians 14: 34-35. With these verses being so similar to I Timothy 2:11-15, they are believed to have been inserted by a later scribe.[11]

The Pastoral Epistles (1Timothy, 2 Timothy and Titus) are narrow, legalistic, chauvinistic, and seriously different from the other letters of Paul. They are called pastoral, because they are written from Paul to two younger pastors of churches, giving pastoral advice about how to deal with problems in their churches. Timothy was the pastor in Ephesus, and Titus was pastor in Crete.[12] These letters are quite forthright in attacking false teachers. Oh my goodness, it appears there was the problem of women playing significant roles in the church. This must be corrected! Beyond the harsh judgments against certain groups, which in general are unlike Paul in the letters of his believed to be authentic, there are other technical or textual reasons for questioning these letters as authentic.

Bart Ehrman, in his textbook *The New Testament*, observes that "apart from personal names, there are 848 different words found in the Pastorals; of these, 306 occur nowhere in the Pauline Corpus."[13] This may not seem that unusual, but a tell-tale sign of a later or different Paul is in Bart's research that, "Strikingly, over two thirds of these non-Pauline words are used by Christian authors of the second century."[14] As Bart writes, "Of even greater importance is the way in which these false teachings are attacked in the Pastorals, for the author's basic orientation appears to be very much like what we find in second century proto-orthodox circles."[15] Therefore, this analysis raises the suspicion of a scribe who edited original letters of Paul and sent them to these churches. There is the possibility that these letters were written later to affirm a form of Christianity that taught that women should be subservient to men, and certainly that they should not hold priestly positions.[16] Whatever the case, the apostolic church, or the proto-orthodox as described by Dr. Ehrman, was well on the path by the end of the second century in formalizing their doctrines as being pure gospel truth and establishing a male system of clergy and bishops to lead the church.

The concept that women should not be priests was adopted early in the development of the church. The layman and lawyer, Tertullian of Carthage, was a brilliant apologist for the literalist interpretation being applied to the Pastoral Letters.[17] He was considered a church father and lived from 160 CE to 240 CE.[18] Strangely, he would later reject what he called the "Church of the Bishops" and change to a charismatic movement called Montanism that embraced speaking in tongues, faith healing, etc. Before his theological shift, he was a warrior for the apostolic church's developing positions. Being second only to Irenaeus as an opponent to the Gnostics, in his book *Prescription Against Heretics*, he rails, "These heretical women–how audacious they are! They are bold enough to teach, to preach, to take part in almost every masculine function — they even baptize people."[19] Good grief! From the writings of Tertullian, Irenaeus, and all who would be considered proto-orthodox, it is clear they loved the Pastoral Epistles as they quoted them often to give evidence that St. Paul affirmed their strict beliefs and positions.[20]

The tradition of Paul, as being the statesman for the lowly place of women at home and in the church, does find relief by this proposed evidence. By two different persons writing the Pauline letters in the Bible, this is crucial, because it frees interpretations. Disconnecting the image of a Paul who is judgmental, and particularly harsh on women, allows one to reconsider whether Paul's theology is so straightforward and unbending as has often been taught.

For sure, the fundamentalists have had their stamp on Paul as their spokesman all the way back to the victorious literalists, but with a better understanding of the Gnostics, the question of Paul's total alliance to the literalists is now uncertain. The find at Nag Hammadi, along with the evidence of their being two Biblical' Pauls, or that some of St. Paul's writing were later edited, radically challenges what has been the fundamentalist way to understand and preach Paul.

With that information, additionally, something else startling happens; Paul becomes more than the exclusive property of the literalists and fundamentalists. The Gnostic Gospels present factual information that the Gnostics claimed that Paul was also their saint. This suggests that both the literalists and the Gnostics used the letters of Paul to promote their own particular positions and theologies.

Paul — a Gnostic — that couldn't be! Not even reasonable or conceivable to many Christians today was that the Gnostics could have appreciated Paul. Now there is strong evidence to the contrary. What follows are books found at Nag Hammadi that support Paul as representing gnostic positions.

The Nag Hammadi Library begins with ***The Prayer of the Apostle Paul.***[21] This short prayer found at the beginning of the Jungian Codex, or Codex I, less than a page in length, has a gnostic orientation, yet it relies on both Psalms and several Pauline letters. One verse is quite similar to what Paul wrote in I Corinthians 2:9 referring to the love of God where it says, "What no eye has seen, nor ear heard, nor the human heart conceived." Dieter Mueller, the translator of Paul's prayer in *The Nag Hammadi Library,* says "The most striking echo to the apostle (Paul) is the request to be granted, what no angel-eye has seen and no archon-ear has heard and what has not entered into the human heart."[22] Not only is the echo similar, but the respect for Paul is clear. This piece closes, "Prayer of the Apostle Paul, In Peace, Christ is holy." [23]

The Revelation of Paul is another gnostic book of Nag Hammadi.[24] Sometimes translated as *The Apocalypse of Paul*, it tells of the ascension of Paul through the heavens. In the Bible's book, 2 Corinthians 12: 2-4, there is a reference to Paul's ascent to the third heaven. Here, this account takes him up to the tenth heaven. Christ is his escort, and in the tenth heaven, Paul is greeted by his fellow spirits.[25] With this special journey with Christ, Paul's status as an apostle is confirmed and raised to a higher level. Douglas M. Parrott in *The Nag Hammadi Library's* introduction to *The Apocalypse of Paul* writes, "The exalted portrayal of Paul as exalted even above the other apostles is at home in second-century Gnosticism."[26] Obviously, this story is a bit mythical, as is Paul's sojourn to the third heaven in the New Testament, but the enhancement here is that Paul, as Dr. Parrott explains, is given the highest status of all the saints.

A third book in the Nag Hammadi collection directly uplifts and praises Paul. By its title, Paul's importance could be overlooked as its name is ***The Interpretation of Knowledge.***[27] Not only does it bring Paul back to earth, but it is packed with teachings from Paul for the church. Absent are the harsh dictates of the Pastorals and the judgment of others. This book is a lengthy expansion or a similar rendition of Paul's letter in the Bible's I Corinthians 12th chapter on spiritual gifts.[28] Proclaiming the church as the body of Christ, as does I Corinthians 12, this new book teaches harmony and respect for differences, reaffirming the Biblical message of a variety of spiritual gifts. It teaches that as there is a harmony among the limbs of the physical body, which work together, so it should be for members of the church. For those who are jealous and hateful, they are ignorant of the "grace that dwells within."[29] *The Interpretation of Knowledge* has gnostic overtones, and its message is in line with a verse in Corinthians, which the gnostics would applaud, "But strive for greater gifts and I will show you a more excellent way."[30]

Beyond these books within the Nag Hammadi writings, there are many verses in the Biblical books that the Gnostics would have claimed gave support to Paul's affinity with them. Elaine Pagels' *The Gnostic Paul* is a book filled with specific examples of how the Gnostics derived theology and perspectives from the Pauline letters of Romans, 1 Corinthians, 2 Corinthians, Galatians, Ephesians, Colossians and Hebrews.[31] All these are books or letters of Paul in the Bible, but instead of just being the sole property of the literalists, Pagels supplies evidence of how the Gnostics used these letters to bolster and argue their positions. Her book is not well known as it is written more for the Biblical scholar than the public though it is now available in paperback. Its full title is *The Gnostic Paul, Gnostic Exegesis of the Pauline Letters.*[32] Yes, the Gnostics as well as the literalists claimed Paul as their own.

Viewed from the gnostic perspective, the primary message of Paul was about experiencing Christ and the Christ who is alive.[33] Fundamentalist Christians might say, "Amen," but there is a problem. Paul's conversion on the Damascus road was more of an experience of enlightenment than a message that all had to be "born again" in order to be a Christian.[34] Paul, before his conversion to Christianity, was known as Saul of Tarsus, a city highly respected like Athens and Alexandria for its embrace of learning and education. Paul was a Roman citizen and a Jew, and a member of the Pharisees with whom Jesus had several encounters and differences. Paul's original disdain with Christianity was because of his belief that Jesus and his followers were a serious threat to the laws of Moses, which was central to the Pharisees.[35] In the Book of Acts, in the Bible, it says that Paul was gathering letters from the synagogues apparently to persecute "any who belonged to the Way."[36]

Interesting is the name, "the Way," to describe these Christians who Paul was ready to persecute. The Way might better describe how Gnostics defined Christianity rather than a religion of required beliefs. Unexpectedly, on his journey to Damascus to persecute those who were following the

Way, Paul encountered a blinding light that brought a message of enlightenment from God.

Paul's conversion was by a vision, which as in the case of Mary Magdalene' visions, was a way of learning from Christ. Paul's conversion on the Damascus Road was not a logical, rational decision to believe in Jesus, but rather came as a bolt from a light that temporarily blinded him. The Book of Acts reports, "approaching Damascus, suddenly a light from heaven flashed around him."[37] He fell to the ground, and Jesus spoke directly to him. Those with him heard the voice but saw no one. Jesus tells Paul to go to the city and added, "you will be told what you are to do."[38] Jesus then spoke again through a vision to a disciple named Annaias, who laid his hands on Paul so that he could regain his sight after being blind for three days. Paul regained his strength and was baptized, presumably by Annaias, who related the message that Jesus had told him that Paul was the one chosen to "bring my name before Gentiles and kings and before the people of Israel."[39]

For fundamentalist Christians, this story known as the conversion of Paul, is often cited to support their believing to be a true Christian and be saved that one must be born again or have a conversion experience. For the Gnostics, Paul's change from persecuting Christians, to being one, was obviously a change of mind, but more importantly the deeper message was that Paul was awakened to the *light of God.*[40] As the text says, "A light from heaven" embraced him.[41] Jesus spoke to Paul directly as he had with Mary Magdalene. Paul was a man who clearly was struck with a new seeing and experience that led to his worship and his relationship with Christ. Thus, in the gnostic understanding, the meaning of the conversion was an *enlightenment*, which allowed Paul to broaden his vision of God. The result was a transformation of how Paul viewed himself, the world, Christianity, and God.

When the story, told in the Book of Acts, is read recognizing the visions, the divine light, and the experience of Paul, the message isn't that Jews and others will go to hell if they don't believe in Jesus. Rather, belief in Jesus opens a relationship to God, beyond the boundaries of religious or pagan beliefs and laws, to the *light of God.*[42] Read through the lenses of the Gnostics, Paul was not simply the property of the literalists who taught the only way to faith was by conversion or verbally confessing what one now believed. Not read as a formula as to how one had to believe in Christ, an embracing of Christ was a spiritual experience as was Paul's. Paul's experience was exceptional, but the Gnostics didn't believe all had to be struck blind, literally, or even metaphorically, by a bolt of lightning. Well, in today's language, one didn't have to be born again, necessarily, in order to believe in Jesus and experience his light.

St. Paul was an inspiration to the Gnostics. They were moved by his conversion from a form of legalistic Judaism. They also did not interpret Paul, as an unrelenting warrior, whose conviction was that those who did not believe as he did were false believers. Not denying his forthrightness, the gnostic Paul was more gentle and loving. Thus, the Gnostics would have read Paul's letters not as rules, regulations, and unbending doctrines; they would have read them foremost as exhortations to live in freedom and love because of Christ.

Paul, for example, asked persons who were believers in Christ, to look at the world, differently, and beyond the strict classifications, of "us" and "them." He teaches in a famous passage in Galatians 3:25-28, "But now that faith has come, we are no longer subject to a disciplinarian, for in Christ Jesus you are all children of God through faith. As many of you were baptized into Christ, you have clothed yourselves with Christ. There is no longer Jew or Greek, there is no longer slave or free, there is no longer male or female; for all of you are one in Christ." This teaching from one of the undisputed letters of Paul seems a far cry from the misogyny, household/church rules and cultural prejudice preached in the Pastorals. From the perspective of the Gnostics, Paul was not one whose role was to establish the strict doctrines and beliefs that would define Christianity, but he advocated freedom in Christ.

Beyond the gnostic understanding of Paul as being a more inclusive Christian, one issue stands out as being a significant theological divide with the bishops hard line teachings — the issue of the bodily resurrection. The importance of this doctrine as it relates to Paul is that it is a prime example of how the literalists and the Gnostics interpreted Paul quite differently. For the literalists, the belief in a physical, bodily resurrection for those who believed in Christ was not only paramount but required. Tertullian wrote, "Anyone who denies the resurrection of the flesh is a heretic, not a Christian."[43] That explains things pretty clearly! Further, Bishop Irenaeus in *Against Heresies* uses the Pastoral Letters, and 1 Corinthians 15, to give *proof* that Paul taught the doctrine of a bodily resurrection. His proof, as he argues in a circularly manner, is that since Christ's resurrection was physical and bodily, so too it will be for those who believe in him![44]

On the other hand, the Gnostics read the same chapter in 1 Corinthians 15, and believed Paul strongly argued for a spiritual resurrection. The whole chapter is fairly complex but teaches quite explicitly in several of its verses a spiritual resurrection. For example in verse 44, "It is sown a physical body, it is raised a spiritual body," and in verse 50, "What I am telling you brothers and sisters, is this flesh and blood cannot inherit the kingdom of God." Then, in a verse sometimes used comically as a quote today in church nurseries, verse 51, says, "Listen, I will tell you a mystery! We will not die, but we all will be changed." Of course, no one knows the how of a resurrection might be. For the literalists, because the Gnostics would dare believe it was spiritual, such a belief was proof of their heresy and their disrespect for Paul.

The evidence presented above of Paul's relation to the Gnostics is not to convince one that Paul was either a Gnostic or a literalist. In today's world, this may seem to be dodging the bullet. Beyond the need for either/or, it appears that both used the writings of Paul to make their case. Although Paul has conventionally been known as the champion of the orthodox, the Gnostic Gospels bring a new challenge to this long held assumption. Apparently, there were early gnostic Christians, who like Peter, also viewed Paul as representing their positions. However, in spite of new controversies, most scholars believe there was an Apostle Paul who lived, and, interestingly, his actuality isn't questioned as often as that of Jesus. The majority of gnostic scholars believe both lived historical lives, but the gnostic writings raise the level beyond the question of their existence.

The critical question becomes how one interprets Jesus and Paul, as one's interpretation also becomes a dimension of reality, as well. History does have verifiable details such as there were writings from someone named Paul, but as with the Bible, interpretation of what Paul wrote and taught is required. Historically, the literalists won the interpretation of Paul, and as many have suggested, and as Dan Brown stressed so well in *The Da Vinci Code*, winners write history. In the book, he quotes Napoleon saying, "what is history, but a fable agreed upon."[45] As regards religion, however, it might be more accurate to say that the winners were those who not only recorded what was historical, but more importantly, won the battle of *interpretation*!

In Biblical studies, what is known as redaction criticism is often applied.[46] Redaction criticism is trying to understand how authors edited or redacted their sources in view of their own vested interest and concerns.[47] Clearly, the literalists had their agenda and won the impression that St. Paul was theirs alone, but there was an additional, different redaction of Paul that cannot be neglected in the study of early Christianity and Paul. A notable Christian group named Marcionism also claimed Paul spoke for them.

The idolization of Paul as a superior saint was not limited to the Gnostics and literalists because another highly popular movement, Marcionism, lifted up Paul for their viewpoints and theology.[48] A priest named Marcion taught his followers that Paul was the sole authority, teacher, and hero for Christian faith. Marcion, born in 85 C.E. to a wealthy family in Sinope on the Black Sea, was becoming in the East an extremely popular preacher and theologian. Very few classify Marcion as a Gnostic as he had quite a different theology, did not accept the Gnostic Gospels, and his beliefs were solely dependent upon Paul and his letters. Marcion, early in his ministry, traveled to Rome and gave the church 200,000 sestercees–a large sum of money, but there was a condition.[49] His proposal, which credits him as being the first person to suggest there be a Christian canon, was that a collection of holy books for a canon should contain only ten of the letters of Paul and the Gospel of Luke.[50] Luke was the traveling companion of Paul as reported in Acts and so the authority for this gospel.[51] Notably, the three Pastoral Letters of Paul were excluded by Marcion as well as all other gospels.[52] In addition, the Old Testament need not be part of any Bible. Why?

Marcion taught that these proposed books for a canon forthrightly sent the message that the God proclaimed by Jesus was merciful, forgiving, peaceful, just, and all loving. In contrast, the God portrayed in the Old Testament was violent, unjust, tribal, jealous, and wrathful. Because of its concept of an angry God, the Old Testament should not be a part of the canon![53] God was a God of love and not hate. Particularly, God's love was not limited to those who were a chosen few, nor vengeful against those whom he disliked, which was the God of the Old Testament.[54]

St. Paul, according to Marcion, was the prime example of understanding that God was a God of love. Paul had given up his hate, the strict rules of his religion, his vindictiveness against enemies and had embraced the loving God of Jesus. Marcion's emphasis was that the message that Paul received from Jesus was that God's love should be spread to all, so Paul's letters and the Gospel of Luke should be the Bible; they best taught this truth that the true God was a God of love.

Although the Bishops of Rome would disagree with Marcion's canonical selection and would begin the church's own selection of a canon, his theological teachings were well received in Asia Minor (now Turkey) and were believed to be quite widespread in the Eastern Empire.[55] Marcion's view of Jesus' God might have been accepted, and his appreciation of St. Paul praised by the church in Rome and the West, but there was a greater problem for the apostolic church than neglecting the Old Testament.

On the basis of Paul and Luke, as he interpreted them, Marcion further taught that Jesus was not a real person — that he did not have a flesh and blood body.[56] This belief, as noted earlier, became known as doceticism from the Greek word, "dokeo," which means "to seem or appear."[57] This concept was strongly advocated by Marcion, arguing that Jesus only seemed to be human and was totally a spiritual being. Often, because of Marcion's doceticism, persons believe that docetic believers and Gnostics were one and the same. Again, this charge is another simplified criticism used to dismiss the Gnostics and categorize them as a whole or one group. Some of the gnostic works do have docetic elements, but this is a misleading charge if all of the Nag Hammadi books are read.

Docetism was not the message of the Gnostics, as it was for the Marcionites. Apparently, not any one of the books of Nag Hammadi was direct or bold enough in their belief of doceticism to be a part of Marcion' proposed canon. Marcion, who would totally separate his followers from the church in Rome, is not mentioned in the gnostic writings. The literalists and a majority of the Gnostics did not accept Marcion's vested view of Paul that his teachings were only about the risen Christ and not his reality as Jesus. To be clear, a common misperception has been that the Gnostics and Marcions were one and the same; they were not. However, there was a common ground between them created by the literalists. The Gnostics and the Marconites were both heretics! The church in Rome excommunicated Marcion as a heretic and expelled him in 144 C.E. Well, not all was forgotten. The Church returned his 200,000 sestercees! [58]

That there was a battle over St. Paul and what theological position he represented has not been commonly known. The winners of interpretation, the literalists, from whom today's fundamentalists owe their legacy, were so victorious that the Marcion view of the superiority of Paul over all other apostles has been known only to a small degree. With the assumption that the teachings of Paul were straightforward and totally supported literalists' theology, the idea that Paul could be understood as a Gnostic also has hardly been considered.

However, there is now evidence that the gnostic view of Paul was not just a minor theological variance but a serious threat to the authority of the literalists. The depth of this threat is revealed in a writing of a Bishop, who will be presented in the next chapter as one of the principal architects of Christianity after Peter and Paul. Bishop Irenaeus' unbelievable harsh words illustrate the literalists own redaction of Paul, and the hard insistence that only they understood his theological truth. This Bishop declares quite directly,

> … it is necessary to examine (Paul's) opinion, and to expound the apostle, and to explain whatever passages have received other interpretations from the heretics, who totally have misunderstood what Paul has said. Further (it is necessary) to point out the madness of their interpretation, and to demonstrate from that same Paul, from whose (writings) they raise questions for us, that they are indeed liars, but the apostle was a preacher of truth, and he taught all things consonant with the preaching of truth.[59]

These heretics "raise questions" and are "liars." Wow! Words of love for those who believed differently? Obviously, there were other interpretations, but the Bishop lays it on the line quite effectively when he points out other interpretations of Paul are simply "madness." Effective words because for centuries there has been little doubt, as the Bishop's states, "Paul was a preacher of truth." Not only that, Paul taught "all things consonant with truth." Of course, what is truth assumes to be pretty well set. Clearly, "the meaning of truth" was whatever agreed with the teachings of the apostolic church — and the bishop makes it clear — Paul did!

The Gnostics believed in truth but in a wider and different perspective than the bishop and his church. They too would have agreed that Paul was a preacher of truth but not only as the Bishop explained. In fact, there is a beautiful concept of Jesus as the truth that was not known because the *Gospel of Truth* would be one of those interpretations known as madness. This so-called false gospel presents truth as a joy in knowing the Father of the one, as they said, who was nailed on the tree — "Jesus, the Christ."[60] As this gospel further says, Jesus was one who enlightened those who were in darkness and ignorance, and made known to them that "the way is the truth."[61] Then, in a form of metaphor, it explains this "way" was in a form of a living *book*. The metaphor becomes clearer in a verse within the 20th passage. It says, "For this reason the merciful one, the faithful one, Jesus, was patient in accepting sufferings until he took that *book*, since he knows that his death is life for many."[62] Then, in the 23rd passage, it explains that this living book is not "vowels" or "consonants," but they are "letters of the truth."[63] Truth, here, is not as expected — arguing for their doctrines against the literalists. Rather, as Harold Attridge and George MacRae in their introduction to this gospel attest, rather than dry accounts of the gnostic systems, these letters of truth, which are published on the cross, bring "genuine religious feeling."[64] In this remarkable gospel, Christ's truth was a realization of knowing the presence of his spirit, or as stated in this gospels' opening paragraph, was a "discovery for those who search for him."[65] Words of madness? Surely, there could be no truth in these words as the Gnostics were all mythical and evil interpreters of the word.

Undeniably, the Gnostics would agree that Paul was a "preacher of truth." They too held him in high respect. Paul was an example of their belief that Christian truth was that more than beliefs but an honest relationship with Christ. This relationship was led by always seeking both the truth and God. Unfortunately, those in power of the prominent Christian church that was developing in the Roman Empire had little regard for even debating truth, as their mission was to declare it.

Declare it they did! Envisioning Paul as a warrior of truth and Christ, they, too, took up his mantle, as they understood it, and became the strident defenders of the new faith. Those who took the lead were several bishops of this developing church who would become like soldiers of the cross. There was a battle to be won, first against those who just didn't understand Christ, and secondly to set the record straight, over all others, as to what were the true beliefs of Christianity.

As setting the record straight, they did! What they stood for and believed would become known as the orthodox view of Christianity. These bishops were the fathers of orthodoxy. Many might assume that the Emperor Constantine was the father of orthodoxy by his calling the Nicene Council in 325 C. E., but a century before his time, the beliefs and form of the church that he would bless was being built and established as the only true voice of Christianity. Constantine's choice of Christianity in its orthodox form cannot be minimized in its becoming a world religion, but now with the Gnostic Gospels a new figure rises in prominence before Constantine. Constantine, certainly, overshadows this church father, but at the turn of the second century, Bishop Irenaeus, fought to establish the beliefs of the apostolic church as no other. He led the battle against all heresies. He penned in five volumes what he believed were the fundamental doctrines and truths of Christianity. After Peter and Paul, this little known bishop stands out as the key figure in why Christianity is understood the way it is today.

* Comment on the Pastoral Epistles of Paul and the Deutro-Pauline Epistles.

In addition to the Pastoral Epistles, the authenticity of three more of the thirteen letters of Paul in the Bible is also questioned. These three are referred to as Deutro-Pauline Epistles. Like the Pastoral Letters, they have some passages belittling women, but they too could be insertions or the position of a second writer other than St. Paul. Ephesians, Colossians, and 2 Thessalonians are called "Deutro" because many scholars believe they were written by a second Paul – another person. Linguistic studies reveal a different style of writing from those of the corpus. The different authorship of the Deutro-Pauline letters is debatable, and many argue for their authenticity, but there is little argument that the Pastoral Letters were written by a different person than those in the Corpus by someone who wanted to use Paul's authority to assert his own positions.[66]

Notes: Chapter 13: St. Paul – a Founder of the Church – a Gnostic?

[1] Elaine Pagels, *The Gnostic Paul*, (Harrisburg, Pa.: Trinity Press International, 1975), 162.
[2] A. N. Wilson, *Paul*, (New York: W.W. Norton & Company, 1997), 14.
[3] Ibid.
[4] Wilson, *Paul*, 258.
[5] Wilson, *Paul*, 150.
[6] Wilson, *Paul*, 15.
[7] Bart D. Ehrman, *The New Testament,* (Oxford: Oxford University Press, New York, 2000), 293.
[8] Ibid.
[9] Ibid.
[10] Ibid.
[11] Ehrman, *The New Testament*, 410.
[12] Harry Hampton Halley, *Halley's Bible Handbook*, (Grand Rapids, Mi.: Zondervan, Revised 2000), (Timothy),835 and (Titus),846.
[13] Ehrman, *The New Testament*, 397.
[14] Ibid.
[15] Ehrman, *The New Testament*, 396.
[16] Ehrman, *The New Testament*, 393.
[17] Tim Dowley, Ed., *Introduction to The History of Christianity*, (Minneapolic: Fortress Press, 2002), 112.
[18] Ibid.
[19] Elaine Pagels, *Beyond Belief*, (New York: Random House, 2003), 159.
[20] Ehrman, *The New Testament*, 401.
[21] James M. Robinson, Ed., *The Hag Hammadi Library in English*, hereafter noted as *NHL*, (San Francisco: HarperSanFrancisco, 1978), *The Prayer of the Apostle Paul*, 27.
[22] Ibid.
[23] Robinson, *NHL*, *The Prayer of the Apostle Paul*, 28.
[24] Robinson, *NHL*, *The Apocalypse of Paul*, 256.
[25] Robinson, *NHL*, *The Apocalypse of Paul*, 259.
[26] Robinson, *NHL*, *The Apocalypse of Paul*, 256.
[27] Robinson, *NHL, The Interpretation of Knowledge*, 472.
[28] I Corinthians 12: 8-10.
[29] Robinson, *NHL*, *The Interpretation of Knowledge*, 478.
[30] I Corinthians 12: 31.
[31] Elaine Pagels, *The Gnostic Paul*, (Harrisburg, Pa.: Trinity Press International, 1975).
[32] Pagels, *The Gnostic Paul*, 1.
[33] Robinson, *NHL*, *The Interpretation of Knowledge*, 473.
[34] Pagels, *The Gnostic Pau*l, 160.
[35] Dowley, *Introduction to The History of Christianity*, 62.

[36] Acts 9:2.
[37] Acts 9:3.
[38] Acts: 9:6.
[39] Acts 9: 15.
[40] Acts 9: 3.
[41] Ibid.
[42] Ibid.
[43] Elaine Pagels, *The Gnostic Gospels*, (New York: Random House, 1979), 50. Also Leonard Shlain, *The Alphabet and the Goddess*, (New York: Penquin Group, 1998), 240.
[44] Irenaeus, *Against Heresies*, 5: 7.
[45] Dan Brown, *The Da Vinci Code*, (New York, Anchor Books, 2003), 256. Dan also adds, "By its very nature, history is always a one sided account.", 256.
[46] Ehrman, *The New Testament*, 144.
[47] Ibid.
[48] Dowley, *Introduction to The History of Christianity*, 104.
[49] J. Michael Matkin, *The Gnostic Gospels*, (New York, Alpha Press, 2005), 43.
[50] Dowley, *Introduction to The History of Christianity*, 104.
[51] Halley, *Halley's Bible Handbook*, 645.
[52] Dowley, *Introduction to The History of Christianity*, 104.
[53] Ibid.
[54] Ehrman, *The New Testament*, 3.
[55] Ibid.
[56] Matkin, *The Gnostic Gospels*, 44.
[57] Matkin, *The Gnostic Gospels*, 21.
[58] Matkin, *The Gnostic Gospels*, 43.
[59] Pagels, *The Gnostic Paul*, 161.
[60] Robinson, *NHL, Gospel of Truth*, 42.
[61] Robinson, *Gospel of Truth*, 41.
[62] Robinson, *Gospel of Truth*, 41.
[63] Robinson, *Gospel of Truth*, 43.
[64] Robinson, *Gospel of Truth*, 39.
[65] Robinson, *Gospel of Truth*, 40
[66] Ehrman, *The New Testament*, 393.

Chapter Fourteen

Bishop Irenaeus – Unknown Hero of Christian Orthodoxy and Creeds

> Irenaeus was the most important and influential of the orthodox Christian writers in the second century. His monumental work, *Against Heres*ies, almost single-handedly defined the shape of orthodox Christian faith. [1]
>
> -J. Michael Matkin, *The Gnostic Gospels*

St. Augustine, St. Thomas Aquinas, Dante, Martin Luther, and John Calvin are considered as some of the essential designers or architects of the Christian Church. Because of the Gnostic Gospels another historical cleric can be added to their statue and fame. Bishop Irenaeus is no stranger for those who have read the previous chapters. With the discovery of the Gnostic Gospels causing new perspectives on early church history, this rather unknown, or at best, little known bishop, comes to the forefront in establishing the apostolic concept of the church and making firm what are considered the orthodox beliefs of Christianity today. Beyond leading the attack on the heretics, and particularly, the demise of the gnostic perspective, a serious factor in his importance is that Irenaeus was the first voice insisting that there be only four gospels in the Bible. Also, he had a direct influence on the content or doctrines within creeds of the church. As stated in the introductory quotation, Irenaeus was the most influential church father and was without peer in the establishment of what generally is now accepted as Christian orthodoxy and theology.

Who was Bishop Irenaeus? Irenaeus was the Bishop of Lyons whose wider parish was the region of Gaul. Irenaeus was one of the most prolific writers among the church fathers and a strong visionary. Because he established more boldly than any other church father, not commandments, but the fundamental articles of Christian belief, he bears a comparison to the Biblical Moses. This may seem a bit radical, but as Moses was critical in the establishment of Judaism, Irenaeus was pivotal in the establishment of Christianity in its orthodox form. Moses, of course, will always remain better known than Irenaeus, but there is an analogy.

Moses was the well known champion of the Hebrews who established them as a distinct group and led them forth from the slavery of Egypt into the promised land of Canaan.[2] Irenaeus was a champion in establishing the proto-orthodox as a distinct group and leading them forth from the slavery of sin into a new promised spiritual land, heaven. Reaching heaven would require more than following the Hebrew law, and it would be achievable only for those who accepted Jesus as the Messiah. Just as Moses delivered the Ten Commandments and established the first five books of the Bible as the holy Pentateuch, so Irenaeus was central in choosing and establishing the four gospels as holy for the canon of the Christian Bible.[3] Much like Moses taking the reins from Abraham, so Irenaeus took the lead from Peter and Paul to establish in the Roman Empire what he believed were their true teachings of Christ and his church. Because of his paper sword, five volumes known as *Against Heresies*, he became best known as the slayer of heresies, primarily, due to the volumes' title.[4] However, not to be overlooked, much as Moses had his lasting influence, so the theological doctrines and ecclesiastical positions he passionately promoted within his books are still the essential or fundamental beliefs of Christendom.

To summarize, what is only an analogy, just as Moses was critical in establishing the covenant God made with Abraham, so Irenaeus was critical in establishing the new covenant with Christ. These covenants established how humankind could relate and know God, and for Irenaeus, the new Christian covenant included doctrines that he declared Christ had taught and passed on to his apostles.

Certainly, other church fathers were part of the establishment of Christian orthodoxy and the formation of the early church, and although

Irenaeus was central, he did not do it alone. As with Irenaeus, other father's writings also survived, and some of their names are more recognizable. Some of these prominent fathers preceded Irenaeus, who lived from approximately 130 to 202 C.E.[5] These earlier fathers helped set the stage for many of Irenaeus' beliefs and positions. Ignatius, a Bishop of Antioch (50-110 C.E.), emphasized the high calling and reverence for those named bishops, and was one of the first to condemn those who didn't believe Jesus was a real person.[6] He wrote seven famous letters while on his way to Rome to be executed as a martyr for his Christian faith. Justin Martyr (C.E.?–165 C.E.), consider the first Christian philosopher became a martyr, and so Justin received his commonly known last name.[7] Justin was a literalists who had some variation in his belief because he proclaimed Christianity, not just a great religion, but the perfect and final philosophy.

Another early church father, Polycarp (C.E? - 156 C.E.), was martyred at the age of 86 by the Romans.[8] Polycarp, the Bishop of Smyrna, also is not well known, but his distinction is twofold. First, he was a close friend and confident of Ignatius and had received some personal letters from him before his martyrdom.[9] Secondly, Polycarp's influence on Irenaeus, who was born in Smyrna, was believed to be immense and was considered critical in Irenaeus accepting a position as a priest in Gaul.[10] Polycarp claimed a friendship with Jesus' disciple John, and he held John's gospel in highest esteem.[11] Irenaeus, thus, would have known this gospel well and perhaps favored this gospel because of because of his special teacher and mentor. With the persecution of Polycarp and his martyrdom, Irenaeus' faith was said to waver, but he remained a young priest in Gaul. Even more disturbing, and yet again, a challenge to his faith, was the martyrdom of Irenaeus' own Bishop in Gaul. Little is known of Bishop Pothinus, but in the wake of growing violence toward Christians in Gaul, Irenaeus stood up even more boldly for the truth of his church. Irenaeus accepted the church's calling to follow the martyred Pothinus as the Bishop of Lyons and the region of Gaul.[12] Obviously, these early church fathers were to have direct influences on Irenaeus and the establishment of the apostolic church.

Contemporary with Irenaeus were the church fathers, Hippolytus and Tertullian. Hippolytus (170 C.E.?-235 C.E.), a Bishop of Rome, was known for his attacks on heretics, and as related earlier, was central in the development or promotion of instructional questions at baptism.[13] Tertullian (160 C.E.-240 C.E.), also mentioned earlier, was a layman from

Carthage who wrote in Latin and was a strong advocate of the literalist understanding of Christ — until he later joined the heretical Montanist movement.[14] Another famed father, Origen (185 C.E.-254 C.E.), a fairly well known church father, out-lived Irenaeus and was to become famous for attacking Gnostics and other heretics. However, because he did not follow the exact teachings of the majority of bishops, his writings were declared heretical by the church after his death.[15] Clement of Alexandria (150 C.E.-210 C.E.) was central in establishing orthodoxy in Egypt.[16] He wrote several works including a book titled *Paedagogus* (The Teacher). In this book, Clement refuted gnostic teachings and claimed the "true gnostic" would be what he stated would be the "perfect Christian."[17] Clement does not define "perfect Christian," but obviously, it was not those whom he called Gnostics.

From this selection of those commonly referred to as church fathers, it is clear others, as well as Irenaeus, had pivotal roles in creating Christian orthodoxy and an institutionalized church. However, with the discovery of the Gnostic Gospels, Irenaeus' importance rises to a higher level. Irenaeus, historically in the middle time frame of the fathers, was to become the bishop whose influence would have the most specific and direct imprint on Christianity today. Along with his charges of heresy, which have been widely accepted as truthful charges, in his writings he also states and explains explicitly many theological doctrines that would find their home in both the Apostles' and Nicene Creeds. Further, to stress Irenaeus' importance in the formation in early Christianity, he was central in demonizing gospels that had gnostic elements and makes it clear the reason that they were unworthy was because they varied from the apostles' beliefs. Already acquainted in earlier chapters with his most famous book *Against Heresies*, (also referred to as *Against All Heresies*), a lesser known book by Irenaeus, *Proof of the Apostolic Preaching*, argues another orthodox position, held almost without question today, except by Judaism, that the Christian faith fulfills the story of the Old Testament.[18]

Bishop Irenaeus' handprint on Christianity has not been highly recognized in Christian history or at least not by those in the pew. Perhaps, if he had become a Pope, he might be remembered better. In the early development of the Papacy, the Bishop of Rome had the inside track, and the chance of a cleric from a foreign Province like Gaul becoming Pope was less than slim. His name is also a bit unusual, and scholars often pronounce his name differently. (Some say, "I- re- knee'- us," and others, "I-ra-nay-us"). However, in spite of these small issues, with the new knowledge and challenge of the Gnostic Gospels, the central place of Irenaeus as the defender and promoter of orthodoxy becomes paramount. In addition to his successful crusade against heresies, which was illustrated in Chapter Seven, Biblical scholars ascribe to Bishop Irenaeus the honor and credit of being the father of their being only four authentic gospels — those that are now in the canon of the New Testament.[19]

Although most scholars believe the four gospels included in the Bible were becoming the favorite of the church fathers, it is only Irenaeus who made the written argument that the Gospels of Matthew, Mark, Luke and John, should be known as holy, sacred, canonical, and from God. In *Against Heresies,* Irenaeus argues,

> It is not possible that the Gospels can be either more or fewer in number than they are. For since there are four zones of the world in which we live, and four principal winds, while the Church is scattered throughout the world, and the pillar and ground of the Church is the Gospel and the spirit of life, it is fitting that she should have four pillars, breathing out immortality on every side.[20]

In the formation of the Bible, this strange explanation, although clearly convincing at its time, is considered one of the serious, historical reasons for the choice of the four gospels for the Bible! Because the Gospels of Matthew, Mark, and Luke are remarkably similar, and therefore, are known as the synoptic gospels, it is understandable how these three books were chosen for a canon. [21]

However, the Gospel of John is different in its style and format, and one reason for its inclusion could have been, as mentioned, that Irenaeus' mentor, Polycarp, had revered John so highly.[22] Of course, John's gospel is beautifully written, yet, it contains serious contradictions in some of the details with the other canonical gospels.[23] Also, it presents in the 14th chapter, the hard line, exclusive position, not in the synoptic gospels, that the only way to know God is through Jesus. Not so boldly presented in the other gospels, and certainly not in the *Gospel of Thomas*, this concept would become a favorite of the literalists and could have been a reason why this different gospel was included in the canon.[24] Not that the Gospel of John should have been excluded. Just as the Gospel of Luke was Marcion's favorite, there would be little doubt that John's would have been Irenaeus' choice over the *Gospel of Thomas.* Well, there was only room for four!

Although it would be difficult to give credence to Irenaeus as an astute scientist, with his belief that there were only "four zones" and "four winds" in the world, there is no question his position as a theologian was influential and pivotal! Against these geographical and cosmic assumptions of his time, this head-strong man's conviction, based on his scientific understanding of the world, convinced Bishops who followed him, and eventually the world, that for Christians, there were only four gospels that were holy and spoke the word of God.

The problem with other gospels, according to Irenaeus and the fathers, was that they promoted heretical beliefs, which Bishops believed threaten one's salvation and eternal life in heaven.[25] In *Against Heresies,* building his case against these gospels that contained unorthodox doctrines, Volume 2, Chapter XXXII, is titled, "Further Exposure of the Wild and Blasphemous Doctrines of the Heretics."[26] He expresses alarm to other bishops that the distribution of these blasphemous gospels, full of false doctrines, had spread beyond the Roman Empire; in fact, he says they were being read as far as his own outlying province of Gaul.[27] Therefore, in Volume 3, Chapter II, he reiterated his verdict, "The Gospels are Four in Number, Neither More nor Less."[28] The bishops heard his plea that heresy existed in all other gospels and accepted his wisdom that God's truth was revealed in four particular gospels. So his claim stands today!

Beyond Irenaeus being the chief prosecutor of heretics and the champion of the four gospels chosen for the Bible, there is another significant reason to grant him exceptional status and fame. In his writings, his direct influence on two primary creeds of the church, the Apostles' Creed and the Nicene Creed, is evident. In the earliest church records, there is no mention of a creed by the apostles but often mentioned is what is called the "Rule of Faith." Many believe this Rule, which has never been found as an original written document, is the precursor of the famous Apostles' Creed. Referring to the Rule of Faith, Irenaeus writes in *Against Heresies,* Volume 2, Chapter XXVII, that it is "the teaching of the church preserved unaltered and handed down in unbroken succession from the apostles."[29] Certainly, this Rule's association to the apostles is direct! At least, according to Irenaeus, this Rule of Faith was that of the apostles.

Irenaeus then shared in Vol. 2, Chapter X, what many believe is the closest record of what the earlier Rule of Faith might have contained. This Rule clearly bears some association to the earliest baptismal questions.[30] However, Irenaeus' comments are written, not as questions but as statements, and therefore, in the form of a creed. As reported in *Introduction to The History of Christianity*, edited by Tim Dowley, "Irenaeus, is the first writer to record a clearly identifiable Rule."[31] Dr. Dowley then summarizes the rather lengthy teachings of the Rule of Faith with its primary statements of faith:

> There is one God, who made the heaven and the earth. There is one Christ Jesus, the Son of God, who was made flesh for our salvation. Jesus was born from a virgin, he ascended bodily into heaven his home. His future coming again would raise up the flesh of the human race to his heavenly home.

The full translation of this rendering by Irenaeus of the so-called Rule may be read in its entirety in Appendix C. Some translators refer to this section of *Against Heresies* as also the Rule of Truth, as Irenaeus often calls it.[32] "Rule of Faith," or "Rule of Truth," the early baptismal questions, which contained these same beliefs, now took on the earliest known form of confession or creed.

Interestingly, anyone who has read or voiced the Apostles' Creed knows there is a similarity. This better known Creed than the Rule, in essence, reiterates these same beliefs. (See Apostles' Creed in Appendix A). Perhaps, an Apostles' Creed by document or oral tradition was his source. Irenaeus does not refer to such by name — as being the Apostles' Creed or even the Apostles' Rule. However, if such a creed did exist beforehand, Irenaeus would have sworn by this creed. Why? He would have praised and lifted it up as divine truth because it implies by its name that it expressed the consensus of beliefs from all the apostles. Therefore, he would have said such a creed from the apostles contained the direct teaching of Jesus. Then, Irenaeus would have declared that these true teachings, taught by Jesus to his apostles, were passed on to leaders in his church.[33] These teachings expressed the precise beliefs about Jesus. Whether, Rule of Truth, or Apostles' Creed, both has a ring of authority.

Quite often in his writings, Irenaeus referred to the wisdom and authority of the apostles and argues that is the reason why his church possesses the truth. In Volume 3, Chapter I, of *Against Heresies* he states as its title **"Apostles Received the Holy Spirit; Possessed Perfect Knowledge."**[34] Perfect knowledge? What could be better than perfect? Irenaeus' further message in the text is that these apostles passed this perfect knowledge on to Peter, and then his knowledge was passed on to the Bishops of Rome, reiterating, or establishing the doctrine of what Irenaeus penned as "Apostolic Succession." [35]

Thankfully, Irenaeus gives more detail or information. In Volume 3, Chapter III, he presents a list of the Bishops of Rome who followed St. Peter, which is helpful for the historical record, and then he adds his reason for doing so.[36] After sharing the bishops' names, he says;

> In this order, and by this succession, the ecclesiastical tradition from the apostle [Peter], and the preaching of truth, came down to us. And this is most abundant truth that there is one and the same vivifying faith, which has been preserved in the church from the apostles until now, and handed down in truth. [37]

In addition to the historical list of succession of Bishops of Rome, who followed Peter, the power of these words is that they rely on the authority of the apostles to affirm the church's beliefs. Again, in his writing, he uses the apostles to discount others. In Volume 3, Chapter IV, the heading is "**Heresies are of Recent Formation and Cannot Trust their Origins to the Apostles."**[38] In other words, the church's beliefs were not heresy because their origins were from the apostles. The argument is forthright. If the twelve disciples, or those apostles, who knew Jesus, believed and taught these truths, what could be more convincing than that these doctrines were those which Jesus himself had blessed. Irenaeus was certainly so convinced, and his writings are filled with the reason that the church's teachings are iron-clad because who would know better than those who knew Jesus and were apostles.

As with the Rule of Faith, no document named the Apostles' Creed and dated before Irenaeus has been found. The oldest, complete Apostles' Creed dates about 300 C.E. — close to 100 years after Irenaeus.[39] Evolving from baptismal questions to a confession to a clear and concise statement or creed of the true and essential beliefs of Christians seems probable. Therefore, could the Apostles' Creed have been crafted as a written document after Irenaeus? Maybe so, but it appears that this summary of Christian beliefs rose more out of the early baptismal questions. Then church fathers, particularly Irenaeus, lifted the authority of the apostles as proof of why their beliefs were infallible. Whether such a creed existed before Irenaeus or was created after him, one fact is evident. His writings, as will be illustrated below, promote the articles of faith within the Creed, not just as a summary of Christian doctrines, but as the standard and hallmarks of Christian beliefs. These doctrines are what the true Christian needs to believe, precisely because these were the beliefs of the apostles.

The Apostles' Creed is now one of the best loved statements of Christianity. Folklore has suggested that all twelve of the disciples had a hand in its creation because there are twelve sentences. Ha, not bad logic, but an argument more than bizarre with the knowledge from the Gnostic Gospels of the differing positions on some of these beliefs among apostles. Some have argued St. Paul's theology is so well formulated that he was involved in its creation, but one would think its formulation would be in his letters, which it is not. However, this Creed is short, poetic, easy to recite, and to memorize. Saying together these holy teachings in unison by worshipers has a certain beauty and presents a strong affirmation of faith. Many Christians, it appears, recite, in church, the words of the Creed without thinking what they are voicing or being bothered that the creed may express beliefs they just don't believe.

Certainly, the Apostles' Creed does provide the basic story about Jesus, but what is often overlooked is that it also further affirms, as literal facts, orthodox beliefs, such as the virgin birth, a bodily resurrection, and that Jesus is now sitting at the right hand of God, ready to come and judge the quick and the dead. Of some interest, the phrase of Jesus descending into hell, that is often a part of the statements, is not found in the earliest Creeds.[40] Rather exceptionally, The United Methodist Church's version does not add the phrase.[41] This motif was used often in the popular Passion Plays of the Medieval Period, and perhaps, only as a conjecture, this trip to hell was added to enhance their drama and excitement! At least, this sojourn explains why Christ didn't rise from the dead until three days after the crucifixion.

As research on the Apostles' Creed provides no evidence that the apostles ever penned or agreed as a group on such a statement, and because no written records exist of Peter passing on these beliefs, other than the tradition stated by the church, a better name for the Apostles' Creed might be the Bishops' Creed! Certainly, the bishops gave endorsement to these beliefs. For sure, Bishop Irenaeus and other second century bishops would be quite proud that the beliefs within the Apostles' Creed are still considered the primary articles of Christian faith.

What follows is remarkable. The beliefs, and nearly exact wordings of the Apostles' Creed, are found as the titles of chapters in Irenaeus' *Against Heresies*. Irenaeus' five Volumes, composed around 190 C. E., are written in a very orderly and organized fashion. He titles the chapters with bold theological statements or doctrines, which he believes express the literal truths. Within in his Volumes, following the titles are a few paragraphs, not included here, which further explain why Irenaeus believes they are true. Here are some examples, of the similarity of titles, to the Apostles' Creed:

> The Apostles' Creed begins, **"I believe in God, the Father Almighty."**
>
> Irenaeus writes in Volume 1, Chapter XXII, "**The Rule of truth which we hold is that there is <u>One God, Almighty.</u>"**[42]
>
> The Apostles' Creed says, "**born of the Virgin Mary."**
> Volume 3, Chapter XXII, the title is: **"Actual Flesh, Conceived and Born of the Virgin"** [43]
>
> The Apostles' Creed says, "**I believe in the resurrection of the body."**
>
> Volume 5, Chapter VII, the title is; "**Christ Rose in the Flesh – So will We"** [44]

The Apostles' Creed says, **"I believe in the holy catholic Church."**

Volume 3, Chapter V, **"The Truth is to be Found Nowhere but in the Catholic Church, the sole Depository of Apostolic Doctrine"** [45]

The argument is *not* that Irenaeus wrote this Creed himself, because it was well representative of other orthodox writers. More than likely Irenaeus built his beliefs and doctrines on the earlier baptismal questions, referred to in Chapter Eight, as they are clearly represented in his writings. However, his expansion of the themes, such as "Christ Rose in the Flesh — So Will We," and his elevation of his church being the only true "Depository of Apostolic Doctrine" suggest that he was a key figure in building and developing these beliefs as the binding truths of Christ and Christianity. With Irenaeus' titles of these chapters being almost verbatim to some of the doctrines that were to be in the Apostles' Creed, his role was at least substantial in the formalization of what this Creed would confess in its final or later forms.

Whatever led to the official acceptance of the Apostles' Creed, this Confession of Faith as it is sometimes called, in spite of its complex history, has become the defining statement of what true Christians believe — or should believe! The argument is not that it should be abandoned as a hymn or confession for worship because it has a corporate spiritual power, and who knows for sure, all of its sentences may well be true. Not even its critics or Gnostics disagree with all of its statements of belief, but Irenaeus would not be pleased that today for many Christians believing all its details is not viewed as necessary to be a true Christian. Watch out, all you heretics!

Irenaeus' connection to early church creeds does not end with the Apostles' Creed. One more significant comparison supports the argument that this unheralded Bishop from Gaul might have had more influence, than ever imagined, in the establishment of Christian creeds. Next in importance to the Apostles' Creed, only one other Creed has the early history, authority, and clarity to explain Christian truth and doctrine, and is popularly known today, as at it conception, as the Nicene Creed. (See, Appendix B for the Nicene Creed.) Once again, one can find in *Against Heresies* words and phrases which are echoed directly in the Nicene Creed —

a document which was written over one hundred years after the life of Irenaeus, but clearly bears his imprint.

As will be expanded upon in the next Chapter, the Emperor Constantine in 325 C.E. called a conference of all church Bishops in the Roman Empire to be held at the village of Nicaea.[46] The result of this council was the creation of the Nicene Creed. Records show that Constantine had a direct hand in its creation, which is fairly well known, but not that of Irenaeus.[47] Irenaeus, of course, was not present during the writing of this Creed as he was long gone. However, although the Nicene Creed is later than the Apostles' Creed, much longer and detailed, it too adds several beliefs, which also can trace some influence to Irenaeus. His direct mark, as was the case with the Apostles' Creed, is hard to refute as one reads the chapter titles and their content in *Against Heresies*. For example:

> The Nicene Creed begins, **"We believe in one God."**
>
> Volume 2, Chapter I, the title is **"There is but one God"** [48]
>
> The Nicene Creed states, **"we believe ...in one Lord Jesus Christ, the only begotten Son of God, begotten of the Father before all worlds."** Then it adds that Jesus **"came down from heaven, and was incarnate by the Holy Spirit of the Virgin Mary, and was made man."**
>
> Volume 3, Chapter XIX, "**Jesus Christ was very God, Begotten of the Father, Most High, and very Man, Born of the Virgin.**"[49]
>
> (*Begotten was a carefully chosen word because it implied Jesus was not conceived like the rest of us.)
>
> The Nicene Creed declares that Jesus was, **"God of God, Light of Light, Very God of Very God, begotten, not made, being of one substance with the Father."**

Volume 3, Chapter XXIX, is titled, **"Proof From the Apostolic Writings that Jesus Christ was one and the same, the only begotten Son of God, Perfect God and Perfect Man"** [50]

"Perfect God" certainly seems implied in the Creed's statement of "Very God of Very God." "Begotten, not made" is used again. Irenaeus' title teaches "Jesus Christ was one and the same," (as God). The Creed varies this by saying, "being of one substance," a phrase that would become quite debatable in the wording of the Nicene Creed during Constantine's Council.

The Nicene Creed declares, **"We believe in one holy catholic church..."** * (* catholic means universal.)

Volume 3, Chapter IX **"The Universal Church moreover, throughout the World, has received this tradition from the Apostles"** [51]

As these are excerpts from the Nicene Creed, when read separately from the Apostles' Creed, they may be seen as mildly related to the earlier Creed. However, not to be overlooked, many of the same beliefs found in the Rule of Irenaeus' time and the Apostles' Creed, such as the virgin birth, Jesus' suffering under Pontius Pilate, crucifixion, burial, his resurrection on the third day, his ascent into heaven, (hell is also not mentioned) and his sitting at the right hand of the Father to judge the quick and the dead are also found in the Nicene Creed — *and in the same order*! Obviously, this Creed builds on the earlier Creed, and although some of the phrases are not exact, many of them are the exact words found in Irenaeus' work, written a hundred years before the creation of Nicene Creed.

The Nicene Creed directly reaffirms beliefs found in the Apostles' Creed, and it contains another phrase which would surely please Irenaeus. Important? Yes! This particular line is similar to the words near the end of the Apostles' Creed which say, "I believe in the holy catholic church...." The Nicene Creed makes this belief even more refined and adds words, perhaps not that noticeable, that clearly would be important to Irenaeus.

The Nicene Creed ends, "We believe in the catholic and apostolic church." *Apostolic Church*? Yes, the words are an interesting *addition* to this later Creed in light of Irenaeus' emphasis and attention to the apostles. Also, within this new phrase ("We believe in the catholic and apostolic church"), is a curious and telling word, easily overlooked, which will be made known and discussed in the next chapter as it relates directly to Constantine's influence on Christianity. However, what is clear is that Constantine, and the Bishops of his time, carry on Irenaeus' message, intentionally or not, certainly not always exactly, but quite well!

With so much distance between Constantine and Irenaeus, the influence of the latter on the Apostles' Creed and the Nicene Creed has not been widely recognized. Although Irenaeus was not directly involved with these creeds, his influence in their reality and development cannot be neglected. Nor can his significance be overlooked in establishing the orthodox theology as being the truth and truths of Jesus. As J. Michael Matkin remarks, in the quote beginning this chapter, "Irenaeus was the most influential of all the orthodox writers because his work, *Against Heresies,* almost single-handedly defined the shape of orthodox Christian faith." [52]

Bishop Irenaeus' legacy remains extremely strong in Christianity today. The Apostles Creed and the Nicene Creed are hallmarks of orthodox theology and for many define Christianity. Also, his influence went beyond having his beliefs expressed quite explicitly in these creeds. By his battle with those who did not accept his church's beliefs as literal truths, he aided significantly in the establishment that Christianity was foremost about beliefs. Of course, he did not create this perception on his own, but by being the boldest of the church fathers to condemn within his five volumes, the Gnostics, the Marcionites, the Ebionites, the Encratites, the Ophites, to name only a few of those whose theological views he considered false, he laid down the line on what was heresy. Irenaeus successfully made it quite clear what beliefs must be accepted to be a *true* Christian. However, by insisting on his literal theology as Christ's truth and that all other views were heretical, he does raise the question if the message of Christ was limited and directed in a much narrower way than Christ intended?

Whatever the case, Irenaeus' story makes it known that other views of Jesus were eliminated, not by honest dialogue and a search for what was true, but rather by some early Christians who insisted only they had the truth. Irenaeus' problem wasn't whether he was a sincere and authentic Christian, or that he was wrong to believe what he did. The problem was that by insisting on his way, not accepting that there were different ways to believe and be Christian, he fell into a trap of many who have decided their knowledge is equal to Christ and God's.

Today, after many battles as to whom possessed the Christian truth, many are awakening to the realization that faith is more about trust than battling emotionally, or even violently, over a set of beliefs. If it had not been Irenaeus and other church bishops of his time, certainly others would have risen, as history attests, to claim exclusive knowledge of God. Irenaeus and his church did it quite well, and by the time of Constantine, Christ's message had become, not about trust, love, and justice. Rather, with Irenaeus' aid, Christianity had become a religion of beliefs. Faith, rather than being a dynamic process of seeking God, became equivalent to what one believed.

Even the Gnostics were put into that mold of Christianity being about beliefs, but the Gnostic Gospels reveal that they had a wider vision of Christ's message than a battle for beliefs. Today their gospels can support those who are calling forth that Jesus should be met again, as if meeting him for the first time.[53] Marcus Borg, for example, does that in his book with the similar name. In telling his story, he writes, "Now I no longer see the Christian life as being primarily about believing. Rather the Christian life is about entering into a relationship with that to which the Christian tradition points, which may be spoken of as God, the risen living Christ."[54] Sounds a bit gnostic, not Gnostic, doesn't it? It might be better to say that Borg's theme relates well to the gnostic message, because the power of the Gnostic Gospels is that they encourage Christians to look back to Jesus, to understand and forgive the sins of the past, and then in the present, to move forward with the living Jesus.

After Irenaeus' time, the establishment of the apostolic church was to grow stronger in its institutional form and organization. Without question, with the aid of Constantine, the victory of the interpretation of Jesus, as the apostolic church explained it, was all but established as the Christian truth. So accepting of this church's prominence and popularity in his Empire, even the church buildings under the bishops' rule were allocated funds for repair by Constantine.[55] More beneficial to Constantine than the church buildings, which he would add to in the Roman Empire with his own treasury, was the system of bishops which was ready made for Constantine. To assemble this fast, spreading group of church's leaders would assist considerably in his announced political ambition to bring harmony, including religion, to the Empire.

In doing so, the face of Christianity would be set for centuries to come, and its expansion as the major religion of the West began in earnest. In Bart Ehrman's words, "What is beyond dispute is that Constantine's conversion was one of the most significant events in the history of Western civilization."[56] The choice to bless and condone the apostolic church as the true voice of Jesus and Christianity was sealed by this Roman Emperor, who used the power of the state to affirm its validity and superiority for Western civilization.

Irenaeus' dream that his vision of Christianity, and particularly his version, would be the universal truth for believers in Jesus had come true! Although Irenaeus and the Emperor Constantine lived nearly one hundred years apart, they were monumental giants in establishing what would become the Christian Church, but even more significantly, what most know as Christianity today. Irenaeus' influence is much less known than Constantine's, but it is clear that Constantine rather innocently inherited an apostolic form of Christianity that he would further promote as the orthodox beliefs and positions of Christianity. Irenaeus' interpretation that Christ's gift was a system of beliefs from God was totally to silence the Gnostics and the theme that they heard from Christ. This theme, which Constantine would never hear or understand, was that Jesus taught and preached that his followers were *more* than just those who were believers, but were honest Seekers of God."

Notes: Chapter Fourteen: Bishop Irenaeus – Unknown Hero of Christian Orthodoxy and Creeds

[1] J. Michael Matkin, *The Gnostic Gospels*, (New York: Alpha Press, 2005), 22.

[2] Henry Hampton Halley, *Halley's Bible Handbook*, (Grand Rapids, Mi.: Zonervan, Revised 2000),137.

[3] Elaine Pagels, *Beyond Belief*, (New York: Random House, 2003), 111.

[4] Elaine Pagels, *The Gnostic Gospels*, (New York: Random House, 1979), XVII.

[5] Tim Dowley, Editor, *Introduction to The History of Christianity*, (Minneapolis: Fortress Press, 2002), 56.

[6] Dowley, *Introduction to The History of Christianity*, 83.

[7] Dowley, *Introduction to The History of Christianity*, 94.
[8] Dowley, *Introduction to The History of Christianity*, 92.
[9] Dowley, *Introduction to The History of Christianity*, 83.
[10] Dowley, *Introduction to The History of Christianity*, 100.
[11] J. Michael Matkin, *The Gnostic Gospels*, 22.
[12] Williston Walker, *A History of the Christian Church*, (New York: Charles Scribner's Sons, 1959), 63.
[13] Matkin, *The Gnostic Gospels*, 29.
[14] Dowley, *Introduction to The History of Christianity*, 112.
[15] Dowley, *Introduction to The History of Christianity*, 107.
[16] Matkin, *The Gnostic Gospels*, Pg. 31.
[17] Ibid.
[18] Dowley, *Introduction to The History of Christianity*, Pg. 100.
[19] Pagels, *The Gnostic Gospels*, Ibid., Pg. XV.
[20] Bart D. Ehrman, *Lost Christianities*, Oxford University Press, Oxford, 2003, Pg. 239.
[21] Halley, *Halley's Bible Handbook*, Pg. 560.
[22] Maktin, *The Gnostic Gospels*, Pg. 23.
[23] Bart D. Ehrman, *Misquoting Jesus*, HarperSanFrancisco, 2005, Pg. 60.
[24] Pagels, *Beyond Belief*, Pg. 30.
[25] Pagels, *The Gnostic Gospels*, Pg. XVII.
[26] Irenaeus, *Against Heresies*, referred hereafter as *AH*, Vol. 2: XXXII.
[27] Ibid.
[28] Irenaeus, *AH*, Vol. 2: XI.
[29] Irenaeus, *AH*, Vol. 2: XXVII.
[30] Dowley, *Introduction to The History of Christianity*, Pg. 115.
[31] Ibid.
[32] Irenaeus, *AH*, Vol. 1: X.
[33] Irenaeus, *AH*, Vol. 3: III.
[34] Irenaeus, *AH*, Vol. 3: I.
[35] Irenaeus, *AH*, Vol. 3: IV.
[36] Irenaeus, *AH*, Vol. 3: III.
[37] Ibid.
[38] Irenaeus, *AH*, Vol. 3: IV.
[39] Dowley, *Introduction to The History of Christianity*, Pg. 117.
[40] Ibid.
[41] *The Methodist Hymnal*, The Methodist Publishing House, Nashville, Tennessee, 1964, Pg. 738.
[42] Irenaeus, *AH*, Vol. 1: XXII.
[43] Irenaeus, *AH*, Vol. 3: XXII.
[44] Irenaeus, *AH*, Vol. 5: VII.
[45] Irenaeus, *AH*, Vol. 3: V.
[46] Walker, *The History of Christianity*, Pg. 114.

---

[47] Ibid.

[48] Irenaeus, *AH*, Vol. 2 : I.

[49] Irenaeus, *AH*, Vol. 3: XIX.

[50] Irenaeus, *AH*, Vol. 3: XXIX

[51] Irenaeus, *AH*, Vol. 3: IX.

[52] Matkin, *The Gnostic Gospels*, Pg. 23.

[53] Marcus Borg, *Meeting Jesus Again for the First Time*, HarperOne, New York, 1995.

[54] Ibid.

[55] Pagels, *Beyond Belief*, Pg. 169.

[56] Bart D. Ehrman, *Truth and Fiction in The Da Vinci Code*, Oxford University Press, 2004, Pg. 13.

Chapter Fifteen

Defining Jesus — The Privilege and Power of Constantine

> Immediately upon coming to power as the sole ruler of the empire, but only then, Constantine asserted the right to exercise absolute authority over the entire Church. [1]
>
> -James Carroll, *Constantine's Sword*

The victory for the definition of Christianity in what would be known as its orthodox form, or as the correct message of Jesus, was not secured until the time of Constantine. With its organization and zeal, the literalist interpretation was becoming the most powerful of the Christian voices, and as such, it was most helpful to Constantine to have bishops whom he could call together and use for his own agenda. It is unlikely that Constantine ever read any of the gospels, but his personal involvement in establishing both the Bishops' Church and their theology was enormous. With his power and might as the world's foremost secular leader, Constantine, by calling a Church Council to define who Jesus was, hoped to bring theological consensus and harmony to Christianity. The result was that certain theological beliefs were affirmed and established by a new creed. With Constantine's choice of Christianity over other religions, another milestone was to be reached. The message of Jesus in its literalist form was to be blessed by an Emperor as the true religion.

As Christianity had been attacked by so many previous Roman Emperors, it is rather ironic that it was an Emperor who led the way for Christianity to become the official state religion of the Empire. Constantine had to know and experience the rise and popularity of this religion, which many Emperors had said was atheistic. Of course, atheistic meant that its followers did not believe in the Emperor as a god.[2] Emperor Worship, and the belief that the Emperor was god, went back to the days of the Roman Republic, but this Roman religion was beginning to falter by the time of Constantine, and Christianity was gaining in popularity.[3] In addition to Christianity, other religions inspired by Greek and Ancient gods were beginning to reemerge in new Latin or Roman forms. Particularly, a major religion named Mithraism was immensely popular within the Roman Army.[4]

Mithras, was originally known as a Persian god, but by the time of the Roman Empire, this same god was called by the Romans, "Sol," or the "Sun god."[5] Some of the Emperors before Constantine had referred to Mithras as the "Sol Invictus" or the "Unconquerable Sun."[6] Mithraism taught that if one would participate in the rebirth of the soul through Mithras, the believer would overcome death and have salvation. This rebirth would happen with one raising and dying with Mithras, as did the sun each day. In some similarities to Christianity, the participant could partake of Mithras through a shared symbolic or communion meal.[7] There was also a most interesting ritual for cleansing from sin. This cleansing took place in a ceremony called Taurobolium.[8] One entered a pit below a bull that was being slaughtered. Then one was "washed by the blood of the bull," and the initiate was "reborn forever."[9] The religion taught, for its constituents, there would be a happy future, whether in this life or in death. Therefore, it was quite attractive to those who were risking their lives in battles. As Williston Walker in his classic book, *A History of the Christian Church*, writes, "the Sol Invictus, Mithras was widely worshiped, and this cult was popular in the army and favored by the Emperors who rose from its ranks." [10]

Mithras was the god of Maxentius, who was a contender for Emperor after the death of Constantius I, the father of Constantine.[11] To settle the issue of whom would be the new Emperor, Constantine and Maxentius met in 312 C.E. for battle at the site of the Milvian Bridge, located over the Tiber River, several miles North of Rome.[12] Constantine later reported to the historian Eusebius, that just before the battle at Milvian that he had seen a vision of a Christian cross in the sky with the words below the cross, "By this sign, you will conqueror."[13]

Conquer he did as Maxentius was killed in the Milvian Bridge Battle on October 28th, 312 C.E.[14] Then, in 323 C.E., Constantine defeated

Lincinius, once his ally, who would have held the title, "Emperor of the Eastern Empire."[15] Now, Constantine was the Emperor of both Empires and his allegiance was with the Christians.

It was to his advantage that the more popular religion, not of the Army, but of the Empire was becoming Christianity. Why Christianity was growing so fast, is an open and intriguing question. It appears the Christian message of love, forgiveness, and a God who loved people and would give eternal life to them was desired. That the God of Jesus loved all, not just a few, and this God would work to overcome evil was a needed message. Even in its orthodox form, it must be admitted that there is a tremendous attraction to Christianity and that it meets many human needs. However, for Constantine, it was fairly obvious his social and political needs were greater than his own personal, religious need.[16]

Although questionable in his motives, few doubt that Constantine's personal vision of the cross and his embrace of Christianity were not sincere, at least, in his own mind. In 313 C.E., Constantine was critical in achieving religious freedom for Christians by helping to create the Edict of Milan — sometimes known as the Edict of Toleration. Clearly supporting the Christians and opening the door to their acceptance, some have questioned his total commitment because he also never gave up his title, "Pontifex Maxiumus," which signified that he considered himself, as previous Emperors, "the high priest of the pagans."[17] He also allowed coins to be minted with heathen emblems on them.[18] Further, he did not condemn those who favored or believed in the "Unconquered Sun," or "Sol." In fact, it was Constantine who made the first day of the week a holiday in his Empire and called it "the venerable day of the Sun." So it is that Christians still call this day, Sunday![19]

Constantine was the consummate politician. He first moved the Capital of the Empire from the West to the East, or from Rome to Constantinople (which he first called New Rome) in an effort to show he wanted a unified Empire.[20] In fact, unity was a driving force in all he did because he wanted what he called harmony in his Empire, and promoting Christianity was part of his plan for unity. Williston Walker explains, "To Constantine's essentially political mind, Christianity was the completion of the process of unification which had long been in progress in the Empire. It had one Emperor, one law, and one citizenship for all free men. It should have one religion."[21]

Certainly his desire for religious harmony was his primary motive in deciding to gather the Christian bishops, from East and West, in a Council that was held in the island community of Nicaea (located in modern day Turkey).[22] The Church was developing some serious theological differences over the divinity and the nature of Jesus. Obviously, Christianity being his choice for the one religion, Constantine thought it should be one body and speak as a united voice. If Christians believed the same, it would help bring harmony to the Church and Empire. Therefore, as Emperor, he convened what was to be known in Christian history as the First General Council of the Church.[23] At least, two hundred bishops from all the Empire, and perhaps according to some sources, as many as three hundred, came to Nicaea to attend the meeting financed and presided over by Constantine in 325 C.E.[24]

The issue was a bit complicated because the bishops involved were believers in Jesus as the Christ, but some saw the need to believe that Jesus was God, not simply divine.[25] Furthermore, this belief was necessary in order to gain salvation.[26] The theological battle was becoming quite intense; the essence of the battle was over the form or nature of Jesus' divinity. The church had become seriously divided between followers of the Bishop of Alexandria, named Alexander, and a Presbyter, a popular priest named Arius. Bishop Alexander believed that the historical Jesus was actually the embodiment of God. In simple terms, Jesus was God.[27] Arius, however, disagreed, but not totally. He believed Jesus was the Son of God, indeed divine, the Savior, yet not quite the almighty God himself.[28] Jesus was sent more as a divine gift in the form of a son from God to share the news that God loved us. Because several Emperors had claimed they were the incarnate God on earth, these Arian Christians found it difficult to say that was to be now the nature of Jesus.[29] In other words, the model for the pagan Emperors should not be transferred to Jesus.

Both of these Christian leaders had dedicated followers, but by the end of extensive debates at the Council, Constantine sided with those in the majority. By vote of the bishops, Jesus became fully man — to clarify any misgivings that Jesus wasn't a real person — also fully God.[30] Undoubtedly, Constantine would have said that it was the bishops, not he, who voted for this belief and gave it veracity. Technically, Constantine would be right, but his personal influence was preeminent and direct.

Eusebius, considered the Christian Church's first historian and present at the Council, noted that the debate was intense and that it was Constantine who insisted the words "of the same substance," or in Greek "homoousion," be in the Creed.[31] Constantine believed that this phrase or word would help the sides to compromise in the debate, as it intimated that Jesus was God without directly saying so. Being of the same substance made Jesus fully divine and equal to God, but not exactly God Almighty. The bishops from the East were divided on the issue, and although not totally opposed to Jesus being of the same substance of God, their concern was that it did open the uncomfortable position of declaring Jesus not just divine, but God himself."[32] Bishops of the West were nearly unanimous in support of homoousion being included in the Creed as they believed that would help their argument that belief in Jesus as God was essential for faith and salvation.[33]

The result of the final vote was that Constantine's solution of using the term homoousion helped only in part and did not achieve a full consensus. With some needed votes from the Bishops of the East, the majority vote would be to include the word, homoousion. This meant to accept the final wording of the Creed, much as it is in today's form, as believing in "one Lord Jesus Christ, being of one substance with the Father." Also, the concern of some of the Eastern Bishops became valid, as Christ being "fully God" was added.[34] Although not a perfect resolution, Constantine hoped the Creed would help bind the division between the East and the West. Indeed, with the vote completed, temporarily, Christians were one because the Council had produced a Creed that was agreed upon by a majority of bishops. This creed called the Nicene Creed was now the official statement by the church for the true understanding of Jesus and Christianity. [35]

The report from the Council was that the Nicene Creed was adopted unanimously.[36] Well, that wasn't exactly the case; Arius and two Western Bishops who voted against the Creed were excommunicated from the Church. If that wasn't enough, they also were exiled from the Empire![37] In essence, when the Council approved the Nicene Creed as the truth of Christianity, the effect was to say that those who disagreed should be silenced.[38] Once again, as in the early formation of the church, one voice ruled over another in declaring what was the sole truth of Christ and Christianity. Significantly, this time, the power and wisdom of the state was added to bless theological truth. As J. Michael Matkin explains about

Constantine's authority, "For the first time, the power of the state was brought to bear in order to support one group of Christians against another." [39]

Constantine was pleased because it appeared that Christians were united in belief, which would help bring harmony to his Empire. Of significance, often overlooked or not realized, is a subtle fact, which was mentioned in the last chapter, regarding the opening phrase of the Creed. The Nicene Creed does not begin, "**I believe**," as did the Apostles' Creed; it begins with the words, "**We believe**."[40] This simple change spoke volumes in that the word, "we," had the power to say these were the beliefs that all Christians held or should believe. Of far more reaching consequence, "we" meant that both the Church, by majority vote, and now the State had approved and blessed what was orthodox truth in Christianity.[41] What became known as orthodox theology for Christianity was settled by the state. As James Carroll in *Constantine's Sword,* explains:

> For the first time in history, the universal Christian Church was set to explain orthodoxy, a word derived from the Greek word meaning right-thinking. [Carroll then argues] that orthodoxy was neither defined by the Lord, nor by a Jew who identified with dissenters, nor by the apostles, nor by evangelist who produced four gospels, nor by theologians, nor by preachers, but by an all-conquering emperor for whom one empire had to equal one religion.[42]

Constantine ordered both heretics, and the schismatics, as he along with the priests began to call those who were not members of the church, to surrender any church properties to the Roman Catholic Church.[43] This judgment of heresy now included the Arians. As a matter of record, only the bishops who had supported the Nicene Creed were given special favors by Constantine and exempted from taxes and compulsory civic duties.[44] Furthermore, Constantine, not yet baptized, established his ecclesiastical authority by declaring that he was the "Bishop of those outside of the Church."[45] Constantine – a bishop? Not many have referred to him as Bishop Constantine, but it didn't hurt. Beautiful churches, the Vatican in Rome, and the Holy Sepulcher in Jerusalem were first built with financing from Constantine.[46] Unbelievably, maybe to his credit, understanding himself, not as God, as earlier Emperors had done, he declared that he was the "Vice Regent of God."[47] With this less than humble title and the power of the written creed, he was able to silence the followers of Mithras and let the bishops strongly condemn others like the Gnostics, who saw the meaning and purpose of Christ, differently. Christianity in its orthodox form seemed all but sealed, but there is more to the story.

Constantine's personal involvement in religion, and particularly in Christianity, was critical to its success; most believe Christianity would not have been established, as strongly as it was, without him. However, there is little indication that his deeper motive was to be a follower or disciple of Jesus. Rather, as so many political leaders have learned, he recognized that to support a popular religion would help his standing and power.[48] His vision of the cross did lead to military victory, but the details of his leading a Christian life are questionable. After a rather unscrupulous life — killing his eldest son and second wife — his baptism was on his death bed.[49] Interestingly, Constantine's baptism was administered by an Arian Christian, which one would not expect.[50]

Baptism, by a follower of Arius, now a schismatic and a heretic — how could that be? Baptized by an Arian? After all, their understanding of Christ had been dismissed by the action of the Council at Nicaea, and Constantine had given his blessing and special privileges to the bishops who voted for the Nicene Creed. Why the switch? Most know the story of Constantine's baptism on his death bed, but the reason it was done by an Arian is a critical part of the story and the conflict ahead.

For a deeper understanding, one must go to events, not that well known, shortly after the Council of Nicaea. Although the Council was called to bring harmony to both the Christian Church and Constantine's empire, harmony in neither would last long! Most bishops must have been thrilled with the support of the Emperor; however, there was one bishop that was to be Constantine's thorn in the flesh and problematic in his spirit for his dream of Christian unity. Bishop Athanasius is not well known in the annals of history, much like Irenaeus, but he also is pivotal in the story of Christian orthodoxy being established by the Nicene Creed. The beliefs of this Creed may have never been made permanent without this bishop's fanatical insistence that it held the total truth, and nothing but the truth, of Christ.

Three years after the Nicene Council, the Bishop of Alexandria named Bishop Alexander, who was present and had led the vote for the Creed, died in 328 C.E.[51] The priest who became the new Bishop of Alexandria was Athanasius. Athanasius had been a secretary to Bishop Alexander at the Council of Nicaea, and as the new bishop was a vehement supporter of the Nicene Creed, which one would think would please Constantine.

However, Athanasius' personal crusade for the literal truth of the Nicene Creed and his unrelenting and vicious attack, against those who opposed the theology of the Creed, was without mercy. With his new found authority, he punished and exiled any priest who continued to be an Arian or those who did not totally accept the Creed.[52] Constantine was not pleased with Athanasius' intolerance and was appalled at his abuse of power. In fact, Constantine became so upset with Athanasius' uncompromising stance on the Creed that he did something quite unexpected. Perhaps with the power of his being the Emperor, or with his new found status within the church, he instructed that Arius be returned from exile.[53] Athanasius, as a bishop of the church, refused the order![54] A bishop disobeying the Emperor? This accelerated the conflict between the two, with records showing that Constantine banished Bishop Athanasius five times, but only with limited degrees of success.[55] So who is in charge? Constantine and Athanasius' conflict would become political, as well as religious, in what might be called the genesis of many future power struggles between Church and State.

Because of his continuing frustration with Athanasius, Constantine ordered, for the final time in 336 C.E., that Arius, over Athanasius' unrelenting authority, be returned from exile.[56] However, what happened was incredible, and for the bishops who were supporting Athanasius, a sign of God's will. On the evening before the formal and official celebration of his return, Arius, now an aged man, died suddenly.[57]

One year later, on May 22th, 337 C.E. Constantine died. Before his death, baptism was administered by Eusebius of Nicommedia, as stated, an Arian![58] Because of the change of mind of Constantine, some perhaps hoped that Arianism might be established as the interpretation of who Jesus was. Such a heretical interpretation was not to be, and the hard line literal interpretation of the Nicene Creed as championed by Athanasius was to rule as the truth. After the death of Constantine, Bishop Athanasius' power within the church would grow significantly. Now, to take one back to the earlier part of this story, Athanasius was indeed the hard line bishop who had sent the Festal Letter of 367 C.E. to the Pachomian monks living near Nag Hammadi. Athanasius had given the official Order that books with gnostic leanings be purged.[59] As this letter was sent after the death of Constantine, the Order gives a strong clue that Athanasius' power in the church would have the last word over Constantine's desire for harmony and tolerance.[60]

Indeed, after Constantine's death, the Nicene Creed and its literal interpretation won the support of future Emperors who were Christian. Although Christianity became the primary religion of the state under Constantine, interestingly, it wasn't until the time of Emperor Theodosis I that Christianity became the official religion of the Empire.[61] Theodosis, ruled from 379 C.E. to 395 C.E., and in 380 C.E., made the declaration that Christianity was the "Official" religion of the Roman Empire![62] Constantine's dream of one religion for one Empire was fulfilled, but again only temporarily, because major divisions between Western and Eastern bishops would develop politically and religiously.

Constantine has commonly been viewed as a culprit by stepping in so directly and boldly with his involvement in Christianity. However, sometimes overlooked, there is another side to his story. Without him, Christianity could have been a lesser force and religion. Had Maxentius won the battle at Milvian Bridge, Mithraism, with its many similarities to Christianity, could have become the state religion. Although Constantine's attempt to use his power to calm the extremism of Athanasius failed, his legacy as a culprit might have been different if his desire for harmony within the church had succeeded — the reason he first called the Council of Nicaea. An irony is that if Constantine had won power and influence within the church, which he did not, other theological views or greater tolerance might have been more widely affirmed, possibly taming the many religious wars, primarily over beliefs, which were to follow. Constantine's legacy of tolerance might have been much more positive than is commonly attributed.

Constantine may have regretted the very creed he established because it did not create "Pax Romana" and his need for unity. Particularly, the words of the Nicene Creed, which defined Jesus as no less than God, or of the same substance, was to create serious controversy in following years. This understanding of divinity would become a contributing factor to the division between the Church in the West and the Church in the East.[63] Even though, the division of these churches was caused as much by geography and politics, there were *seven* more official Church Councils to be held, the last being again in Nicaea in 787 C.E.[64] These Councils, as the first Nicene Council, were held to settled the continuing debate concerning Jesus' divinity. The debates primarily were still whether the nature of Christ was one nature or two, fully man or fully God. As often assumed, the debate didn't end in 325 C.E.! And the debate became even more inflamed in years to come as the issue became more refined over the developing question of the exact relationship of Christ, the Holy Spirit, and God the Father — or the doctrine of the Trinity.[65]

In these rather unknown seven Councils, as compared to the Council of Nicaea in 325 C.E., there was a growing division of theological perspective even beyond the Creeds between the Western and Eastern Empire. A central issue became how salvation was attained. Salvation, for the West, meant getting right with God by "believing" in Christ. The Eastern vision of salvation, perhaps influenced by the *Gospel of Thomas*, was by "joining" ones spirit to God by the Holy Spirit through Christ. The West usually triumphed over the East in the theological debates and in the official decrees which were made as Pronouncements from the Councils. The consequence was that these theological decrees, Williston Walker reports, caused "more division than consensus."[66]

Other serious issues beyond how one could obtain salvation also helped cause the split between Rome and the Eastern Church. In 692 C.E., the East had its own Council which declared it had "equal privilege with the See of Old Rome."[67] Oh my! At this Eastern Council, the Eastern Church separated itself by referring to its own church organization as the "Orthodox Church," and not the "Catholic Church."[68] It also enacted the right of marriage for its leaders.[69] It voted to prohibit a favorite Western symbol of Christ being represented as a lamb.[70] In contrast to the West, it affirmed the symbol of a human figure as the correct representation of Christ or icon to symbolize the incarnation.[71]

Icons were religious images usually painted on wooden panels and were highly respected in the Eastern culture. The use of icons became another cause for the split between Western and Eastern Christianity. In 725 C.E., a dramatic declaration was issued that sealed the division of the one Church as envisioned by Constantine. The Western Pope, Leo, forbade the use of icons in worship! To say the least, in the East, as Walker writes, there was "religious revolt."[72] To this day, although not much is made of it, there are major differences stemming from these Councils in theology, ecclesiastical polity, celibacy of priest, the use of icons, and ways of worship between the Roman Catholic and Eastern Orthodox Churches.

Much of this division was due to the fact that the unified political Empire, which Constantine had hoped to create, was to divide after his death. The regions were to become known as the Western or Roman Empire, and the separate Eastern, or Byzantine Empire.[73] Constantine's dream of one Empire with one religion was not to last. What did last in the Western interpretation of Christianity were the Apostles' Creed and the Nicene Creed, and the insistence that what they stated was the only true way to understand Jesus.

The cost was that those who heard the message and meaning of Christ differently from the literal interpretation of the Nicene Creed were censored, by the most unlikely source, the Roman government! Theodosis, in making Christianity the official religion of his Empire, allowed pagans to worship in peace; however, as a matter of record, he enforced the removal of any remaining heretical Arians and Gnostics from the Church.[74] Wouldn't Bishop Irenaeus be smiling again?

To summarize, after the lifetime of Jesus, St. Paul, St. Peter, and the writers of the New Testament Gospels, two primary architects of the Western form of Christianity were Irenaeus and the better known Constantine. Bishop Irenaeus was more directly involved in the development of the early church by his insistence that there were only four true Gospels and that the literal interpretation of what was shared in these Gospels was orthodoxy. Further, by driving the stake, to use a pun — in holy ground — that all other gospels and interpretations were heresy and that only the bishops possessed the true teachings of Jesus, Irenaeus laid the foundation for Constantine to establish Christianity, in its orthodox form, to be the truth of Jesus. By affirming the status of bishops, calling and financing the Council at Nicaea, and helping to write its Creed, Constantine added the blessing of the state to the growing religion of Christianity. Although the Nicene Creed did not help his goal of harmony and unity, Constantine inadvertently opened the door for the conservative bishops of the Western Empire to declare and affirm what Irenaeus had earlier stated as being the immoveable truths of Jesus and the Church.

Once again, the hard line, authoritarian policy of insisting on one's truth won, politically and religiously over those who had little room to speak or be heard.

Irenaeus and Constantine are often not related together in the development of the church and Christianity because of the many years that separated them, but their connection is more than telling in how the orthodox or fundamental interpretation of Christ came to be known as the normative way to believe and be Christian. Constantine sealed Irenaeus' views, or as he might say the truths of Christianity, with the Nicene Creed, allowed the state's endorsement of one form of Christianity, and opened the door for Athanasius to nail the coffin of the Gnostics. That is until the more inclusive, gnostic perspective of Christ, the Church, and Christianity could be resurrected from its burial and be revived by the find at Nag Hammadi!

The discovery of the Gnostic Gospels, however, bring forth another reason why many did not take these writings as having much to contribute to Christianity. Irenaeus and Constantine cannot take all the blame for the Gnostics not being recognized as legitimate Christians. Something else helped seal their fate of being unworthy to be called Christians, which will be the subject of the next three chapters. Within their own materials, there are wild and unreal mythologies that did not serve them well over time.

Even at the time of their inception, gnostic mythologies would have been considered radical and tainted, as they dared to incorporate and mix different traditions. Roman pagans would have thought that blending Jewish and Christian stories in their mythologies were heresy. The Hebrews would be appalled that they corrupted Jewish stories with classical mythology, and clearly, the literalists were appalled that the Gnostics changed Biblical stories from being interpreted as actual, historical events. Along with such criticisms of cultural assimilation, it was the rumors of ridiculous gnostic mythologies that survived throughout most of history and were used to cast them as mythological Christians who did not know reality or believe in the real Jesus.

Now, with the Nag Hammadi writings, the evidence is that the gnostic mythologies do not dominate all their thinking and that the Gnostics' antagonist used these wild tales, well, to describe and define them as heretical. Although one might think that the mission of the Gnostics was to convince the world that their views were right and all others wrong, their mythological opinions are essentially confined to a few books. In these books, their complex and conflicting tales are quite difficult to explain as being one story, because of their many variations of themes. However, their stories are clearly mythical, and they should be understood for what they are, myths!

A significant point is that seekers don't always find the truth, and it would be hard to argue that the Gnostics found it. The Gnostics themselves are an outstanding example of the need for change of beliefs with new knowledge and the imperative of continual seeking. However, to write them off as irrelevant Christians would be like writing off Christianity today because the Genesis' accounts do not totally agree with new scientific information. In the same tone of Christianity being more than proving that the creation stories of Genesis are total truth, so the myths of the Gnostics should not be read as their scientific answers. Certainly, as mythology gave way to science, and mythology came to mean that which was false, the ridicule of the Gnostics found reinforcement by those who said they knew the true story of creation. Unfortunately, the Gnostics' myths often have come to represent all that they believed; however, in spite of this, their mythical stories are engaging configurations for those who are intrigued by mythology. With much speculation about their myths, the Nag Hammadi books let the gnostic mythologies be analyzed with first-hand knowledge. Beyond whether they are true or not, the key question is, do these myths define their faith in Christ?

Notes: Chapter Fifteen: Defining Jesus–The Privilege and Power of Constantine

[1] James Carroll, *Constantine's Sword*, (New York, Houghton Mifflin, 2001), 188.
[2] Tim Dowley, Editor, *An Introduction of The History of Christianity*, (Minneapolis: Fortress Press, 2002), 82.
[3] Ibid.
[4] Williston Walker, *A History of the Christian Church*, (New York: Charles Scribners' Sons, 1959), 10.
[5] Ibid.
[6] Ibid.
[7] Walker, *A History of the Christian Church*, 11.
[8] Ibid.
[9] Ibid.
[10] Walker, *A History of the Christian Church*, 97.

[11] Walker, *A History of the Christian Church*, 100.
[12] Walker, *A History of the Christian Church*, 101.
[13] Ibid.
[14] Carroll, *Constantine's Sword*, 171.
[15] Walker, *A History of the Christian Church*, 101.
[16] Bart D. Ehrman, *Lost Christianities*, (Oxford: Oxford University Press, 2003), 250
[17] Dowley, *An Introduction of The History of Christianity*, 140.
[18] Ibid.
[19] Walker, *A History of the Christian Church*, 140.
[20] Walker, *A History of the Christian Church*, 105.
[21] Ibid.
[22] Carroll, *Constantine's Sword*, 55.
[23] Walker, *A History of the Christian Church*, 108.
[24] Ibid.
[25] Ibid.
[26] Carroll, *Constantine's Sword*, 190.
[27] Walker, *A History of the Christian Church*, 107.
[28] Ibid.
[29] Dowley, *An Introduction of The History of Chris*tianity, 74. Also see, Marcus J. Borg/John Dominic Crossan, *The First Christmas*, HarperOne, San Francisco, 2007), 63. "The titles of the Roman emperor Caesar Augustus were: Divine, Son of God, God, God from God, Lord, Redeemer, Liberator, and Savior of the World." By the time of Constantine, these titles were not as bold, but they were the tradition granted to former emperors.
[30] Carroll, *Constantine's Sword*, 189.
[31] Walker, *A History of the Christian Church*, 108.
[32] Ibid.
[33] Ibid.
[34] Carroll, *Constantine's Sword*, 191. Here is a discussion of how the Creed was refined after its acceptance at the First Council of Nicaea. Now, in today's Ecumenical version, it states this phrase rather than being of one substance as, "We believe in one Lord, Jesus Christ of one Being with the Father." One substance or one being? Seems the argument continues.
[35] Carroll, *Constantine's Sword*, 188
[36] Carroll, *Constantine's Sword*, 189.
[37] Dowley, *An Introduction of The History of Christianity*, 168.
[38] Ibid.
[39] J. Michael Matkin, *Early Christianity*, (New York: Alpha Books, 2008), 242.
[40] See Appendix B The Nicene Creed.
[41] Carroll, *Constantine's Sword*, 189
[42] Ibid.
[43] Elaine Pagels, *Beyond Belief*, (New York: Random House, 2005), 168.

[44] Ibid.
[45] Paul Johnson, *A History of Christianity*, (New York: Simon and Schuster, 1976), 69.
[46] Pagels, *Beyond Belief*, 169.
[47] Carroll, *Constantine's Sword*, 187.
[48] Carroll, *Constantine's Sword*, 188.
[49] Carroll, *Constantine's Sword*, 203.
[50] Walker, *A History of the Christian Church*, 110.
[51] Walker, *A History of the Christian Church*, 109.
[52] Walker, *A History of the Christian Church*, 110.
[53] Ibid.
[54] Ibid.
[55] Ibid.
[56] Ibid.
[57] Ibid.
[58] Ibid.
[59] David Brakke, *Athanasius and Asceticism*, (Baltimore: John Hopkins University Press, 1995), 320.
[60] Ibid.
[61] Walker, *A History of the Christian Church*, 117.
[62] Ibid.
[63] Ibid.
[64] Walker, *A History of the Christian Church*, 149.
[65] Walker, *A History of the Christian Church*, 115.
[66] Walker, *A History of the Christian Church*, 147.
[67] Ibid.
[68] Ibid.
[69] Ibid.
[70] Ibid.
[71] Ibid.
[72] Walker, *A History of the Christian Church*, 148.
[73] Walker, *A History of the Christian Church*, 111
[74] Dowley, *An Introduction of The History of Christianity*, 149.

Chapter Sixteen

Background to Gnostic Beliefs and Myths

> Myth will be what it always has been: to render in contemporary terms the mysteries of our own inner life, and the relationship of these mysteries to the cosmic life — because we are all part of the cosmos.[1]
>
> -Joseph Campbell, *An Open Life*

After the death of Constantine in 337 C.E., there was a great silence for the Gnostics. In contrast, there was a roar of prestige and power for the church that now could be called the Roman Catholic Church, as its seat of power was truly in Rome. However, the serious division of churches in the West and East would accelerate, especially, as Constantine's united Empire would begin to unravel. Bishops in the West, with the prestige of the Church in Rome, gained primary rule over churches in all the Empire. This privileged position also gave them the ability to increase their belief that their interpretation of Christianity was what all Christians should accept. However, in spite of their effort to be the universal church, all was not calm with the on-going issues of ecclesiastical authority, icons, priestly marriage, and theology. In the Eastern Empire, thirty years after Constantine's death, and perhaps not totally a surprise, Arianism became the preferred doctrine of their bishops and was not considered heresy![2] In the West, Arianism, which did not die out overnight, became the serious threat within the church replacing the Gnostics as their primary foe.[3]

With the Gnostics all but being eliminated for any discussion involving theology, Athanasius' Order in the Festal letter of 367 C.E. to destroy books with gnostic influences, becomes more understandable. With the Apostles' Creed and the Nicene Creed as his swords of truth, these other minor gospels had no worth in the true interpretation and understanding of Jesus or his message. However, within his charge that books with gnostic leanings were "defiled, polluted, full of myths, and empty," there was one solid truth.[4] The writings did contain myths.

Myths have come to mean stories that are false. However, Joseph Campbell, through his various books, has helped open a wider understanding that myths do carry significant meanings and messages. More precisely, he says regarding myths, "They don't represent answers but are attempts to express insights."[5] Myths often speak to mysteries that cannot be explained with pure logic. Most myths, like dreams, are not literal, nor coherent, and they delve into knowledge that is beyond rational and scientific proof. As Campbell once explained, "Myth is a metaphor. We must not confuse mythology with ideology. Myths come from where the heart is. The myth does not point to a fact: the myth points beyond facts to something that informs the fact."[6] Many cultures, traditions, and religions have used myths to inform and explain the world's creation; the Gnostics also join the procession to tell their versions of the story.

As expected from the criticism of mythical thinking in the writings of the fathers, the gnostic creation myths develop primarily from the stories told in Genesis, highlighting the Biblical characters of Adam, Eve, Seth, and the Serpent.[7] In one way, they accept these characters as real or actual worldly beings, and then in the same story, they describe them as supernatural realities. This perception of them being both real and spiritual beings is where it gets fascinating and the imagination of the Gnostics soars.

In a general overview of their mythology, Gnostics believed both the material and spiritual worlds were real, but ultimately, the spiritual was more important than the physical world.[8] Good and evil existed in both worlds. There was one true God, who was often called Father, also known as Mother/Father, and at times was called the Divine Parent.[9] From the Divine Parent came forth emanations, or what they called "aeons." These aeons were divine extensions, usually spiritual, of the Godhead that included the Holy Spirit and Christ, and in contrast to the theology of the church, God's manifestations were not limited to a trinity or three beings.[10] From this basic belief of emanations from the Parent, there is a variety of stories of how these celestial beings or gods fulfilled their divine functions both in the heavens and on earth.

A central theme in most of the gnostic myths is that the creator of our world was not one of the divine gods but was created by a "mistake" by one of the divine beings. Therefore, the creator was a Demiurge.[11] In Plato, a Demiurge is the source that fashioned the world from preexisting ideas, forms, or materials of the chaos.[12] This may explain why two pages of Plato's Republic constituted one of the texts found in the Nag Hammadi discovery.[13] The use of the term, "Demiurge," may also be why some once believed that the Gnostics were stronger believers in Greek philosophy than in Christianity. The opposite was true. The Gnostic Gospels reveal that Christianity dominated their assimilation of Greek philosophy and myths because all the stories lead to Christ.

The assimilation of Greek mythology, itself, was only partial as the Gnostics developed new gods and characters not in classical mythology. Importantly, their Demiurge was *different* from that of Plato or the Greeks. Their Demiurge was an inferior, evil subordinate created outside of the heavenly realm.[14] Before Adam and Eve, the Demiurge had cursed the Supreme God, who was filled with goodness, and in the process of rebellion, the Demiurge created the material world.[15] This malevolent Demiurge's creation of the world explains how evil was created and came into this world.

Because of the Demiurge's direct participation in creation, some Gnostics believed everything in the material world was evil.[16] In the literalist story, the one true God was perfect and made everything good before Adam and Eve took the fall, bringing forth continual sin.[17] By contrast, in the gnostic myth, the lowly creator of the world, who was less than the supreme God, was evil; therefore, his creation was evil. Importantly, everything being evil wasn't the end of the story. In creation, something positive was infused, particularly, in the creation of mankind. The Gnostics believed humankind was a part of the Demiurge's evil creation, but humans were born with a gift described as a spark or seed.[18] In essence, this spark was the spirit of God which persons could find within themselves.[19]

This spark was a gift from the true God and was delivered to Adam and Eve through the divine beings of the spiritual world. Probably, in its most acceptable version, this divine spark came from the eternal or divine

Christ.[20] Upsetting to some, but exciting for others, this divine seed also came through the divine Sophia.[21] In other words, the spiritual or positive, or whatever one wishes to call the spark, was a part of mankind's creation. Then, to make it clear that there was a true God who loved humans and had placed his spirit within their creation, Jesus, the embodiment of the divine Christ, entered the world as a person.[22] His message was that individuals needed to awaken to the spirit within, the Holy Spirit.[23] This awakening would bring wholeness or completeness to one's life. By Jesus' death and resurrection, he became the Savior on earth, and today is the living and eternal Christ.[24]

This thumbnail sketch does not explain the complicated, illogical, imaginative, and differing details that are found in the gnostic myths, but this summary reveals that there is a combination of Greek and Hebrew sources. In doing so, the rejection of the literalist interpretation is clear; the Gnostics did not read the stories of Genesis as a literal, historical, or scientific account. Indeed, they may have been first in line to differ with what is popularly called today, creationism, or that God's process of creation was precisely as told in the Bible. In spite of the orthodox claim that the stories of Genesis were records of what actually happened, the Gnostics would have claimed that the two differing, conflicting creation stories in Chapters 1 and Chapter 2 were both myths. Also, they would claim as mythical, the story of the snake tempting Eve, which resulted in sin entering the perfectly good world.[25] The Gnostics take these same stories and tell them differently. Of course, this is upsetting to those who take the literal interpretation as the truth, but even more disturbing is the common charge that the Gnostics believed in many gods![26]

Many gods? How could that be? What is often misunderstood is that the gnostics did believe in one true or supreme God.[27] They also believed in angelic spirits, divine forces and lower gods, but as stated above, all these were extensions of the one true God. In that sense they were monotheist, but because they had not given up the Greek belief in lesser gods, the charge was that they were simply polytheist. Well, not completely so. God the Father/Mother, the Divine Parent was One.[28] However, their conception of the Supreme God was not totally the same as the traditional Jewish and the orthodox Christian God.

There was a more perfect God beyond the demiurge who created the earth. This Supreme God's purpose was beyond the role of observing and judging all the good and evil on earth, blessing some and cursing others. This God was unknowable, yet always deserving of awe; they criticized those who didn't believe there was a God beyond the idols which men created for themselves.[29] As the theologian Paul Tillich expresses, there is a "God Beyond God" or a God beyond the one whom most people assume they know or create in their minds.[30] In other words, the God we imagine, or think we know, is too small!

Although the world of angels and spirits are acceptable to many today, and the idea of lower gods is not, the real challenge isn't to accept the Gnostics' version of gods, creation, or the cosmos, as the truth. They do not imply that believing their myths is a requirement for being a believer and follower of Jesus. Because they had various myths, this was not a reason to conclude that one view was right, and the other wrong; the different stories were considered a natural part of the nature of myths.

In the context of their time, myths for the Gnostics were not just false stories, nor were they rational facts. Myths unfolded wisdom beyond human understanding and were the way for centuries that mankind had made sense of the world. Myths were not laughable tales but were serious efforts in the quest for an explanation of how things were in the earthly world, why evil existed, and how life might be in the spiritual and eternal realm. Myths were not history but were about things eternal. As Andrew Welburn in his book *The Beginning of Christianity*, says, "Under the sway of mythological forces, ancient man had little awareness of time and history."[31] The cycle of life was eternal expressed, perhaps best, by the Egyptian practice of burying favorite items with the dead. For the Gnostics, the mythical world had a reality as many believed before them. Something, however, with the concept of myths was about to change with the Hebrew God.

Leonard Shlain, in his book *The Alphabet Versus the Goddess*, believes it was the Hebrews who made a startling discovery — language — and then history![32] The Hebrew book of Genesis was presented not as myth, but the history of creation. Their story was not myth; it was historical. All the gods, particularly the goddesses of the past, were false imaginations and untrue, because they were outside history.[33] Their God had entered into their history and had chosen them as being blessed as the true people of God; yet, there was a condition. They would be blessed only if they followed the commandments of the one God. This God, much like the gnostic concept of the Invisible Spirit, was unnamable but could be worshiped as Yahweh or Jehovah.[34]

The Gnostics, however, had a problem. It was not that there was one God, and this God had entered into the reality of the Hebrew world. A serious issue was that this God was presented as being only male. This was unacceptable to gnostic Christians. They believed God was One, both male and female, and most of all a Spirit.[35] Therefore, their interpretation of the one true God went beyond that of the Hebrews.

The Gnostics, thus, had some differences with the Hebrew tradition, so all was not pleasant, but their greater differences were with those Christians who took over the Hebrews' stories and made them exclusively their own. Obviously, the Gnostics would be in agreement with several reformed groups of Jews today who believe that such stories, as the creation in seven days, the details of Adam and Eve, and their encounter with the serpent could be understood beyond a literalism. The Jewish books of the Old Testament were revered by the Gnostics, but their value was far more than proving, by their prophecies, that Christianity was now the true religion and only valid religion over Judaism.[36] As will be seen in the Sethian account, they have an answer to the question, what about the salvation of those in the Bible who came before Jesus? Overall, the Gnostics, as opposed to the proto-orthodox, used Jewish stories, not to prove Christianity was the only true religion, but to take many of their stories to build upon and expand their mythological view of the world.

In the time period of the gnostic writings, the creation story told in Genesis wasn't the predominantly accepted version of creation in Roman society as for many Christians today.[37] One might have thought the Gnostics would have rejected the Genesis story altogether, as did the Marcions.[38] Accepting of the Old Testament, they applied the standard for their day, myths. They not only added myths to the Hebrew version of creation but expanded it with the new story of Christianity. Within their stories are different words or terms, which reflect the combination of pagan and Christian ideology, and need explanation. Some are: "aeon" — an eternal emanation of the Supreme Being; "archons" — angels, but often as evil ones; "autogenes" — one who is self begotten or begotten; and "pleroma" — fullness or the heavenly realm of the spiritual.[39] For a full glossary of terms, see the Appendix in Meera Lester's *Everything Gnostic*

Gospels Book or the glossary of this book. All of these unusual terms are used quite often in their differing mythologies.

The two principal schools of gnostic myths, of how the world was created and how man came to be, are those of the Valentinians and the Sethians. There were other gnostic creation myths, but these are the prominent ones from which many pick out themes, and say, "this is what the Gnostics believed." These two myths are similar in some ways, but they don't always agree and often take conflicting paths. They do represent the struggle mankind has been involved with from the time of intelligence to make sense, or explain how, and/or why, we are here. Particularly, in the realm of religion, they attempt to address what happened before our births, and what will happen after our deaths. For sure, these mythical stories are not always easy to understand as they are quite complicated. These myths have many cross references, similarities, and have many places where logic and rational thought are thrown to the wind.

In spite of their complication, there are patterns that have led scholars to identify certain books within the Nag Hammadi writings as Valentinian or Sethian.[40] Although some texts can easily be identified as to which schools they belong, there have been conferences held over the positions of several of the writings; even today, there is not total consensus.[41] Then, there are books like the *Gospel of Thomas* and the *Gospel of Mary* in which many see both views, or some who see neither gospel as related to a certain school. The complete picture is a puzzle, but the next two chapters give a more detailed overview to help understand these two primary gnostic myths. Clearly, the gnostic stories should be understood for what they are, myths! They do not tell the whole story or the most valuable part of the Gnostics' story — their dynamic faith in Christ. These myths do perk interest, are fascinating, and like so-called themes of Gnosticism in the media, can be entertaining. Perhaps, by their association to Christianity, their imaginative tales can help revive some studies in traditional, as well as other religious myths.

Notes: Chapter Sixteen: Background to Gnostic Beliefs and Myths

[1] Michael Toms, *An Open Life*, (New York: Harper & Row, 1989), 117.
[2] Williston Walker, *A History of the Christian Church*, (New York: Charles Scribners's & Sons, 1959), 118.

[3] Walker, *A History of the Christian Church*, 13.
[4] Elaine Pagels, *Beyond Belief*, (New York: Random House, 2003), 177.
[5] Toms, *An Open Life*: Joseph Campbell in conversation with Michael Toms, 23.
[6] Toms, *An Open Life*, 21.
[7] Elaine Pagels, *Adam, Eve, And The Serpent*, (New York: Random House, 1998), 57.
[8] National Public Radio Programing, Morning Addition, printed report, "The Spiritual Message of the Matrix," May 16, 2003. "The world we are living in is not the ultimate reality."
[9] Elaine Pagels, *The Gnostic Gospels*, (New York: Random House, 1979), 57.
[10] J. Michael Matkin, *The Gnostic Gospels*, (New York: Alpha Books, 2005), 14
[11] Richard Valantasis, *Gnosticism and Other Vanished Christianities*, (New York: Doubleday, 2006), 148.
[12] Matkin, *The Gnostic Gospels*, 176.
[13] James M. Robinson, editor, *The Nag Hammadi Library in English*, referred hereafter as *NHL*, "Plato, *Republic*," (San Francisco: HarperSanFrancisco, 1978), 318.
[14] Matkin, *The Gnostic Gospels*, 181
[15] Ibid.
[16] Bart D. Ehrman, *Lost Christianities: Christian Scripture and the Battle over Authentication*, (Chantilly, Virginia: The Teaching Company, Part I, 2004), Pg. 55.
[17] Genesis 1: 31.
[18] Matkin, *The Gnostic Gospels*, 42.
[19] Robinson, *NHL*, the *Gospel of Thomas*, Pg. 126.
[20] Matkin, The Gnostic Gospels, 41.
[21] Ibid.
[22] Matkin, *The Gnostic Gospels*, 179.
[23] Matkin, *The Gnostic Gospels*, 42.
[24] Matkin, *The Gnostic Gospels*, 124.
[25] Creation Stories: Genesis 1:1 to 2:3. Genesis 2:4 to 4:6 The Snake: Genesis 3: 1 to 24.
[26] Ehrman, *Lost Christianities*, 21.
[27] Matkin, *The Gnostic Gospels*, 178.
[28] Matkin, *The Gnostic Gospels*, 238.
[29] Robinson, *NHL*, the *Gospel of Philip*, Verse, 72, 152.
[30] Pagels, The Gnostic Gospels, 39.
[31] Andrew Welburn, *The Beginnings of Christianity*, (Edinburgh: Floris Books,1991), 39
[32] Leonard Shlain, *The Alphabet and the Goddess*, (New York: Penguin/Compass, 1998), 71.
[33] Wellburn, *The Beginnings of Christianity*, 39.
[34] Henry Hampton Halley, *Halley's Bible Handbook, Revised*, (Grand Rapids, Mi.: Zondervan, 2000), 1020.
[35] Pagels, *The Gnostic Gospels*, 56-57.
[36] Valantasis, *Gnosticism and Other Vanished Christianities*, 18

[37] Pagels, *Adam, Eve, and The Serpent*, 41.
[38] Bart D. Ehrman, *The New Testament,* (Oxford: Oxford University Press, 2008), 200.
[39] Meera Lester, *The Everything Gnostic Gospels Book*, (Avon, Ma., Adams Media, an F+W Publication, Inc., 2007) 268.
[40] Karen L. King, *What is Gnosticism?,* (Cambridge, Ma.: Harvard University Press, 2003), 153.
[41] King, *What is Gnosticism?*, 156.

Chapter Seventeen

The Valentinian Myth

> The Valentinians are considered those who have found an answer and stopped there to be far inferior to those who sought a deep knowledge and found true rest in their seeking. [1]
>
> -Richard Valantasis,
> *Gnosticism and Other Vanished Christianities*

The Valentinian school of gnostic thought was headed by a popular teacher named Valentinus, a native of Alexandria, who lived from 100 C.E. to 165 C.E. Most scholars think his movement, more so than the Sethians, was the biggest gnostic threat to the apostolic church.[2]

The basic theological concepts that Valentinus taught, first began with the belief that God the Father/Mother is good, without evil![3] For sure, that is a significant variation from the assumption that the gnostics believed God was bad and evil. No, not so. The Demiurge, not the Father/Mother, was the evil creator.[4] Indeed, as the literalists, the Valentinians believed that the really true God was good and One.[5] Valentinians also believed human ignorance of their being a loving God was corrected by the sending of his Son, Jesus.[6] The crucifixion and resurrection of Jesus was a revelation, or in Valentinian terms, a "publication" as they expressed it, of his knowledge of God the Father.[7] Salvation was achieved by awakening oneself to a relationship with the Father through the living Jesus rather than accepting beliefs.[8] A major difference from the literalists was that the Valentinians believed other divine beings existed.[9] In spite of this basic disagreement, they believed that the primary Savior for the world was Jesus the Christ.[10]

Some of these Valentinian positions may sound somewhat related or similar to the traditional story of Jesus. As Dr. Karen King says, "Valentinian myth and thought are more decidedly Christian than is Sethian mythology."[11] Some believe this is so because one of the Valentinian books, The *Gospel of Truth*, was probably written by Valentinus, who was believed to have been earlier in his career, more closely aligned with the literalists.[12] Scholars believe this gospel was a sermon written or preached in order to appease an audience of both Gnostics and literalists.[13] As far as convincing the literalists, his sermon apparently was not a success, because Valentinus — as you well know — although nearly a Pope, was eventually excommunicated and declared a heretic by the apostolic church.[14] As for his followers and their relationship to the church, Richard Valantasis of Illif Theological Seminary in Denver, explains, "The Valentinians never left the church; rather, the church kicked them out." [15]

More than Valentinus' slightly different theological wordings, such as the expression "publication" for the term "revelation," there were some distinct teachings. These different conceptions of God and the spiritual world clearly set him apart from the literalists and had to anger them. For example, the Valentinians believed in a One, unknowable God, who could be compared to a Divine Parent, but also could be understood as a Monad. Monad was a term also used by the Sethians meaning the One.[16] However, to complicate their understanding of God, one school of Valentinian thought, taught that the supreme God should be understood as a dyad as well. The dyad implied a paired being, or a masculine-feminine pairing.[17] In other words, the Divine was a single being whose nature was both masculine/feminine. From this almighty source came emanations known as aeons.[18] Aeons were divine like beings with positive characteristics that flowed or emanated from the One. As pairing was a part of the Divine being's nature, so the characteristics of the aeons were also in pairs. Thus, one emanation was the Primal Depth, which was masculine, and his counterpart was Silence, which was feminine.[19] From these aeons there came forth other aeons that were also pairs such as Intellect and Truth, Word and Life, Son and Church. All together there were fifteen male/female pairs or a total of thirty different aeons.[20]

As emanations, it is important to understand that these aeons, sometimes identified as gods, but most often as pure, divine realities, helped make up the plemora. Plemora was a term implying the fullness of the spiritual world or the divine fullness of the true God and Father.[21] A good example of this emanation is in the Nag Hammadi book *The Tripartite Tractate*, considered Valentinian. Verse 2, says, "The Father is a single one. Yet, he is not like a solitary individual. For whenever there is a 'father,' the name 'son' follows. But the single one, who alone is the Father, is like a root with trees, branches and fruit."[22] In other words, the divine world flows from the true God.

A related part of this divine extension, according to the *Tractate*, is the pairing, the Son and the Church. So it says, "Not only did the Son exist from the beginning, but the Church too existed from the beginning."[23] Obviously, the Church was held in high regard! Later, it even declares, in praise, that the Church is the "aeons of the aeons — forever and forever."[24] Surely the apostolic church, although disagreeing with this concept, must have liked this expression of respect for the Church! As for the Son, the *Tractate* teaches "the Father rests upon the Son."[25] Then, it explains a somewhat different fall from goodness than is traditionally told for humankind, and this story of the fall uses a variation on the theme of logos or the word.

This *Tractate*, a religious epistle or pamphlet, teaches that the aeon, Logos or Word, falls from grace.[26] His fall, interestingly, is the result of this Word's "abundant love" in accordance with the Father's love.[27] Further, it teaches all who are dependent upon Logos share his quality of "free choice."[28] Remember, the literalists taught there was no need for free choice as that was heretical![29] Perhaps because this aeon had free choice, for the Valentinians, exactly where Logos falls from grace is not explained explicitly. Most assume it was to the created world; definitely, it is somewhere outside the plemora — or the divine realm of the aeons.

After this fall, Logos, or the Word, returns to the plemora to redeem himself, is forgiven and becomes the Savior.[30] He is also known as the aeon who reveals the Father to others, and particularly, to those outside the plemora.[31] Thus, Jesus becomes the Word.[32] As the Word, Jesus comes as Savior to our world to reveal the abundant love of God. One can see in this Valentinian myth with Christ coming to this world as Jesus, a decidedly Christian bias, but a different interpretation of how Jesus entered the world as Savior.

This story of the Word sounds like a reflection from the Bible's Gospel of John, which by its philosophical inclusions, has been considered to have some gnostic leanings.[33] That is a different perception! There are some resemblances in *themes*. In John's gospel, the eternal Word becomes flesh in Jesus; and as with the Gnostics, Jesus is taught as preexistent as the Word.[34] The Gospel of John has been the flagship for believing that Jesus as the Word became flesh in this world. However, Jesus' coming is as the Nicene Creed explains, with the emphasis being that God and Jesus are one and the same. The Valentinians believed in Jesus as the Word, and his coming into this world as Jesus to publish God's love, but with a more mythological rather than a historical interpretation of Jesus. In other words, in John's version, Jesus comes straight from God, being of the same substance, as Constantine insisted. Whereas in the Valentinian story the coming of the preexistent Christ in the person of Jesus is more complicated and is not as direct. First, there is the fall of the Word by his free choice, then the fall from grace, and then his repentance before coming to the world as Savior. Maybe the Valentinians were trying to fill in the story of what happened before the pre-existing Christ came into the world, but the Word comes to the world as Jesus the Christ.

Although the next version of Jesus coming into the world is not totally separate from the story of the Word, it could appear to be a different creation story that leads to Christ. Far more controversial, and some would say more exciting than the aeon, "Word," is the last aeon who was emanated from the Father. Her official name is Wisdom, but most people know her as Sophia![35] The complex myth of Sophia in its Valentinian form provides an explanation, particularly for the fall, unlike the story of the Word's fall, told in *The Tripartite Tractate*. This adds a conflicting twist to the story, but it helps to explain where the aeon, "Word", may have fallen — to a physical world created by a Demiurge.[36]

Sophia is crucial to the creation of the world. For an unexplained reason, Sophia or Wisdom, attempted to create the world on her own without the Father's approval.[37] Her attempt failed because of her arrogance and her neglect to work with others who made up the plemora. The result was that she created not another aeon but something that was outside the plemora.[38] She created a lesser or lower god, or in most interpretations, a being lower than a god, a Demiurge.[39] This Demiurge, not Sophia, created a world.[40] This world is now our earth that was created as material and devoid of spirit or soul.[41] Thus, the support comes for the popular theme that all Gnostics believed the material world was totally evil. Although some

Gnostics, such as the writer of a gnostic book called *Thomas, the Contender* would support that all flesh is evil, there is more to the story. Clearly, the story of the Demiurge makes it rather simple to say everything on earth was evil, but often not recognized is, for some Gnostics, the story does not end here. Indeed, there is more to the story than the debate as to whether the earth was created either all good or all bad.

In the expanded and often conflicting story, in simplified terms, there will be a bad Sophia and a good Sophia. Sometimes, this is referred to as a lower Sophia and a higher Sophia.[42] In her lower form, she is sometimes known as Achamoth.[43] In the higher account, she is the blessed and godly Sophia, who in positive terms represents the divine feminine. She is a source and spirit from on high, which resides in us now, not just in females, but in both males and females.[44] In the lower form, it is Achamoth who brings forth the Demiurge who created the material world.[45] Somehow, not fully explained in this story, the higher Sophia's spirit invests itself in the world despite the fall, symbolized in the lower Sophia.[46] Because of the ignorance of people about the spiritual dimension of life and the knowledge of the one true God, the pair of aeons, who are Christ and the Holy Spirit, were sent to this poorly created world. Their task was to restore people who had not awakened to the spirit of God and spiritual salvation.[47] The essence of the story was that the higher Sophia was the means by which persons within the created world could possess within themselves a divine spirit, seed or spark.[48] By awakening to that reality, one could be brought fully alive by their belief in Jesus and then develop their relationship with Christ.[49]

This is a highly simplified telling of her story, and Sophia will appear even more significantly and central for the need of spirituality in her Sethian version. In the complexity of her story, and in many variations of her myth, she has been described in several ways by several sources. Some have presented Sophia as being preexistent with Christ — as both were aeons, the creator of the questionable God called Yahweh, the prototype of the human soul, the consort of Jesus and sometimes as his sister, and as being equal with the Holy Spirit. Sound confusing? Yes, with her many titles and functions, yet, in spite of the different descriptions, the one central accumulative image or message is that she represents the *divine feminine* in humankind. In essence, she elevates the feminine dimension that many see or believe is essential to the very nature of God.[50]

Jacob Boehme, the seventeenth century mystic, might have caught her Valentinian essence as he saw in her the idea that a man must discover and unite with his inner Sophia to be whole.[51] Carl Jung certainly echoed this message in his teachings of the feminine and masculine in both male and female. So it is that many hold her as a positive revelation of God and a spirit in their life. Of course, the duplicity of Sophia in the Valentinian story serves to underscore the complexity of trying to get a totally clear understanding of myths. Indeed, searching for meaning beyond their details is the challenge to the modern mind.

We will return to Sophia in her Sethian version, but beyond the Valentinian's varying themes in their creation myths, there are some noteworthy rituals which are helpful in understanding their related practices and sacraments. Because of these rituals, there is reason to believe that the Gnostics formed a separate church. This may have happened to some degree, but it appears with limited success. Of course, the church fathers would have no room for such unapproved rituals, and for the ones that were similar to their own, there was no room for different interpretations. Today, some want to revive these rituals and make them the religion of Gnosticism, but even though there is evidence of rituals in both Valentinian and Sethian schools of thought, the challenge to modern Christianity is greater than recreating their rituals as if they are the true and mystical way to God.

Rituals have a place in religion, but as with beliefs and myths, faith is greater than many religious practices that have gone on for many centuries in various forms. If Christian faith is more than rituals, there is room for different rituals, as well. The Valentinians had rituals, as did the Sethians, and the message becomes as with beliefs, rituals are essential and vital to the exercise of faith. The *Gospel of Philip* is the primary source for five specific sacraments promoted by the Valentinians. In their variation of some conventional rituals, and with some different and unique new ones, they are intriguing. The Valentinian sacraments are Baptism, Eucharist, Chrism, Redemption, and the Bridal Chamber.[52]

In *Baptism*, an unusual element was added to the symbolic cleansing of the soul with water. There was an emphasis on receiving resurrection and living as a new person in Christ.[53]

In the *Eucharist*, sometimes known as Communion, eating the bread and wine took on a spiritualized body and blood. This sacrament was also known as taking in the Word and Holy Spirit.[54]

Chrism was an anointment with oil, usually in conjunction with baptism, signifying Jesus was the Anointed One, and that his divine light is now revealed to the believer.[55]

Redemption, a sacrament, celebrated the release from the bonds of the Demiurge. As Irenaeus explains it, which was meant to be sarcastic, that redemption for the Gnostics was "to be regenerated into the power which is above all."[56] The most intriguing and least understood is the sacrament of the Bridal Chamber.[57]

The name *Bridal Chamber* alone raises curiosity. Not unexpectedly, Irenaeus in *Against Heresies* charges that the Bridal Chamber was a place where women could be and were physically seduced.[58] The Nag Hammadi books reveal a higher purpose and vision. The *Gospel of Philip* makes it clear that union in the Bridal Chamber was entirely spiritual — at least in its intent! As Dr. Valantasis says, "the Bridal Chamber celebrated the complete union of the Gnostic with the divine realm, a permanent and immutable status of perfection and rest which characterizes the good of a Valentinian life."[59] In other words, its purpose was restoration of one's spirit with the plemora or divine realm.

A totally different perspective than Irenaeus' is that the Bridal Chamber allowed one to be free of the sexual act. What? Although a passage in Philip understands that "without marriage the world would not exist," sex was sometimes understood as supporting or giving into the material world.[60] According to this interpretation, the experience of the Bridal Chamber allowed one to rise above and opt out of the evilness of sex.[61] Now — that is a different twist!

As can be imagined, the apostolic bishops had to be outraged, particularly at the different sacraments. Interestingly, they are all Christ-centered, but the variations of theology and the extension of the rituals had to be maddening for the literalists. As Meera Lester writes in *The Everything Gnostic Gospels Book,* "The bishops were intent on guiding the church in a direction of universal acceptance of converts of varying degrees of knowledge and understanding and would not tolerate challenges to their doctrine, hierarchy or ritual."[62] Variation in rituals — how could that be? Of course, Roman Catholics today believe in five sacraments and the Protestants only two, and so the argument isn't all that new to Christianity.

With this information, the question can again be raised what if Valentinus had become Pope? Perhaps, assuming that he could have had some influence, there could have been more rituals or sacraments and a different understanding of the theological term, "Word." Perhaps Valentinus' Christ-centered mythology would have been the standard of the day or more highly accepted. Of course, Valentinus was much closer to becoming a Pope than Mary Magdalene, but evidence from her gospel is that she would have liked the Valentinian emphasis on Sophia and the divine feminine dimension of God! To be fair, Valentinian mythology, although quite different, has some thoughtful and creative designs of theology and provides interesting variations on traditional Christian beliefs. Indeed, their myth also has some bizarre, imaginative, twist and turns, but not nearly as much as those found in the Sethian mythology.

Notes: Chapter Seventeen: The Valentinian Myth

[1] Richard Valantasis, *Gnosticism and Other Vanished Religions*, (New York: Doubleday, 2006), 48.
[2] Valantasis, *Gnosticism and Other Vanished Religions*, 47.
[3] J. Michael Matkin, *The Gnostic Gospels*, (New York: Alpha Books, 2005), 41.
[4] Matkin, *The Gnostic Gospels*, 176.
[5] John T. Robinson, Editor, *The Hag Hammadi Library in English*, referred hereafter as *NHL*, *The Tripartite Tractate*, (New York: HarperCollins, 1978), 60.
[6] Karen King, *What is Gnosticism?*, (Cambridge, Ma. Harvard University Press, 2003), 159.
[7] Robinson, *NHL*, the *Gospel of Philip*, 150.
[8] Matkin, *The Gnostic Gospels*, 127.
[9] Matkin, *The Gnostic Gospels*, 122.
[10] King, *What is Gnosticism?*, 159.
[11] King, *What is Gnosticism?*, 154.
[12] Meera Lester, *The Everything Gnostic Gospels*, (Avon, Ma., Adams Media, 2007), 175.
[13] Matkin, *The Gnostic Gospels*, 125
[14] Matkin, *The Gnostic Gospels*, 41.
[15] Valantasis, *Gnosticism and Other Vanished Religions*, 45.
[16] Matkin, *The Gnostic Gospels*, 238.
[17] Ibid.
[18] Michael Allen Williams, *Rethinking Gnosticism*, (Princeton, N.J., Princeton University Press, 1996), 15.
[19] Ibid.
[20] Ibid.
[21] Matkin, The Gnostic Gospels, 291.

[22] Robinson, *NHL, The Tripartite Tractate*, Verse 2, 60.
[23] Robinson, *NHL, The Tripartite Tractate*, Verse 35, 63.
[24] Robinson, *NHL, The Tripartite Tractate*, Verse 58, 64.
[25] *Robinson, NHL, The Tripartite Tractate, Verse 59, 64.*
[26] Robinson, *NHL, The Tripartite Tractate*, Verse 80, 74.
[27] Robinson, *NHL, The Tripartite Tractate*, Verse 59, 64.
[28] Robinson, *NHL, The Tripartite Tractate*, Verse 85, 76.
[29] Matkin, *The Gnostic Gospels*, 287.
[30] Robinson, *NHL, The Tripartite Tractate*, Verse 86, 77.
[31] Robinson, *NHL, The Tripartite Tractate*, Verse 90, 79.
[32] Robinson, *NHL, The Tripartite Tractate*, Verse 95, 82.
[33] Pagels, *The Gnostic Gospels*, (New York: Random House, 1979), 143.
[34] John 1:14.
[35] Matkin, *The Gnostic Gospels*, 122.
[36] Williams, *Rethinking Gnosticism*, Pg. 17.
[37] Williams, *Rethinking Gnosticism*, 16.
[38] Ibid.
[39] Ibid.
[40] Ibid.
[41] Williams, *Rethinking Gnosticism*, 17.
[42] Matkin, *The Gnostic Gospels*, 122.
[43] Ibid.
[44] Williams, *Rethinking Gnosticism*, 17.
[45] Matkin, *The Gnostic Gospels*, 124.
[46] Williams, *Rethinking Gnosticism*, 17.
[47] Matkin, *The Gnostic Gospels*, 122.
[48] Williams, *Rethinking Gnosticism*, 17.
[49] Matkin, *The Gnostic Gospels*, 124.
[50] Matkin, *The Gnostic Gospels*, 193.
[51] Elaine Pagels, *Beyond Belief*, (New York: Random House, 2003), 75.
[52] Robinson, *NHL*, the *Gospel of Philip*, 141.
[53] Matkin, *The Gnostic Gospels*, 136.
[54] Matkin, *The Gnostic Gospels*, 139.
[55] Matkin, *The Gnostic Gospels*, 138.
[56] Matkin, *The Gnostic Gospels*, 140.
[57] Matkin, *The Gnostic Gospels*, 141.
[58] Matkin, *The Gnostic Gospels*, 143.
[59] Valantasis, *Gnosticism and Other Vanished Christianities*, 53.
[60] Matkin, *The Gnostic Gospels*, 143.
[61] Ibid.
[62] Lester, *The Everything Gnostic Gospels*, 176.

Chapter Eighteen

The Sethian Mythology

> The Sethians were like many people I know today who are spiritual seekers, who restlessly travel from one religion or spiritual tradition to another in search of wisdom." [1]
>
> -Richard Valantasis,
>
> *Gnosticism and Other Vanished Christianities*

In the Nag Hammadi Library, there are more books assigned to the Sethians than to the Valentinians, and by its mythological terminologies, the newly published *Gospel of Judas,* clearly, is of Sethian influence. The classification of books as being Sethian is easier than being Valatintian, because in the Sethian writings, they use certain, unusual, and distinctive names. They are called Sethian because in their myths they trace their roots names to Seth and identify themselves as being children of Seth.

Seth was the third son of Adam and Eve in the Hebrew story of the creation of humankind, and according to the Sethians, he was the most important of their sons.[2] In the Hebrew account, the story goes that Adam and Eve's first son, Cain, killed the second son, Abel. Therefore, according to the Sethians, the mantle of sharing God's spirit in this world was placed squarely on Seth.[3]

Before getting further into Sethian mythology, it must be reiterated that their mythology is much more complicated than that of the Valentinians – as if that were good news. Sethian paths have many more turns, details, and mythological characters, making the Sethian's literature more difficult to follow and understand. Many verses have words and terms that cannot easily be understood without an overall picture of their mythology.

As with the Valentinians, God the Father is mysterious and unknowable.[4] The Sethians, however, often refer to the true God as the Invisible Spirit.[5] God is also One, and before emanations of aeons, the Sethians teach that there are three dimensions to the Invisible Spirit. The set of powers of this Spirit are the Father, Mother, and Son, which seems to contradict God's mysterious nature, but it is an attempt to be descriptive.[6] Interestingly, some believe this configuration helped to accelerate the creation of the orthodox doctrine of the Trinity in order to separate themselves from the Sethian triune belief.[7] However, unlike the orthodox Trinity, aeons, again spiritual extensions of the one God, extend beyond the triune Godhead.

Often, as in the Valentinian myth, the Invisible Spirit is also called the Divine Parent or Father/Mother. It is a bit confusing, but in this Divine Parent configuration, the Father is the Invisible Spirit, the Mother is named Barbelo, and the Son is known as the Autogenes, which meant "the self generated one."[8] The Son is sometimes equated with the earthly Christ, but he is believed at this stage to be a higher reality or force, and particularly, known as the *light*.[9]

Many aeons proceed from the Divine Parent in the Sethian's version of the Trinity. These extensions are complex and include four basic "luminaries" who are assisted by at least sixteen attendants.[10] Most importantly, one of the aeons who comes into existence is the divine Christ, not yet the Jesus Christ of earth, but a preexisting and eternal being called the Invincible Power![11]

In the myth, there are additional cycles of emanations from the supreme God, and in one of these, lo and behold, who comes forth but the enigmatic Sophia. As in the Valentinian myth, she figures in the creation of our world. As an aeon, some versions have her as the female consort of the divine Christ, but even though paired with Christ, she makes a mistake and falls from her godliness.[12] Her fall is much more dramatic than in the Valentinian version. Again, a notable part of this Sethian version is, after her fall, she does repent of her error, much like the Word repented in the Valentinian mythology. In the Sethian version, the fullness of the divine realm or the Divine Parent directly hears her repentance and prayer, forgives her, and offers her praise once again.[13]

The story of Sophia's fall is explained best in the Sethian text named *The Apocryphon of John*, also translated as *The Secret Book of John*.[14] It reports, "Now Sophia, who is the wisdom of insight and who constitutes an eternal realm...she wanted to bring forth something like herself, without her partner and his consideration. The male did not give approval. Nonetheless, she gave birth. Something came out of her that was imperfect and different in appearance from her."[15]

Her story here is similar to the Valentinians' Sophia in that she tries to self create without the assistance of other aeons, disrupting the balance and harmony of the plemora.[16] However, in this account she literally "aborts," and the result is an incomplete god or Demiurge, which the Sethians give the name Yaldabaoth, meaning "child of chaos."[17] Yaldabaoth, whom some scholars translate as Ialtabaoth, is also called Sakla, meaning "fool," and sometimes called Samuel, meaning "blind."[18] This chaotic, foolish, and blind god is the craftsman or creator of the material world.[19]

Because of the supposed creation by this child of chaos, many assume that the material world for the Gnostics was all evil, but in the Sethian story, the main problem was that it was "flawed." It was incomplete and chaotic. In Sethian texts, the word "deficiency," which is also sometimes translated as "lacking," is often used to describe the material world's creation.[20] The problem with this world is that there is a deficiency within, and something is lacking to make it full or whole.

The Sethians are hard on the evilness in the world, and on its creator, or the Demiurge, because his work is flawed and incomplete.[21] Evil abounds. Nevertheless, to say that all material is evil overlooks that within humans, there is some part of them that allows them to know and experience God. This gift comes in a complex path from Christ and Sophia. Beyond this gift, the message is that the awful evil that exists in the world needs to be opposed and overcome through self examination, insight, and wisdom.[22] Life without our awakening to the spiritual world and its fullness is a choice, and without it, results in one being lacking in life, or not being whole in one's living. Although there is much darkness and evil on earth, the Sethians preached that "hope" can overcome the world's deficiency.[23] This theme of deficiency in one's life may appear to be sensible and intriguing. At this juncture, however, Sethian mythology becomes quite complex, especially, when they explain how hope came into the world.

Hope becomes possible because there was an aeon named Adamas who enters the story of mankind's creation. In the *Gospel of the Egyptians*, also known as *The Holy Book of the Great Invisible Spirit*, it says that Adamas "came down from above for the annulment of the deficiency."[24] Adamas, not be confused with the earthly Adam, is an emanation from the divine Christ. Here things get a bit dicey. Adamas, an aeon, is like a perfect or incorruptible human, and he makes a request for a child who "may be the father of the immoveable generation."[25] This earthly son is called Seth, sometimes the Great Seth, and just to add to the puzzle, this earthly Seth is also sometimes presented as equal to the divine Seth of the plemora.[26]

The earthly Seth can trace his ancestry to his father Adamas, who importantly in the story came forth from Christ. Seth becomes the father and savior for those who would become the incorruptible race, and who would be God's blessed ones.[27] Although the story is incomplete, which challenges a clear understanding of this mythology, the tale of Adamas develops further. As Adamas was the father of the earthly Seth — he was the good seed.[28] Adamas was not the father of Cain — the bad seed.[29] So who was the father of Cain–the bad seed? Well, it is no other than the Demiurge or the one named, Yaldabaoth, or also the foolish Sakla, or the blind Samuel, or whatever the name, the source of evil.[30]

Of course, this is getting more complicated, so no wonder the short stories told in Genesis, are better appreciated as simply a straight forward description of what literally happened. To this point it would appear that Adam and Eve were bypassed in the story of the creation of humans. Not so.The Sethians have a different twist on their story, and it returns us to the blessed Sophia and the evil Yaldabaoth.

The reason Adamas, and then Seth, his earthly son, are sent to the world is because someone in the heavenly fullness heard the blind god, Yaladaoth, the Demiurge, make the claim, "I am God and there is no other besides me."[31] Well, the reason Yaldabaoth would make such a claim was that he was ignorant, and being ignorant, this made him, arrogant! His blindness in believing that he was the only god is unacceptable to the plemora, so a voice from above speaks. Shocked by this voice, Yaldabaoth along with those called "archons," a term meaning evil, angelic rulers, who now control the created world, look up to see whose voice this could be.[32] They all see a reflection on water beneath Yaldabaoth, and he responds, "Come, let us create a human after the image of God and after our likeness."[33] Giving in a bit to goodness, in the same passage, the Demiurge says "that his image may become a light for us."[34] The result is that Yaldabaoth and this voice from above create the physical, human body,

Adam.[35] Adam, being created by both good and bad forces, inherits both qualities. With enumerated detail to his many specific bodily parts, which are assembled by a throng of angels, Adam lies on the ground, unable to stand or move.[36] Different spirits, altogether, 365 of them, create, separately, everything from the spleen to his toe nails, and in this writing there is an amazing list of all the body parts directly created by these different celestial beings![37] Indeed, for them, creation was direct, not evolutionary! In spite of this careful creation, something was still missing.

Therefore, those from on high urged Yaldabaoth to breathe some of his spirit into Adam.[38] So this foolish Demiurge does and what happens is astonishing! The breath that he sends into Adam's limp body is the feminine divine Spirit that he possessed from his mother, Sophia.[39] Adam arises, moves, and breathes, and from that time of awakening, all the descendants of Adam will be blessed and have the capacity to know God because of the divine spirit that has come to them, thanks to Sophia.[40]

There is still something lacking so here comes Eve![41] The story is similar to the details told in Genesis, Chapter Two, but there are definitely innovations!

Because Yaldabaoth is jealous of Adam's powers and fullness, he pulls the feminine aspect out from Adam and creates a woman who is Eve.[42] In Greek, her name is Zoe, which means life.[43] Adam and Eve are happy together in spite of Yaldabaoth's action because they both now have the gift of life. Adam recognizes her as his feminine counterpart, and the two of them live in perfect wholeness.[44] Now comes the snake, who speaks to Adam and Eve, bringing them great wisdom, and as might be expected, this serpent's story is different!

The serpent, instead of being a tempter to Eve, is a teacher who instructs both Adam and Eve to resist the Demiurge's (Yaldabaoth's) continuing jealousy.[45] The snake is described as "wiser than all the animals that were in Paradise."[46] We have heard that before, but this time the snake is a positive creature because the "female spirited principle" has come into the snake.[47] As in the traditional story the serpent teaches that they would not die if they ate from the special tree in the middle of Paradise.[48] This wise female snake, a description that continues a long history of being a positive feminine force in mythology, says that when Adam and Eve eat from the tree, "the eyes of your mind will be opened."[49] Eve takes the bold step and gives the fruit of the tree to her husband, a positive gift! As Elaine

Pagels says, in her book *Adam, Eve and The Serpent*, "gnostics often depicted Eve — or the feminine spiritual power she represented — as the source of spiritual awakening."[50]

The Demiurge is furious that Adam and Eve ate from this tree and were able to have minds like the gods, and now possess knowledge that allows them to recognize good and evil.[51] The Demiurge kicks them out of the Garden of Eden.[52] Some things never change!

The monstrous nature of the evil Demiurge gets worse! Yaldabaoth rapes Eve![53] Yes, a bit bold, and it turns out that Eve has two children from the rape. These children are Cain and Abel.[54] If that isn't enough, the teaching states that this is where sexual intercourse originated, in other words, it did not have a pleasant beginning.[55] Oh my! Now, the story turns again to Seth and how the good seed finds its rest in him.

A gap in the story, which may be due to incomplete texts, occurs with the gift of the good seed. Here, the higher divine Sophia embeds the spiritual seed into Seth.[56] First, at the time of her repentance, her spiritual seed is passed on to the divine Seth.[57] Then, somehow this seed flows in the plemora from the divine Seth to the divine Adamas, the father of the earthly Seth.[58] The earthly Seth is a gift from Adamas to Adam and Eve, and their third son is an extremely special child. He is special because he is the embodiment of the divine aeon, Seth.[59] So they name this human child after his "godfather" — to use a pun. Seth, the earthly one, becomes the beholder of the spiritual seed that is passed on through his descendants, especially to the heroes and prophets of the Old Testament.[60] This answers the question about how those who came before Jesus attainted salvation. For those saved, Seth possessed the source of redemption. Seth had spiritual knowledge, and those of his seed were worthy of eternal, incorruptible life and calling.[61]

Finally, the story comes to its basic finale; now comes the explanation of Jesus. Sethians believed Jesus was the incarnation of Seth, both of the divine and earthly Seth.[62] That ought to turn some heads! In the majority of the versions, more than the human Seth, the spiritual dimension of Seth creates a seed of spirituality that particularly came forth in persons like Noah, Moses, David, and most powerfully, in Jesus.[63] Jesus is the fulfillment of the Old Testament. In a new twist on the lineage of Jesus, he becomes the representative of Seth, and in so doing, Jesus becomes the

Savior.[64] Jesus is more important than Seth because Jesus the Christ is now the Savior for the world, but his spiritual history traces back to Seth.

With this basic sketch of the Sethians' mythology, an understanding of what some believe was a unique ritual of theirs may be better understood. Sethians may have accepted some of the rituals of the Valentinians, but there is no direct evidence. Whatever the case, the Sethians may have had an unnamed ritual which was more pertinent to them. It has been described as something like "Ascent and Descent."[65] In essence, it would teach that the Savior's descent to this world calls for seekers' ascent also to the divine world.[66] Unlike the Saviors' ascent, the seekers' ascent is not direct and final. For the seeker, it is a process of both ascent and descent, which are both spiritual journeys.

As with the mystics and Buddhists, oneness with God is achievable, but for these Gnostics, the ascent is never complete. Enlightenment for the ascent does come through prayer and praise, so there are hymns and prayers, such as the beautiful book in the Nag Hammadi collection, *The Thunder: Perfect Mind.*[67] It elevates the feminine divine power but also exhibits what is called negative theology. Negative theology?[68] It is not as bad as it sounds.

For example, it would say God is good, but the negative is that the goodness of God cannot be attained, and that expresses the negative aspect. Dr. Valantasis explains the concept in his book, *Gnosticism*, that "God is good, and then negating it – that God far surpasses every known good."[69] In other words, God can be known, but God surpasses that which can be known. One can experience the Invisible Spirit, but the negative is that knowing and experiencing God is limited.

Beyond realizing that the negative is that God cannot be totally known, the emphasis in this ritual is one's spiritual ascending and descending. A book in the Nag Hammadi collection explains it well and is named the *Three Steles of Seth.* This book contains seven hymns of praise and it says, "For together and alone they sing praises, and they become silent. And just as they were ordered, they ascend. After they become silent, they descend...."[70] So although there is no specific named ritual in their writings, their teachings encourage a mystic ascent to the plemora using hymns and prayers. Then, a descent that calls for another or new ascent – a fascinating visualization! As Dr. Valantasis writes, "Sethian prayers and hymns expressed both the mystery of negative theology and the wonder of ascent."[71]

The Valentinian and Sethian mythologies are different stories, but they have several similarities, with intertwining words and themes. Most would describe both as wild, strange, and bizarre. However, although there is no evidence to support their stories, they make some points that must be considered as feasible, helpful, or positive. Some of these are the elevation of the divine feminine; creation was not all bad or all good; God is greater than what we think; and there is a promise of hope for those who will awaken to the spirit of God that can be found within. Today, such interesting themes may be far more questions or issues in the spiritual quest than their myths being alternative stories, which belong to spiritual battles.

Most likely, both the Valentinians and the Sethians thought their myths were right and true. However, with their eccentric stories, who today could think they were the pure holders of truth? Could not the same be said for the early Christians who thought only they were right and preached that everyone else was wrong. As stated before, the beliefs and myths of these Gnostics should not be taken as either/or to theological literalism, or as simply alternatives to what is widely now accepted as Christian orthodoxy. The argument of this book is that these gnostic myths were a part of the search in the struggle to be honest to God. Do these gnostic beliefs and myths hold the answer to the way it was, and what is true? Only the invisible, unknowable God might know these mysteries, because, for the Gnostics, religious answers are bound by human nature and limited knowledge; that is why today we are seekers.

Along with the Gnostics, we are part of the ongoing search to understand not only this world and the God or gods that many cultures, societies, and individuals have sensed and believed to exist. Of course, there are those individuals and a few societies that have claimed that no God or spiritual world exists. The Valentinians would call this lack of insight into the existence of the divine world as "ignorance;" the Sethians would call it a lack or "deficiency of knowledge."[72] Perhaps, could they be saying the same thing? Whether it is deficiency of knowledge or ignorance, their myths raise another question about our world today. Obviously, their myths don't make much sense, but the theme of knowledge is relevant for our times. A new realization arising in our culture is that there is a lot we don't know about our world, ourselves, and God.

With the many advancements in knowledge by science, there is a growing confidence in what we know. Indeed we are learning a lot more. In spite of that reality, science today is revealing that even what we think we know or believe may be partial or incomplete. A prime example of partial knowledge comes with the new discoveries in astronomy. One hundred years ago, the common knowledge was that our galaxy was the only one; today, we have the knowledge that there are billions in the universe. In essence, we thought, what we knew and believed, was all but certain.

This same attitude of certainty for religions has been around even before the rise of science, and certainly, that was the case in early Christianity. The Gnostics were charged as those who knew all truth because of their myths. Those who charged that the Gnostics knew it all also boldly stated because of their beliefs and authority, instead, they knew all truth. This claim of certainty did not stop there, as obviously, wars and conflicts have been fought by those who thought they knew it all. Of course, this attitude of certainty will not vanish, but slowly, some are beginning to realize that certainty may not be the true way of faith. Because of this realization, the discovery of the Gnostic Gospels could not come at a more appropriate time in history. Science is changing, and perhaps, Christianity can begin the process, as well. The Gnostic Gospels open that door by raising the question, is faith more about seeking than knowing?

Notes: Chapter Eighteen: The Sethian Mythology

[1] Richard Valantasis, *Gnosticism and Other Vanished Christianities*, (New York: Doubleday, 2006), 36.

[2] Michael Allen Williams, *Rethinking Gnosticism*, (Princeton, H.J., Princeton University Press, 1996), 90.

[3] Genesis 4: 1-25 5:3-8. Luke 3: 38.

[4] J. Michael Matkin, *The Gnostic Gospels*, (New York: Alpha Books, 2005), 102.

[5] Elaine Pagels, *Beyond Belief*, (New York: Random House, 2003), 127.

[6] Matkin, *The Gnostic Gospels*, 103.

[7] Richard Smoley, *Forbidden Faith: The Secret History of Gnosticism*, (San Francisco, HarperSanFrancisco, 2006), 24.

[8] Richard Valantasis, *Gnosticism and Other Vanished Christianities*, 38.

[9] Valantasis, *Gnosticism and Other Vanished Christianities*, 39

[10] Matkin, *The Gnostic Gospels*, 107.

[11] Matkin, *The Gnostic Gospels*, 104.

[12] Matkin, *The Gnostic Gospels*, 180.

---

[13] Matkin, *The Gnostic Gospels*, 181.
[14] James Robinson, Editor, *The Nag Hammadi Library in English*, hereafter noted as *NHL*, (San Francisco, HarperSanFrancisco, 1978), *The Aprocryphon of John*, 104.
[15] Robinson, *NHL, The Aprocryphon of John*, 110
[16] Robinson, *NHL, The Tripartite Tractate*, 181.
[17] Matkin, *The Gnostic Gospels*, 108.
[18] Valantasis, *Gnosticism and Other Vanished Christianities*, 40.
[19] Matkin, *The Gnostic Gospels*, 181.
[20] Karen King, *What is Gnosticism ?*, (Cambridge, Ma.,: Harvard University Press, 2003), 160. Karen uses Yaldabaoth for the Demurige.
[21] King, *What is Gnosticism?*, 159.
[22] Meera Lester, *The Everything Gnostic Gospels Book*, (Avon, Ma., Adams Media, 2007), 82.
[23] Lester, *The Everything Gnostic Gospels Book*, 85.
[24] Robinson, *NHL*, the *Gospel of the Egyptians*, 212.
[25] Ibid.
[26] Robinson, *NHL*, the *Gospel of the Egyptians*, 214.
[27] Matkin, *The Gnostic Gospels*, 107.
[28] Matkin, *The Gnostic Gospels*, 184.
[29] Ibid.
[30] Jean Doresse, *The Secret Books of the Egyptian Gnostics*, (New York: MJF Books, 1986), 162.
[31] Doresse, *The Secret Books of the Egyptian Gnostics*, 163.
[32] Matkin, *The Gnostic Gospels*, 14.
[33] Williams, *Rethinking Gnosticism*, 11.
[34] Robinson, *NHL*, *The Aprocryphon of John*, 113
[35] Ibid.
[36] Matkin, *The Gnostic Gospels*, 182
[37] Ibid.
[38] Ibid.
[39] Ibid.
[40] Williams, *Rethinking Gnosticism*, 12.
[41] Matkin, *The Gnostic Gospels*, 183.
[42] Ibid.
[43] Ibid.
[44] Ibid.
[45] Pagels, *The Gnostic Gospels*, 35.
[46] Robinson, *NHL*, *The Hypostasis of the Archons*, Verse 15, 154.
[47] Robinson, *NHL*, *The Hypostasis of the Archons*, Verse 15, 154.
[48] Ibid.
[49] Pagels, *Adam, Eve, and The Serpent*, 68.
[50] Pagels, *Adam, Eve, and The Serpent*, 69.

[51] Matkin, *The Gnostic Gospels*, 183.
[52] Matkin, *The Gnostic Gospels*, 184.
[53] Ibid.
[54] Ibid.
[55] Williams, *Rethinking Gnosticism*, 12.
[56] Williams, *Rethinking Gnosticism*, 10.
[57] Ibid.
[58] Lester, *The Everything Gnostic Gospels Book*, 184.
[59] Valantasis, *Gnosticism and Other Vanished Christianities*, 41.
[60] Matkin, *The Gnostic Gospels*, 184.
[61] Lester, *The Everything Gnostic Gospels Book*, 188.
[62] Valantasis, *Gnosticism and Other Vanished Christianities*, 41.
[63] Lester, *The Everything Gnostic Gospels Book*, 188.
[64] Ibid.
[65] Valantasis, *Gnosticism and Other Vanished Christianities*, 41.
[66] Ibid.
[67] Robinson, *NHL*, *The Thunder, Perfect Mind*, 295.
[68] Pagels, *Beyond Belief*, 163.
[69] Valantasis, *Gnosticism and Other Vanished Christianities*, 42.
[70] Robinson, *NHL*, *The Three Steles of Seth*, Verse 127, 401.
[71] Valantasis, *Gnosticism and Other Vanished Christianities*, 42.
[72] King, *What is Gnosticism?*, 159.

Chapter Nineteen

The Gnostics' Gift — Fresh Air for Christianity

> America is currently awash in an unpleasant surplus of clanging, clashing certitudes. This is why there is a rhetorical bitterness absurdly disproportionate to our real differences. It has been well said that the spirit of liberty is the spirit of not being too sure that you are right. One way to immunize ourselves against misplaced certitude is to contemplate — even to savor — the unfathomable strangeness of everything, including ourselves. [1]
>
> -George F. Will, *The Oddness of Everything*

Elaine Pagels is the mother of the new interest in the Gnostic Gospels. In gnostic terms, she might better be known as the mother/father of these gospels because their new birth and rise in popularity has opened a window that can continue Christian reform and bring fresh air to today's Christian world. Dr. Pagels, a humble, but brilliant scholar, would be the first to say this isn't about her, but a stirring of those who want Christianity to take a step forward in spiritual understanding and maturity. The Gnostic Gospels present an opportunity for Christianity to move beyond the bottlenecks of history and affirm that Christian faith is not a battle for doctrines, or the superiority of certain churches, but as taught and proclaimed by Jesus, a trust in a loving and spiritual God.

A certain scholar in one of his books reminded both scientists and Christians that Soren Kierkegaard, the Danish Christian philosopher and theologian, once made the statement that the irony of life is that it is lived forward, but understood backward.[2] Certainly, that is the way most Christians have believed in Christianity. Christianity has been about believing in the Jesus of the past, affirming the various events of his life, idolizing persons in the Bible, making its written words holy and eternal, and believing unchangeable doctrines that were established by past theologians as truths for all times. The task for Christians has been to trust the truth of these beliefs from the past, and then live forward with the conviction that they will bring peace, salvation, and eternal life.

The Gnostic Gospels turn this way of belief upside down. The emphasis on faith is on the present and the future, not the past. In these gospels, the task of faith is to trust the presence of Christ and God. In no way does this mean the past is irrelevant and without merit. Yes, there was a historical Jesus, and his story is remarkable and true. More essential, however, than believing all the details of Jesus' life is the task of embracing in one's present life, the living Christ.

These gospels affirm the belief that this incredible man, Jesus, was resurrected as the Christ. More importantly than debating resurrection's possibility, for those who believe, its call is to experience new life and hope, now, for one's spiritual present and future. Christ's life on earth brought a message of God's love, understanding, and acceptance of us, yet, we needed to do our part by awakening to the spirit within us, loving others, and God. God understood our sin, or as Jesus expresses it in the *Gospel of Thomas*, our poverty, or the lack of accepting his spirit for living our lives. Faith, then, is not about having all the answers but living with the trust of God's spirit, both within and without, to make us whole. The task of faith is to seek and develop that spirit as Jesus did and to become Christ-like on earth. As many evangelical Christians understand today, faith is an experience, and knowing is a relationship, not knowledge of unchangeable facts and doctrines. So it is that they might understand more deeply and appreciate the opening verse of the *Gospel of Truth*, which again says, "The gospel of truth is a joy for those who have received from the Father of truth the grace of knowing him."[3] However, for many Christians the greater focus than one's relationship with Christ and others has been a crusade to get others to believe as they do — as if there was no other way. With emotional certainty, their mission is to make their particular church's doctrines and beliefs the exclusive and superior message of Christianity. In spite of their passion, the problem arises that there are too many competing church groups that insist that their own experiences are the only true way to be Christian, and their beliefs are the basic and fundamental truths of Christianity. More precisely, as Karen Armstrong states in her book *The Battle for God*, the problem is that for those in the know, "Each fundamentalism is a law unto itself and has its own dynamic."[4] A kind of absolute certainty takes form within particular groups, and because of their convictions, the religious calling is to convert others to be as they are — right with God. Obviously, the early apostolic church has not been the only church that insisted its ways and beliefs were directly from God, but clearly, they were one of the earliest to promote certainty as the way to be a Christian. Many have followed in various forms of fundamentalism, and today, an overlooked influence that has reinforced the belief that one can possess absolute truth, even in one's religious beliefs, is arguably the field of science.

Although science is often viewed as a detriment to religion, it has given some forms of Christianity encouragement to be certain. For years, unintentionally, the discipline of science has added fuel to the fire that certainty can be attained. Science has described reality as being hard, cold facts that can be proven as true or false. On the surface, this ability to decipher truth from fiction has challenged religious thinking, and for some, its relevance. Particularly, this is true when one considers the corrections science has made to Christian beliefs since the Age of Reason or the period of history known as the Enlightenment. A number of beliefs, which the church had insisted upon as Biblical and worldly truth, have been proven by science as false. In doing this, science has established its own certainties.

For example, there is no question that the earth revolves around the sun, in spite of the church's insistence in the 1600s that the earth was immoveable — based on Biblical texts.[5] Mountains of evidence exist that the earth is older than the six thousand (or so) years that some deduce for its age from the Bible.[6] Clearly, science refutes the beliefs of those who still believe this short time frame is the age of the earth. Nevertheless, many desire to believe science is wrong, and their interpretation of Genesis is all that matters. The fairly new fact that our planet is a part of a solar system and that the sun is only one of four hundred billion stars in the Milky Way has few defectors. Even the Roman Catholic Church has its own magnificent telescopes and astronomers affirming these observations.[7] Visible and detectable evidence also confirm as many as 140 billion galaxies are still expanding along with ours in the universe.[8] The world is no longer a three story universe of hell below, earth in the middle, and heaven above. Indeed, old religious conceptions of the world have faced new challenges with new scientific information. These astronomical facts only scratch the surface of scientific challenges to past Christian beliefs including issues of creation, evolution, and more recently, the role of genetics in life decisions.

One might think many new, nearly undisputable, facts would cripple Christian beliefs. For some Christians, however, in spite of the challenges of modern science, their belief is that Christian doctrines still have the greater truth. The irony is that the success of scientific truth, which they don't totally reject, strengthens their resolve that certainty can be established. Inspired by science, and using the Bible as their authority for pure religious truth, some Christians have made their interpretations of Christianity to be like the scientific facts of life. If there are immutable laws in the objective world, there must be the same in the subjective and spiritual realms, and fundamentalists have been more than willing to explain these laws and facts. One such organization, for example, in their primary pamphlet, has narrowed down the Bible to four spirituals laws.[9] These laws present God's plan and doctrines, which if accepted, guarantee salvation and eternal life. Even others who call themselves Christians need to be converted as these laws are truth, and the experience of being 'born again' is the only way to find and know God. For those, like this group, who believe that Christ preached and taught a very hard and narrow way to believe, their voice will always be present because their pride, as the apostolic church, rests in the certainty of knowing the truths of Jesus and God.

For those who believe Christ taught more than a narrow way, and believe that science can provide corrections and insights even to Christian truth, the Gnostic Gospels bring relief and support. Many Christians, and perhaps the majority, object that Christianity is about accepting fundamental, literal doctrines, and hard clad, immutable truths. Without belittling the Bible, they believe and have experienced a closeness and relationship to God without believing every word in it as literal, or as some say, the gospel truth. Gospel truth is revealed in the Bible, and beyond literal truth, there is spiritual truth that can be realized and experienced metaphorically, analogically, symbolically, and personably.

The Bible is more than a cookbook or a scientific textbook but is a beautiful expression of faith of those who believed in God, his creation of the world, and his reality. The New Testament of the Bible is a witness of those who experienced this God through the messages and life of Jesus. Jesus taught there is a spiritual world, but he left its details of its design to his followers, who had differing opinions, but all had faith and belief in him. He did not put his teachings in writing, but allowed his disciples to tell and share his messages in various ways to those who were Jewish, as he, but also to those who were not. Although accounts varied, and often conflicted, he trusted that the basic message of God's love and reality could be known. Christ's actions were more than words, and the words he spoke and the messages he gave were not limited to singular interpretations. Therefore, being a Christian does not require one to believe everything in the Bible or totally agree with what one's church teaches. In agreement with the Gnostics on these perspectives, a primary message becomes that faith supersedes beliefs and is not limited or bound by them. Faith is more than any fundamentalism, and for the Christian, seeking is a process of trust with openness to what is true for both the material and spiritual world. Because there is not a need for certainty, faith is freed to bring forth an emotion of joy and a continual awakening to the spirit of God.

However, as Jesus' call to faith moved from Christ to Christianity, this higher meaning of truth was reduced to spiritual truth being either/or, and to the necessity of believing certain doctrines. Christ, himself, did not center his teaching on beliefs such as the virgin birth, but as the early apostolic church grew in power, the demand that all Christians believe as they did, became by its victory, the true way to understand Christ and his messages. Something radical happened; Christianity became a religion of beliefs. These beliefs were to become the fundamental truths of Christianity.

Now, something else radical is upon us because of the Gnostic Gospels. With the insight that Christian faith was bound and restricted by one narrow interpretation that became a fundamentalism unto itself, the Gnostic Gospels revive a higher vision and truth for Christ. These gospels encourage faith to become a dynamic process of seeking, and they help Christianity to move beyond being a fundamentalism of unchangeable positions and beliefs.

A prominent scientist has made the case against fundamentalism, whether it was in science or religion. He wrote,

> The characteristic of all fundamentalism is that it has found absolute certainty — the certainty of class warfare, the certainty of science, or the literal certainty of the Bible — a certainty of the person who has finally found a solid rock to stand upon which, unlike other rocks, is solid all the way down. Fundamentalism, however, is a terminal form of human consciousness in which development is stopped, eliminating the uncertainty and risk that real growth entails.[10]

The scientist who wrote these words was Heinz R. Pagels, the husband of Elaine. Heinz wrote three highly popular science books before his death in a climbing accident near Aspen, Colorado in 1988. His first book *The Cosmic Code*, published in 1982, was dedicated to his parents who opened the door of science to him.[11] His second book *Perfect Symmetry*, published in 1985, was inscribed with dedicatory words, "For Elaine," his high school sweetheart whom he had married in 1969.[12] Two tragedies, deeper than any words can express or logic can explain, were to happen to the Pagels' family. Their son Mark, born in 1981, died of a pulmonary hypertension disease at age six. Heinz's last book *Dreams of Reason: The Rise of the Science of Complexity* was published in 1988. The inscription of dedication reads, "In memory of our son Mark. His home is the universe."[13] Within fifteen months of Mark's death, Elaine, as she has expressed it, also was to lose the first love of her life, Heinz. One would think that could be the end of her religious quest, but instead her remarkable faith was focused forward, not just in academic terms but in the experience of living through pain and uncertainty.

Elaine had become famous through her book *The Gnostic Gospels* published in 1979. The book was a shock to many of us who were Christians because of the exposure of new gospels that could be read and studied. Their contents provide some excitement because the new messages and teachings of Jesus encouraged the theology that Christianity was more than a battle for beliefs and that some in the early church had rejected doctrines which didn't make sense today. Then, Elaine's book *Beyond Belief: The Secret Gospel of Thomas*, published in 2003, was powerful as she further explained how these new gospels could refresh and excite faith and Christianity.

Both of these books build on the wisdom of her husband's comments about Soren Kierkegaard. His was the reminder from Kierkegaard, mentioned earlier, that the irony of life was that it was lived forward, but understood backward. Kierkegaard became famous partly because of his statement that Christianity was a "leap of faith." Certainly, a leap of a faith is forward thinking and the Gnostic Gospels support that vision. Faith doesn't yield us from the uncertainties and trials of life, but faith as seeking brings peace at the present and hope for the future because of one's trust and relationship to the living Christ.

The fact that there are no certainties in life has been known for a long time. Although faith has often taken the form of certainty in some religious circles, faith may be able to recapture its deeper and more dynamic meaning because of the Gnostic Gospels. In support of the attitude that faith is more about seeking than battling over answers, once again, surprisingly, is the field of science. A serious shift has occurred in the discipline of science. Whereas many believed that science could provide the answers as to what was real and true in the world, many of the new discoveries have opened more mysteries and unanswerable questions than ever imagined.

Certainly, science of the Nineteenth and Twentieth Centuries brought many new truths to the design, laws, and reality of the world. Along with wonderful inventions, making life more comfortable and manageable, an attitude was also building that science could unlock the mysteries of the world. This optimism was clearly embraced near the beginning of the twenty century by Lord Kelvin, the British physicist, who invented the absolute temperature scale named after him. Science was making incredible advances in the nineteenth century, and so confident in its ability to discover nature's laws and truth, Kelvin made the inference in one of his speeches that science was on the edge of discovering everything about the world that could possibly be known.[14]

Of course, Lord Kelvin had never heard of Albert Einstein or Niels Bohr! With their radical, new perception and insight, understanding the world became much more complex. With Einstein's imagination and theories, the whole cosmic geography of space and time was understood differently. Bohr led the way for the verification of the minuscule world of the atom and quantum physics. Both have blown the lid off of certainty!

Once again, the world, in part due to these scientific minds, is a vast, mysterious abode and not simply understood. Indeed, there are many new solid truths. Modern science has given proof that atoms and other galaxies exist, and many of their details have been verified beyond question by nuclear bombs, computers, and travel in air and space. These discoveries, which have also brought practical and helpful gifts, have opened a new window on the world that makes clear that our knowledge is incomplete. In essence, there is a new story of science that says our search for understanding has only begun.

Much of the world is becoming comprehensible; indeed, there are some answers, but as Einstein suggested, it is "its incomprehensibility that leaves us in awe."[15] Ironically, he also wrote, about our ability to understand the world, that "the eternal mystery is its comprehensibility."[16] Then he adds, "The fact that it is comprehensible is a miracle."[17] Comprehensibility and incomprehensibility, together, is the new model for science, and even that which we can know, which Einstein calls a "miracle," is open to question and change in our understanding of the world.

The world is being better understood, but some of the new knowledge, such as the complexity of the atomic world and the vastness of the cosmos, raises radical, new questions, not only of our survival, but also why such a large and intricate universe even exists? Great advances for civilizations have been made on earth, and understandings of the world have advanced, but a subtle change of attitude is being realized. The change is from a sense of certitude, in part created by science, to a need, enhanced by the new science, to recognize that the world is a fragile, changing home with many uncertainties. Even our personal worlds are being affected.

George F. Will, a conservative columnist, in 2005 at the University of Miami, in a graduation speech titled "The Oddness of Everything" said to the students, "The more they appreciate the complexity and improbability of everyday things — including themselves — the more they can understand the role of accidents, contingencies, and luck have played in bringing the human story to its current chapter." He then makes the remark, "This is so because the greatest threat to civility — and ultimately to civilization — is an excess of certitude."[18]

Of course, the attitude of certainty doesn't apply to all, but, currently, who doesn't' know someone who believes their opinions are the facts. For many, certitude seems to reign, and the sign of confidence is that one knows the truth. Beyond this attitude that George Will seemed to be addressing, something new is happening in science that also might affect personal and even religious attitudes. One of the new dimensions of science is the realization: the more we know, the less we know — or understand.

A major example of this was the discovery, separately, by astronomers Brian Schmidt, and Saul Perlmutter, in 1988, of what is called dark energy.[19] Taken by surprise, their research gave evidence that the universe's expansion of space was accelerating at an incomprehensible rate.[20] Within this expansion, they inferred from their data that everything we observe from people, stars, galaxies, or more precisely, all things known as being material, comprise only 4.6 percent of our universe.[21] By studying supernovas, they calculated that an additional part of our universe is roughly 23 percent dark matter, objects that can be detected only by instruments and not visible with telescopes.[22] Shockingly, 72 percent of the universe is dark energy, or a force that is measurable, but unknown as to its essence, content, or source. Whatever it is, it is an energy that is constantly expanding our universe.[23]

The problem with such information, as reported by Astronomy Magazine's associate editor, Liz Kruesi is that, "In this increasingly accelerated expansion, dark energy would rip the Local Group, rip the Earth from the Sun, and ultimately rip even atoms apart." She concludes, "The big rip would not be before (about) 55 billion years in the future, if at all."[24] Whew! Yes, many details of reality are being discovered, but along with them, are as many questions as answers. No one understands the composition of dark energy, so the rush is on in the midst of mind boggling uncertainty to discover what this force is.[25] Mystery once again trumps complete understanding, and although there may one day be an answer, Lord Kelvin's certainty that everything could be explained by scientific information is now challenged exponentially. The message seems to be without seeking, knowledge and truth would be frozen, and so it is with the search for things eternal.

Therefore, the principal message that the Gnostics heard Jesus preaching might be similar to a lesson found in the Book of Proverbs, in the Old Testament, that teaches, "With all your wisdom, seek understanding."[26] The power of the Gnostic Gospels is that they witness that to be a Christian means to seek understanding rather than to have all of the answers. Indeed, many of the gnostic beliefs and myths, previously assumed to be their declarative truths, were strange and different, but never did they close their books and say, "this was it." Therefore, if one can get beyond their bizarre myths, their style of faith has much to inspire and offer Christians today who now do their own seeking with vast new amounts of information and truths.

Because of increased uncertainty, and the complexity not only of science, but of the challenge of living with new fears and threats in today's world, some may turn to forms of faith that appear to give a sense of security. As confusion abounds, isn't an increase in that style of faith predictable? However, for those who want their faith to be honest as possible, open to change, and, yet at the same time, led by a trust in a God, the Gnostics offer inspiration that faith can be a dynamic trust without the need of certainty.

Therefore, what follows is a basic review of much that has been presented in this book. In doing so, one can begin to grasp why these Gnostic Gospels can transform "what we know as Christianity," as stated by Elaine Pagels in the opening quotation of this book. This transformation is not radical as it relates well to the basic teachings of Christianity. Part of its excitement is because these gospels encourage the spirit of Christ to be revived in a Christianity that has focused on doctrines and differing church proclamations of truths rather on inner and spiritual experiences.

In today's world, many are ignoring the dictates from churches, which proclaim theological and moral absolutes, as if persons can't decide or think for themselves. Many doctrines just don't make sense, and there does not seem to be the freedom to say so. Others are understanding that when the pastor declares, "the Bible says," their word of the Lord can represent various, conflicting, and differing viewpoints, according to the preacher's prejudice. In other words, what was called Christian authority isn't as strong as in the past, and although many still respect different ecclesiastical traditions, the claims to certainty are being questioned. The Gnostic Gospels transform Christian faith precisely because they encourage questioning; they move the goal from being certain to a dynamic trust in a living Jesus and God.

Having faith without certainty does not mean that one gives up all beliefs, but the emphasis is on using one's intelligence, mind, and new knowledge, rather than blindly believing what you are told. Even when one has beliefs, an attitude of seeking and openness to change is greater than the conviction that "I have the truth and you don't." The concept of seeking implies that one is open to all kinds of knowledge, and faith requires one to use their mind in relating to others and God. Particularly, in the gnostic gospels of Mary and Thomas, using one's mind is critical in growing faith.

An example in The *Gospel of Mary* is when Mary Magdalene asked Jesus whether one's vision should come through the soul or the spirit. Jesus answered that it is through "the mind which is between the two."[27] Having faith didn't mean there were no answers to be had, but that the nature of faith is to be open to new ways of thinking and understanding. Why? These gospels teach using one's mind is an essential part of faith; it allows one to grow in faith. Of course, most everyone could say, of course, we use our minds, but, for the Gnostics that meant being open to change.

This concept of using one's mind to seek God is also more than apparent in interpreting the new sayings of Jesus found in the *Gospel of Thomas*. These sayings are not easy platitudes. Only those who are like Yaldabaoth, the blind god — a know it all — discussed earlier, who claimed pure and exclusive divine knowledge, could find a simple meaning to Jesus' words recorded in Thomas' gospel.[28] To understand the messages within these verses requires one to think.[29] Thomas' gospel is different from those in the Bible and certainly challenges those who sometimes like to say, "Jesus said it; just believe it!" The *Gospel of Thomas* moves beyond such simplicity. This gospel does not diminish the four gospels in the Bible, as it contains many of the same verses. However, the sayings of Jesus in Thomas require exercising one's mind, because some of the teachings are so puzzling, that they have been compared to what are known as koans.[30] In spite of there not being direct answers, these verses encourage the unconventional thought that Jesus' teachings and messages were foremost, not about giving answers, but encouraging persons, like the Pharisees, the Sadducees, and us to re-exam how we exercise and live our faith.

As Marvin Meyer says in his introduction to his book *The Gospel of Thomas*, "The readers of the *Gospel of Thomas* are invited to join the quest for meaning in life by interpreting the oftentimes cryptic and enigmatic hidden sayings of Jesus. They are encouraged to read or hear the sayings, interact with them, and discover for themselves the interpretation and meaning."[31] Could this same insight not be applied to the gospels and writings in the Bible? Reading the Bible, as well as the Gnostic Gospels, becomes not finding answers, but a process of becoming closer to God by seeking love and God's spirit within them.

There are further reasons why gnostic Christianity brings fresh air to faith. Beyond upholding the story of Jesus Christ and adding additional insight, also, the conception of God is expanded. With a new liberty, perhaps God can be understood as more than just as a male, but as a Spirit, and the ludicrous image of a grandfather with white hair and a stick can be dismissed forever. Instead of a wrathful God, who is sitting in the heavens, judging those who are naughty, bad, or sinful — or those who don't believe correctly — there is a God who loves and wants a positive relationship with us. Instead of being required to believe in certain doctrines in order to be a true Christian, say for just an example, the popular and rational concept of God as a Trinity, which Sir Isaac Newton disliked passionately, perhaps a less definable, gentle God will dominate our vision.[32] Trusting a loving and accepting God, whose spirit is within this world, but not of the world, will give us strength and hope and guidance in a crazy and challenging world.

Indeed, rather than a judgmental savior, the Gnostic Gospels state that Jesus came to awaken us, as children of God, to the spirit within us. By recognizing that we are made in God's image, we are free to move beyond the poverty of an empty life and do have reason to live and love. Sin is not a state of total depravity; a doctrine that has encouraged persons to demean and believe there is no good in themselves. Rather, sin is missing the mark of living a loving and wholesome life. Yet, as the book of Romans in the Bible teaches, by recognizing our sin, we accept a humbling message; we all fall short of the glory of God.[33] Thus, forgiveness is a reality that can help us move beyond the sins that can hurt and destroys us. Faith moves us to that which we love, and faith makes us whole. That is why the gnostic concept of self knowledge is so critical.

Self knowledge, as part of the meaning of gnosis, is an important concept in helping us to make and correct our decisions in both faith and life, and it leads to making our faith personal and honest. This deeper understanding of ourselves takes us to the heart of gnosis. Gnosis is not simply the same as self knowledge, a doctrine of salvation, nor is it a set of beliefs; all of these have been explained by critics as its meaning. No! Gnosis is our positive relationship to Christ and to God, and that relationship needs, as the *Gospel of Philip* teaches, to "ripen" continually.[34] As one awakens and recognizes this relationship, something remarkable happens. One becomes *spiritually alive*!

Faith, and our gnosis, however, isn't only about ourselves. Bringing forth God's spirit and love calls forth our responsibility not only to ourselves but to our community. Our communal responsibilities can be exercised in places such as in the church, where we may learn each other's concerns and needs as deeply as our own. In community, our challenge is to seek honest understanding of ourselves, others, and the world. How we treat all these, and especially others, not just judge them, is crucial to the message of Jesus. Therefore, being a part of the church and other communities, the gnostic understanding of Jesus isn't as one who allows us to escape the world.

Often, a charge against the Gnostics has been, because they believe ultimately the spiritual world is more important than the material world, the concerns of this world do not matter. The Gnostic Gospels bring an altogether difference understanding.

Being faithful or spiritual isn't to deny the world, nor is it to say that the spiritual world and the earthly world are two different separate realms. Rather, the realms interact with each other, and our participation, according to the Gnostics, can and should be in both.

Because the Gnostics believed boldly in a spiritual world, two popular misconceptions that have caused some to dismiss them as irrelevant, and simply a secret sect, or cult, can be corrected. First, a charge was that they were pure spiritualists — meaning they believed the only real world was the spiritual. Secondly, they were dualist — meaning there was a drastic separation and a dueling opposition between the two worlds.

Karen King in her book *What is Gnosticism?* goes into considerable detail to illustrate that those conflicting typologies, that only the spiritual is real, and then the spiritual is in conflict with the other material world — is to stereotype or misread their religion or beliefs.[35] Because there was so little information, and so much misinformation before Nag Hammadi, it is understandable why the Gnostics were known as those who believed the material world was totally evil and that the spiritual was all that mattered. Now, there is formidable argument against such classification. Karen writes, "My point: as a group, gnostic texts do not supply consistent evidence of extreme anticosmic dualism for which they so often stand as the most famous example in Western history."[36] In other words, because the Gnostics were known to elevate the spiritual world, the assumption was that didn't care about anything in the material world. Anticosmic dualism meant two worlds basically battling against each other. Again, because of their myths, there is some reason to understand this kind of dualism, but as Karen points out that is not a consistent position, and even within their myths, there is a great deal of interaction between the material and spiritual.

Surprisingly, this same charge of being dualist, or that the spiritual and physical world are separate realities, has not been made for those who teach that the spiritual world is simply in another literal location or place called heaven or hell. The Gnostics did not have a conception that heaven was a specific prized spiritual location that was to be awarded after death for those who lived holy or godly lives. Nor was hell a destination for those who did not believe correctly. Heaven and hell were not denied as spiritual realities, but the concept that they were dueling places for one's soul was not their spiritual focus.

The focus for the Gnostics clearly wasn't about delaying the spiritual until death. Agreeing that there was more than our world, Jesus was in a most powerful way, one who shattered the curtain, or belief, that the only world is the material one. Beyond our limitations of knowledge, the reality of a spiritual world exists, and Jesus' call was not to wait for it later, but to seek, know, and relate to it now. In contrast to past understandings, based largely on hearsay, rather than on firsthand information, the Gnostics believed both the spiritual world and the material world were real and interacted. Resurrection was something we can experience now, as well as in the future. They also believed Jesus was not only a real person, but he now interacts with us spiritually as the living Christ. Such a way to believe changes the focus of faith from beliefs to belief.

Focusing on belief, which is open, honest, and led by seeking, causes something dramatic to change, not only for one's personal vision, but also the understanding of a gnostic way of faith. As might have previously been assumed, agreeing with gnostic beliefs and myths is not the message of the Gnostic Gospels. All beliefs, myths, or doctrines are open to the test of truth. Because someone or some group believes something sincerely doesn't make it the truth, and particularly so, for those who are similar to the stringent faithful whom the Gnostics encountered. Of course, certain beliefs may be true, and to believe in their truth is not wrong, but to insist on one's belief as the only way to relate and know God is not faith. Jesus' call was to faith, and for the Gnostics, foremost that meant trusting a spiritual energy, which may have included beliefs; yet, those could change with new knowledge. Although some beliefs may be helpful and true, spiritual rest, comfort, and freedom come in the process of seeking.

As Christians, the Gnostics were believers in Jesus, but more importantly because of their understanding of Jesus, they were "Seekers of God." Their faith was awakening to the spirit of God, which surrounds them, both within and without; then the task of faith was continually seeking all truth, and particularly, spiritual truth. Gnosis was not a body or set of truths, but a way to seek God with love. In today's world, their way of faith needs to be reconsidered because instead of arrogance it teaches, *always seek the truth, do not declare it.*

Certainly, for those who arrogantly claim their beliefs, for whatever reason, are equal to God's, this way of faith could shift attitudes of certainty to humility and Christian maturity. No better example can be given than the quote noted earlier by the Gnostic, as stated by Dr. Pagels, "We too, have accepted the faith you describe, and we have confessed the same things — faith in God, in Jesus Christ, in the virgin birth and the resurrection — when we were baptized. But since that time, following Jesus' injunction to 'seek, and you shall find,' we have been striving to go beyond the church's elementary precepts, hoping to attain spiritual maturity."[37]

The primary message the Gnostics heard from Jesus, hidden but preserved for our benefit, was seek and you shall find, and even in finding to keep seeking! To identify oneself as a gnostic Christian may seem awkward and heretical; that is not necessary, particularly, if that implies joining another group. However, expressing that one is gnostic in their Christianity, meaning to be a *seeking* Christian, may be a refreshing and honest way to declare one's faith. The greatest shift is more on seeking than believing. Hopefully, this book has helped to gain a better understanding of the Gnostics, and the false stereotyping of these early Christians, which has served to cover over what is far more important, a long hidden, yet deeper, more spiritual message of Jesus. Therefore, be ye not Gnostics, but Seekers of God!

Notes: Chapter Nineteen: The Gnostic's Gift: Fresh Air for Christianity

[1] George F. Will, "The Oddness of Everything," (Newsweek, May 23, 2005), 84.

[2] Heinz R. Pagels, *The Dreams of Reason*, (New York: Simon and Schuster, 1988), 21.

[3] John T. Robinson, Editor, *The Nag Hammadi Library in English*, (San Francisco: HarperSanFrancisco, 1978), the *Gospel of Truth*, 40.
[4] Karen Armstrong, *The Battle for God*, (New York, Random House 2000, Introduction, XII.
[5] Dava Sobel, *Galileo's Daughter*, (New York, Penguin Group, 1999), 7. The primary text for the sun standing still: Joshua 10: 12-14.
[6] www.creationism.com.
[7] www.Vaticanastronomy.org.
[8] John Gribbin, *The Omega Point*, (New York: Bantamm Books, 1988), "The Scale of the Universe," 30.
[9] www.Campus Crusade. Com; Tracts and Booklets.
[10] Heinz R. Pagels, *The Dreams of Rea*son, (New York: SIMON AND SCHUSTER, 1988), 328.
[11] Heinz R. Pagels, *The Cosmic Code*, (New York: SIMON AND SCHUSTER, 1982), 9.
[12] Heinz R. Pagels, *Perfect Symmetry*, (New York: SIMON AND SCHUSTER, 1985), 4.
[13] Pagels, *Dreams of Reason*, Pg. 7.
[14] Marcelo Gleiser, *The Dancing Universe*, (New York: Penguin Group, 1997), 150.
[15] Mein Weltbild, *Ideas and Opinions: Albert Einstein*, (New York: Crown Publishers, 1954), 292.
[16] Ibid.
[17] Ibid.
[18] George F. Will, *The Oddness of Everything*, (Newsweek, May 23, 2005), 84.
[19] Liz Kruesi, "Will dark energy tear the universe apart?" (Our cosmic fate depends on the biggest unknown in science) (Astronomy Magazine, Feb. 2009), 34ff.
[20] Ibid.
[21] Ibid.
[22] Ibid.
[23] Ibid.
[24] Ibid.
[25] Ibid.
[26] Proverbs 4:5 KJV.
[27] Robinson, *The Nag Hammadi Library in English*, the *Gospel of Mary*, 525.
[28] See Chapter Eighteen on the Sethian Myth.
[29] See Chapter Nine on Thomas' Gospel.
[30] Pagels, *Beyond Belief*, (New York: Random House, 2003), 54.
[31] Marvin Meyer, *The Gospel of Thomas: The Hidden Sayings of Jesus*, (San Francisco; HarperCollins, 1992), 7.
[32] James Cleick, *Isaac Newton*, (New York, Vintage Books, 2004), 107.
[33] Romans: 3: 23.
[34] Robinson, *The Nag Hammadi Library in English*, the *Gospel of Philip*, 156.

[35] Karen King, *What is Gnosticism?,* (New York: Random House, 2003), 192.
[36] King, *What is Gnosticism?*, 208.
[37] Pagels, *Beyond Belief*, 129.

Appendix A

The Apostles' Creed

I believe in God the Father Almighty, Maker of heaven and earth. And in Jesus Christ his only Son our Lord; who was conceived by the Holy Ghost, born of the virgin Mary, suffered under Pontius Pilate, was crucified, dead, and buried; he descended into hell; the third day he rose again from the dead; he ascended into heaven, and sitteth on the right hand of God the Father Almighty; from thence he shall come to judge the quick and the dead. I believe in the Holy Ghost; the holy catholic church; the communion of saints; the forgiveness of sins; the resurrection of the body; and the life everlasting. Amen

Appendix B

The Nicene Creed

We believe in one God the Father Almighty, Maker of heaven and earth, and of things visible and invisible; And in one Lord Jesus Christ, the only begotten Son of God, begotten of the Father before all worlds, God of God, Light of Light, Very God of very God, begotten, not made, being of one substance with the Father by whom all things were made; who for us men, and for our salvation, came down from heaven, and was incarnate by the Holy Spirit of the Virgin Mary, and was made a man, and was crucified also for us under Pontius Pilate. He suffered and was buried, and the third day he rose again according to Scriptures, and ascended into heaven, and sitteth at the right hand of the Father. And he shall come again with glory to judge both the quick and dead, whose kingdom shall have no end.

And we believe in the Holy Spirit, the Lord and Giver of Life, who proceedeth from the Father and the Son, who with the Father and the Son together is worshipped and glorified, who spoke by the prophets. And we believe one catholic and apostolic church. We acknowledge one baptism for the remission of our sins. And we look for the resurrection of the dead, and the life of the world to come. Amen

Appendix C

The Rule of Faith

From Irenaeus' *Against Heresies* Vol. I: X:

The Church, though dispersed throughout the whole world, even to the ends of the earth, has received from the apostles and their disciples this faith: In One God, the Father Almighty, Maker of heaven and earth, and the sea, and all things that are in them; and in one Jesus Christ, the Son of God, who became incarnate for our salvation; and in the Holy Spirit, who proclaimed from the prophets the dispensations of God, and the advents, and the birth from a virgin, and the passion, and the resurrection from the dead, and the ascension into heaven in the flesh of the beloved Christ Jesus, our Lord, and His manifestation from heaven in the glory of the Father "to gather all things in one," and to raise up anew all flesh of the whole human race, in order that to Jesus Christ, our Lord and Savior, and King, according to the will of the invisible Father, "every knee shall bow, of things in heaven, and things in earth, of things under the earth, and that "every tongue should confess to Him, and that He should execute just judgment towards all; that He may send "spiritual wickedness," and the angels who transgressed and became apostates, together with the ungodly, and unrighteous, and wicked, and profane among men, into everlasting fire; but may, in the exercise of His grace, confer immortality on the righteous, and holy, and those who have kept His commandments, and have persevered in His love, some from the beginning, and others from their repentance, and may surround them with everlasting glory.

Glossary

Achamoth: The name of the lower Sophia whose fall is part of the creation of the earth.

Aeon: Angelic like beings that emanate from the Supreme God and are expressions of the divine.

Adamas: The divine Adam and the father of the divine Seth.

Androgynous: Being both male and female.

Apocalyptic: Means "Revelation." It can refer to spiritual experience or prophecy of future events.

Apologist: Early Christian defenders of orthodox Christianity.

Apostolic Church: This was a church who claimed its doctrines, beliefs, and ecclesiastical formation were that of the original apostles. As their teachings would become the norm or standard doctrines for understanding Christ and Christianity, they are also referred to as the proto-orthodox.

Autogenes: One who is self begotten or self generated as Jesus in the Apostles' Creed; it also is a description or name of the divine Christ in gnostic literature.

Barbelo: In Sethian mythology, the name of the Divine Mother.

Basilides: Consider one of the earliest gnostic teachers, but his work was overshadowed by Valentinus.

Bridal Chamber: A ritual of the Valentinians in which one becomes emerged with Christ and the divine world.

Church Fathers: Early Christian writers beginning at the Second Century who claimed their knowledge and positions were passed on to them by the apostles. Most were Bishops of the Church but not all, and as strong apologist for their church's beliefs, they often attack those who were heretics.

Demiurge: In Plato, a mediator between the divine and the material world. For Gnostics, a craftsman/creator of the material and evil world.

Docetic: A term meaning only appearing or seeming to be real.

Dualism: Implies there is a spiritual world and a material world but they are separate. Sometimes it means anticosmic or two worlds against each other.

Dyad: Divine beings paired as masculine and feminine partners.

Eschatology: Means dealing with final or last things such as the end of the world.

Gnosis: Is a Greek word that means "knowledge." For the church fathers, it primarily meant the false and secret knowledge that the Gnostics claimed to possess. For the Gnostics, it was a term meaning foremost a relationship as in "knowing" another.

Gnostics: The name given by the church fathers to those who differed with their doctrines and beliefs about the "knowledge of God." The Gnostics, not a name they called themselves, were dissenting Christians who accepted other gospels as having truth and believed the knowledge of God was not limited to the doctrines of the church fathers.

Heresiologists: Proto-orthodox leaders who attacked the heretics as false believers.

Heresy: A word that means "choice," and was considered the sin of those who did not agree with the church's official positions and beliefs.

Irenaeus: Bishop of Lyons and Gaul (130 C.E.—202 C.E.) who led the charge against all heresies, was influential in establishing content of Creeds, and was consider the father of their being only four gospels in the Bible.

Marcion: The leader (85 C.E.—160 C.E.?) of a movement called Marcionism. Most scholars do not consider him a Gnostic as there is no mention or support for him in their writings. Maricon taught that there was no need for the Old Testament because of its cruel God, that only the Gospel of Luke, the Book of Acts, and certain letters of Paul be the canon for the Bible. Most importantly, he preached a docetic Jesus Christ meaning he only appeared to be a real person. Some gnostic texts have a docetic position but it was not anywhere as strong as Marcion taught. His followers in Asia became a threat to the church in Rome so he, like the Gnostics, was condemned as a major heretic.

Monad: A word that means "one," and in gnostic literature refers to the Supreme and One God.

Rule of Faith: Believed to be the forerunner of the Apostles' Creed. Not discovered in its original form, it is believed to have been developed from early baptismal questions. Its earliest written form comes in Bishop Irenaeus' *Against All Heresies*. This Rule, longer than the Apostles' Creed, but similar to it, is found in Appendix C.

Pleroma: The name of the fullness of the divine world.

Sethian: Seth was the third son of Adam and Eve. After Cain killed Abel, the spiritual mantle of the world fell on Seth. Without a major leader like the Valentinians, many gnostic books are considered Sethian because they elevate Seth as the father of the immortal race. In Sethian mythology, Christ, the Savior, is the descendent of Seth.

Sophia: As a feminine aeon, she (wisdom) is the last spirit that emanates from the divine world. Over all, she is a positive force as she breathes into mankind the spirit of God. Her negative side is that she tried to create "something" without the help of other aeons and that something was the evil Demiurge, who became the creator of the evil filled earth. So when she repents, her positive spirit is allowed to enter the world. With many descriptions, foremost she represents the divine feminine principal in life.

Tertullian: An Egyptian layman and lawyer (100 C.E.? – 160 C.E.) who was considered a church father. Writing in both Greek and Latin, he was a powerful apologist for the apostolic church, was very harsh on women, and even more so, the Gnostics. However, he became a heretic as he eventually joined the Montanist movement that believed in speaking in tongues, faith healing, and the imminent Second Coming of Christ.

Valentinus: Almost elected Pope, in 143 C.E., Valentinus (100 C.E – 160 C.E.) was the most important gnostic teacher and his followers were called Valentinians. His teachings were closer to traditional Christianity, but as he moved far beyond the accepted doctrines of the church, he was excommunicated as a heretic. The Valentinian Myth, with its several variations, was named after him, and as he developed quite a following, he was considered the biggest threat to the apostolic church.

Yaldabaoth: The name given to the Demiurge in Sethian mythology. Also his name is sometimes translated as Ialtabaoth. Either way as the evil craftsman, his name means child of chaos. If that is not enough, he also called Sakla – the fool and Samuel – the blind one.

Index

CPSIA information can be obtained at www.ICGtesting.com
Printed in the USA
LVOW070742080812

293451LV00001B/16/P